Language and Image in the Reading–Writing Classroom: Teaching Vision

LANGUAGE AND IMAGE IN THE READING–WRITING CLASSROOM: TEACHING VISION

Edited by

Kristie S. Fleckenstein
Ball State University

Linda T. Calendrillo
Western Kentucky University

Demetrice A. Worley
Bradley University

LEA LAWRENCE ERLBAUM ASSOCIATES, PUBLISHERS
2002 Mahwah, New Jersey London

MW

Lawrence Erlbaum Associates, Inc., Publishers
10 Industrial Avenue
Mahwah, New Jersey 07430

Library of Congress Cataloging-in-Publication Data

Language and image in the reading-writing classroom : teaching vision / edited by Kristie S. Fleckenstein, Linda T. Calendrillo, Demetrice A. Worley.
p. cm.
Includes bibliographical references and index.
ISBN 0-8058-3940-2 (cloth : alk. paper) — ISBN 0-8058-3941-0 (pbk. : alk. paper)
1. Language arts. 2. Imagery (Psychology) in children. I. Fleckenstein, Kristie S. II. Calendrillo, Linda T. III. Worley, Demetrice A.

LB1576 .L283 2001
372.6—dc21 2001033960
CIP

Books published by Lawrence Erlbaum Associates are printed on acid-free paper, and their bindings are chosen for strength and durability.

Printed in the United States of America
10 9 8 7 6 5 4 3 2 1

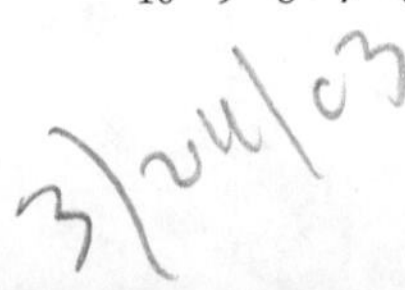

DEDICATIONS

To the women in my life, who have anchored me as I leaned out to look: mothers, sisters, daughters, friends.

Kristie S. Fleckenstein

To my father Anthony Calendrillo, who taught me everything I know about images and gave me the vision to see both inside and out.

Linda T. Calendrillo

For my African-American literature and writing students, who know the power of images and words.

Demetrice A. Worley

Contents

Acknowledgments

We would like to acknowledge the work of our contributors, without whose insights and patience this work would have remained a passing vision.

I would like to thank my undergraduate intern, Megan Pendley, who discovered more about publishing than she ever wanted to learn; my graduate research assistant, Suocai Su, for his unerring eye, patience, and ability to multitask; department administrative assistant, Sandy King, for shepherding draft after draft through the copier; and the English Department at Ball State University for their support. Finally, I would like to thank my daughters, Anna and Lindsey, who have generously offered to draw for me anything I was unable to say.

—Kristie S. Fleckenstein

I wish to acknowledge the help I received with this project from two staff members at two different institutions: Ginny DiBianco from EIU, who helped early in the stages with the prospectus, and Eva Whittle from WKU, who helped late in the process with the final product. I also wish to thank John Guzlowski and Lillian Calendrillo-Guzlowski for all their advice and editing assistance.

—Linda T. Calendrillo

Thank you, Linda T. Calendrillo and Kristie S. Fleckenstein—*We* had a vision, but without *your* work and dedication, this book would have remained a dream.

—Demetrice A. Worley

Introduction: Teaching Vision: The Importance of Imagery in Reading and Writing

Kristie S. Fleckenstein
Ball State University

> *"I don't know what to write next," my 9-year-old complains as she struggles to fashion a story for a Young Authors contest at her elementary school. "Well, why don't you draw your story, then write it," I suggest. "Oh, yeah," she sighs with relief. "I should have done that first."*
>
> *"You want me to draw? In my reading journal," a first-semester composition student asks me, aghast. "I can't draw. Don't make me draw. It just . . . just fouls up my thinking." His panic is not manufactured. It is full blown and real.*

Our elementary schools successfully inculcate in our children the importance of language first and imagery second, if at all. Graphic imagery, mental imagery, and verbal imagery (terms I explore more fully in chap. 1) are merely extras, walk-ons in the educational drama. Because of this training, my fourth grader, an avid drawer, tried to write her story before she drew her illustrations. However, she remained so closely tied to her images that she could greet with relief the suggestion that she use them to jump-start her stalled story. But my first-semester composition student no longer possessed this flexibility. By his 13th year in school, he could only greet with full-fledged terror the suggestion that he draw a reading journal. Although he lived immersed in a highly imagistic culture, he could not comfortably consider the idea of using imagery in his reading–writing activities.

We should not be surprised by his response or his terror. Throughout their schooling, we assess our students' progress on the merits of their linguistic performances, and we teach by analogous linguistic performances. In the reading-writing classroom, discourse is not only the object of study, it is also the medium of study. As our research and textbooks over the past century reflect, reading-writing has typically been conceptualized and taught as an art of language. Thus, it is no wonder that, by high school and college, our students are no longer adept at recognizing the inextricable integration of imagery and language in their learning.

Despite this linguistic orientation in our pedagogy and our theories of meaning, we are gradually coming to a renewed acknowledgment of the importance of imagery in our knowing of and being in the world. Work in cognitive psychology, as well as the interdisciplinary efforts in anthropology, history, and cultural studies, has heightened our awareness of the fusion of image and word in knowledge. We are construing more precisely the ways in which images explicitly and implicitly permeate reading and writing. Such knowledge comes at a crucial juncture in our cultural history. We live in an era in which we are awash by multimodal imagery, inside and out. First, Damasio (1999) connected the continuous stream of mental imagery accompanying our waking and sleeping lives with the development of what he called our core and autobiographical identities. Second, the proliferation of imagery around us—through the hypermedial World Wide Web, computer interfacing, visual media, and virtual reality—highlights the need to attend to the influence of imagery in a networked world. Stroupe (2000) argued that the growing dominance of the multimedia Internet requires of us a multimedia literacy; the hybridization of the "image-word" demands a reconfiguration of what we do as meaning makers and as teachers. Smagorinsky (2000) concurred, claiming that the most significant change literacy teachers will face in the new millennium is the shift dictated by the changes in media. Such shifts in scholarly and cultural perspectives have led the National Council of Teachers of English (NCTE) to establish a committee on visual literacy and to incorporate into their *Standards for the English Language Arts* (IRA/NCTE, 1996), jointly created by NCTE and IRA (International Reading Association), an emphasis on visual literacy. "We must therefore challenge students to analyze critically the texts they view and to integrate their visual knowledge with their knowledge of other forms of language," the *Standards* stated (p. 7). Teaching reading and writing needs to include teaching imagery in its myriad forms.

OVERVIEW OF THE BOOK

Unfortunately, few books on reading-writing pedagogy offer postsecondary teachers explicit and specific strategies for integrating imagery into their pedagogy. This collection begins to fill that gap, providing theory-based methods for tapping the strengths of meaning as a fusion of image and word. The chapters in this book offer concrete answers to the question of how we can use imagery to enrich our teaching of reading and writing. These 15 chapters organize themselves according to two guiding principles. First, each addresses in different ways the inextricable integration of imagery and language in meaning. Although the authors focus on imagery, they do not privilege imagery over language. Rather, they emphasize the fusion. Second, each essay focuses on a specific kind of imagery—mental, graphic, and verbal—describing powerful teaching-learning strategies based on the deployment of that kind of imagery in the classroom. Although we organize this collection around three kinds of imagery, we do so cautiously. As the chapters indicate, particular kinds of images overlap and enfold each other, just as image and word are inextricably enfolded. A graphic image is also a mental image, a mental image is realized and shared through verbal imagery, and a verbal image finds fulfillment in both graphic illustration and mental experience. We can divide them linguistically, but not realistically. When we open the door to imagery, we open the door to the entire family of images, each of which offers gifts that add depth to our teaching. As teachers, we are not limited to one kind of imagery or one kind of language, nor need we limit our students to one kind of imagery, one kind of language. The blend of chapters within this book underscores this.

We open with Part I, Provenance: Authorizing the Image, an introductory section consisting of two chapters that frame the remaining ones. I (chap. 1) begin by defining imagery as a set of relationships, including within this definition a description of the three kinds of imagery highlighted in the collection. I also explore the ways in which imagery and language enfold, concluding with an examination of three gifts—feeling, forming, and transforming—that imagery carries with it into our classroom. Hobbs (chap. 2) traces the historical connections among imagery, language, and pedagogy, highlighting the complicated transactions among technology, cultural orientation, and the weave of word and image through Western history.

Framed by these introductory chapters, the following 12 chapters offer insight into the ways we can use mental, graphic, and verbal imagery in our classrooms. Part II, Mental Vision, focuses on the flash and movement of our interior scenes, which are filled with sights, sounds, textures, smells, and tastes. Pullen Guezzar (chap. 3) extends the reader-response theories of Rosenblatt and Iser by combining them with art psychology to forefront mental imagery in students' writing and reading. She draws on Arnheim's principles of centers and vectors and applies them to students' initial drawings and writings to help students develop their responses to aesthetic texts. Focusing on the interplay of reading and writing, Innocenti (chap. 4) addresses students' apathetic attitudes toward reading and writing. She advocates engaging students in writing assignments that facilitate a physical relationship with the words on the page. Innocenti offers memory work and sensory vignettes as two ways to link the sensual experience of daily living with the texts students read and write. She demonstrates that this linkage affects students' ability to craft abstract as well as concrete texts. Mylan (chap. 5) explores the possibilities of visualization activities for encouraging students to see themselves as writers and overcome writer's block by assisting them throughout their writing processes. Highlighting somatic and enactive imagery, Worthman (chap. 6) describes an approach to writing that draws from his work with an inner-city teen theater group. Imagery, he argues, helps teenagers address their and others' real-life situations and develop their own writing voices based on their experiences.

If mental imagery permeates our interior lives, then graphic imagery bombards us from the outside. We live in a world and culture that are increasingly dominated by images layered on images. Advertisements in magazines come with visual images, scratch-and-sniff strips, and texture. Information on the Internet is offered in audio as well as textual sound bites. Arcade experiences include virtual rollercoaster rides, car races, and laser tag. Our realities and knowledge are hypermediated. The chapters in Part III, Graphic Vision, focus on this array of imagery, offering us ways to use and critique its power in our classrooms. A trained artist as well as a writing teacher, Hobson (chap. 7) argues that all writing that incorporates visual techniques, especially sketching, can benefit visually as well as linguistically oriented students. Hobson provides examples of visual approaches to writing that can serve the interests of all students. Fox (chap. 8) turns to imagery-rich advertising, arguing that advertising, from magazine ads to TV commercials, offers accessible texts for classroom use. Focusing on five high school English as a Second Language (ESL) students, Fox illustrates how students' exploration of media texts motivates them to address complex issues such as power and ideology, nonverbal communication, stereotyping, and emotional appeals. With the guidance of mystic-poet William Blake, Hecimovich (chap. 9) helps his students understand and use the fusion of medium and meaning in Web pages. Hecimovich uses Blake's worldview and artistic mix of the verbal and visual to lead students in his technical writing class to a similar integration in their own learning. Using only materials available in their immediate environments, students create new media and messages as a prelude to creating Web sites that capitalize on the multimedial elements of the computer. Smith (chap. 10) explains that a common problem confronting writing teachers who encourage their students to tap electronic media for information about world events is that students frequently produce discourse that resembles aphoristic or proverbial thinking. The source of that problem can be traced to the visual noise infiltrating electronic media. Using advertisements, Smith provides a description of classroom practices that help students deconstruct images and adapt them into heuristics for socially pertinent discourse.

As each essay illustrates, imagery and word cannot be separated. Word, seemingly so divided from image, is, in fact, soaked in imagery. Image, to be used, must be named. Nowhere is this mutual constitution more evident than in the verbal images we create in our reading and our writing. Therefore, we conclude our collection with Part IV, Verbal Vision. Sheridan-Rabideau (chap. 11) opens this section with a focus on verbal imagery in our natural language, our daily discourse. Sheridan-Rabideau argues that verbal imagery is a necessary ingredient in helping girls and women envision themselves as political and personal agents. Drawing on Goffman, Sheridan-Rabideau suggests ways that classroom assignments and classroom talk can be structured to offer opportunities for the creation of positive verbal images of girls and women. Friend (chap. 12) continues this exploration of verbal imagery in everyday discourse by examining the verbal images that frame conceptualization of teachers; she explores the formative power of that imagery as it guides what can and cannot be done in the classroom. Analyzing the interviews and focus group conversations of students gathered together to discuss teaching and teachers, Friend highlights three dominant images that organize teacher–student interactions, suggesting the necessity of attending to these images as a prelude to improving classroom dynamics. Images written and printed on a page also serve as sites of power in our literate culture. Worley (chap. 13) examines one such site in literature written by African-American women. She explores how students of color and White students use writing and imagery to construct images of themselves as readers, writers, and agents of change. By focusing on their acceptance, rejection, and redefinition of the *other* as presented in contemporary African-American women novelists' texts, Worley argues that teachers can help students transform images of self and other. Her classroom approach relies on an amalgamation of literary metaphor and student illustrations. Concerned with breaking down the artificial distinctions between creative writing and expository writing, Teich (chap. 14) taps the imagistic richness of Wordsworth and Basho, a 17th-century Japanese haiku master. He asks his students to attend to Wordsworth's concept of spots of time, illustrating such spots through both Wordsworth's poetry and Basho's haiku. Students create their own spots of time—their own verbal imagery—to foster greater understanding of the poetry and greater awareness of themselves.

To invite further exploration of imagery and language arts beyond the parameters of these essays, the anthology concludes with Calendrillo's

Afterimage, a bibliographical listing of sources that merit teachers' attention. Pushing beyond the sources cited in the individual references pages, this listing includes books, articles, journals, and websites that explore imagery from myriad angles.

The word grows out of the image, Langer (1942) wrote, and can never be severed from its matrix. We need to integrate imagery and language into our teaching because it is by means of such integration that we create, transform, and live in our world. To teach shorn of imagery is to teach shorn of vision. These 15 chapters offer new ways to see our teaching of reading and writing.

REFERENCES

Damasio, A. (1999). *The feeling of what happens: Body and emotion in the making of consciousness.* New York: Harcourt.

International Reading Association/National Council of Teachers of English. (1996). *Standards for English language arts.* Urbana, IL: Author.

Langer, S. K. (1942). *Philosophy in a new key.* Cambridge, MA: Harvard University Press.

Smagorinsky, P. (2000). Snippets: What will be the influences on literacy in the next millennium? *Reading Research Quarterly, 35,* 277–278.

Stroupe, C. (2000). Visualizing English: Recognizing the hybrid literacy of visual and verbal authorship on the Web. *College English, 62,* 607–632.

I

PROVENANCE: AUTHORIZING THE IMAGE

1

Inviting Imagery Into Our Classrooms

Kristie S. Fleckenstein
Ball State University

> *All thinking begins with seeing.*
>
> —Langer (1942, p. 224)

We wake up in the morning with the afterimages of dreams fading behind our eyes. We decorate, or shave, the face reflected in the mirror. In the kitchen, as we reach for the milk, we open a refrigerator festooned with snapshots, stick figures, and lopsided rainbows. We rattle the last bit of Cheerios into a bowl and begin preparing a mental grocery list, traveling up and down the aisles of our memory. On the way to work, we stop, turn corners, and park on autopilot, relying on responses to images that seemingly bypass consciousness. We climb the stairs to our building without looking at either feet or risers, depending on a body image that fails us only when we dance. The screensaver on the computer greets us. We shake the mouse awake, double click on the icon for Internet access, and enter cyberspace via a gateway of pictures. Finally, we gather our books, papers, and dry-erase markers; head out the door; enter our class; and begin—to talk. We banish our images to the nether regions and attempt to weave solely out of language a world that we call *language arts*.

A continuous stream of images marks our waking and sleeping lives. Yet, paradoxically, it is language that we use to define our humanity and measure our sophistication. Benchmarks of our development as a species are tied to language. The great leap theory of anthropological evolution ties our mutation into *Homo sapiens* to the development and use of the larynx to create spoken words (Diamond, 1998). The great divide theory of human civilization, introduced by Levi-Strauss (1966) and applied to 20th-century literacy by Ong (1982), asserts that the development of complex thought is tied to the development of written words. Intellectual children—such as philosophy, logic, and politics—are tied to a culture's ability to write. Even individual psychological development is linked to language. Perhaps because of this, articles asserting our various literacy crises have always defined those crises in terms of language: words that Johnny cannot read or write, words that Johnny can decode but cannot comprehend. It is the word, after all, that Vygotsky (1962) identified as the smallest unit of meaning.

The scales of meaning and teaching need to be balanced so that word no longer eclipses image. Language is not the sole, perhaps not even the primary, means by which we create meaning of our worlds. Imagery arises within and around us, marking indelibly the linguistic fabric we weave. We cannot separate our development as a species or as individuals from imagery. As Langer (1942) argued, "Images are . . . our readiest instruments for abstracting concepts from the tumbling stream of actual impressions" (p. 128). Therefore, any theory of humanity's intellectual evolution must include the pictures on the walls of Lascaux Cave in southwestern France. Graphic and mental images serve as precursors to and mutual participants in the cultural development of humankind. Such images "make our primitive abstractions for us," Langer wrote. "[T]hey are our spontaneous embodiment of general ideas" (p. 128). The development of the larynx means nothing if we have nothing to say. Langer (1962) pointed out, "The great step from anthropos, animal to man, was taken when the vocal organs were moved to register the occurrence of an image, and stirred an equivalent occurrence in another brain, and the two creatures referred to the same thing" (p. 50). The great leap was propelled by the kick of imagery. The great divide theory of cultural evolution is similarly marked by imagery. Imagery is the bridge joining orality and literacy. Tannen (1989) long argued that the characteristics of oral language and written language, especially in terms of their joint reliance on imagery, speak more to their similarities than to their differences. Thus, the intellectual sophistication ascribed to the shift into written language is presaged and reflected back to us in our oral traditions where images dominate.

Graphic imagery, verbal imagery, mental imagery—we rely on these images, consciously and unconsciously, in every aspect of our lives, and we can trace their influence in our evolutionary and individual histories. Yet when we enter our classrooms and begin to teach composition, reading, and literature, we rarely reference the rich variety of images infusing our worlds. Instead, we reference language, using language to do so. We turn our backs on imagery. Yet imagery, from the kinesthetic imagery of muscle and bone to the graphic imagery of girders and stick figures, cannot be choked off so easily. Imagery sneaks into our classrooms through metaphor, simile, and description. It erupts from websites, computer icons, illustrations, body language, and student artwork on chalkboards, desks, and margin doodles. It rips through the illusion that words are all, tying us to the immediacy and materiality of the moment, fusing thought and feeling. Because we cannot separate our words from images without wrenching away meaning and meaningfulness, we need to open the door to imagery. By doing so, we can better understand and teach the difficulties and exhilarations of writing, reading, and literature. By focusing on the play of language and image, we can help our students resonate to, rather than resist, language arts. Such an endeavor does not require that we attend to imagery to the detriment of language. Rather, such an endeavor requires that we nuance our sense of meaning by welcoming into our classrooms the necessary transaction between imagery and language.

The purpose of this chapter and this book is to edge open that classroom door a bit by providing a rationale and flexible framework for integrating imagery into our language arts teaching. As a teacher who actively incorporates imagery in my writing-reading pedagogy, I cannot offer a single, definitive answer to the question, "How should we teach fusing imagery and language?" Instead, I believe there are many answers, as the chapters in this book indicate—answers that individual teachers must evolve, working both top-down from an understanding of imagery and language and bottom-up from the give-and-take of each classroom performance. Rather than offering a definitive answer to the question of how we should teach using imagery, I suggest a starting point—a launching pad for investigation and experimentation. The question I explore in this chapter is as follows: To integrate imagery into our reading-writing pedagogy, what do we need to know about imagery and its potential for enriching our students' language experiences? I answer that question in two parts. First, we need to know what imagery is and how it enfolds language. Therefore, I open with a description of three kinds of images—mental, graphic, and verbal—following that with a working definition of imagery. I conclude this first section with an explanation of the reciprocal movement of imagery and language in meaning. Second, we need to know what gifts imagery brings into our classrooms. I respond to this by exploring three ways that imagery can enrich our teaching. I conclude with a vision of multimodal teaching.

DEFINING VISION: THE FACETS OF IMAGERY

Isodora Duncan supposedly said that if she could say what she meant, she would not have to dance it. Dancing was her response to the recalcitrance of language. Defining imagery offers us a similar conundrum: To explain imagery, we must use language, thereby boxing imagery in the constraints of language. Mitchell (1986) neatly captured the difficulty in his book *Iconology*. Every definition of imagery necessarily reflects the language of the disciplinary community from which it issues, Mitchell pointed out. I, too, am bound by the language of my academic specialty. Unfortunately, I cannot dance imagery between the pages of a book even if I could dance. But I can pry open my linguistic box by giving a face to imagery that complements (and contests) the face that my disciplinary language chisels for me. Therefore, I wish to anchor my descriptions and definition of imagery with the image of Georgia O'Keeffe's *Black Iris,* a painting that communicates the lushness and ambience of a deep purple iris by folding folds within folds. Not a single element of the flower stands alone. Instead, the image exists within and by means of its relationships. This is also the linguistic definition I wish to offer of imagery: An image—regardless of whether it is mental, graphic, or verbal—consists of an array of relationships that marks or punctuates an unknowable reality in a particular way. Counterintuitive though it may seem, neither graphic, mental, nor verbal imagery is a thing; instead, all imagery consists of a pattern of mutually creating folds crafted by a metaphoric logic. Let me anchor my definition of imagery in a description of the three kinds of images featured in this anthology.

The Three Faces of Imagery

Imagery offers us a cornucopia of richness. Not only does it deepen our understanding of what it means to mean, it also does so in three different forms. We are not limited to inviting merely one kind of imagery into our classrooms. We have the opportunity to invite in three incarnations of imagery: mental, graphic, and verbal. In this section, I describe each kind of imagery, but with a caveat. Beware of taxonomies, Britton, Burgess, Martin, McLeod, and Rosen (1975) warned us in the first chapter of *The Development of Writing Abilities,* a study based on taxonomizing thousands of writing samples taken from British schoolchildren. That same warning applies here. I have divided imagery into three categories—mental, graphic, and verbal. But they cannot be so neatly separated outside of the parameters of language. A graphic image is also a mental image in that we perceive it by means of internal processes. A mental image is also a verbal image, however, in that we must name it to use it. Similarly, a verbal image, although couched in language, exists within the mental image we construct cued by language or within the graphic image we sketch to illustrate language. Thus, the borders among these three kinds of imagery are always blurred and osmotic. Writing and reading are likewise intertwined. We might be able to read without physically writing, but someone has to write for us to read. Also, we cannot write without reading what it is we write (see Kucer, 1987; Tierney & Pearson, 1983, on the similarities between reading and writing). Thus, categories and processes overlap, offering us both frustration and possibility. With that caveat in mind, let me begin with mental imagery—what Damasio (1999) called the core to consciousness.

Mental imagery consists of that never-ending stream of sights, sounds, and sensations circulating within us. It can manifest itself as a static visual representation or as a series of frames fading into each other like a film where smells, sounds, and feelings interweave. Ostensibly private and idiosyncratic, mental imagery relies on the same relationships and neurophysiological processes that yield perceptual images. For instance, the areas of the brain involved in sight are also those involved in the evocation of mental visual imagery (Aylwin, 1985). Regardless of its omnipresence in our lives, scholars have attended only sporadically to imagery over its 2,500-year history. According to Simonides, mental imagery first came into prominence in Greece when an Athenian dinner party went awry. Supposedly the roof fell in on the guests, mangling the bodies beyond recognition. A survivor (in some accounts, Simonides himself) identified the bodies by referring to a mental schema of the seating arrangements. From this beginning, mental imagery has been historically privileged as a mnemonic, as a tool of memory, not unexpected in an era when rhetors (and poets) were required to orate elaborate speeches from memory. As print technology increased in sophistication, reliance on mental imagery waned and interest in it languished. It was not until the rise of cognitive psychology within the last 50 years that interest in mental imagery experienced a renaissance.

Unlike mental imagery, graphic imagery has always been of interest, from the early work of classical Greece on viewing (Goldhill, 1996) to our current concern with our graphic-rich culture. Graphic imagery refers to that loose category of material images that permeates our society. This includes photographs, architecture, art, film, and computer iconography, ranging from Power Point presentations to web-page special effects. Historically, graphic imagery has exercised a powerful influence on human societies, reflected by efforts to control, repress, or use graphic imagery to solidify power for a particular group in a culture (Mitchell, 1986). Because graphic imagery seems to be lodged in a visual field outside of the boundaries of blood and bone—it exists out there, not in here—it offers us the strength (and the dangers) of position. Such is the truth that Rose (1989) captured in his autobiographical work, *Lives on the Boundary*. Speaking of the poverty of his childhood environment, Rose noted, "It is an unfortunate fact of our psychic lives that the images that surround us as we grow up—no matter how much we may scorn them later—give shape to our deepest needs and longings" (p. 44). The graphic images surrounding us are also part of us. The power and ubiquity of graphic imagery in Western culture has led the National Council of Teachers of English (NCTE) to establish a standing committee on visual literacy and incorporate into their *Standards for English Language Arts,* jointly created by NCTE and International Reading Association (IRA, 1996), an emphasis on visual literacy. Graphic images represent a force that we need to both understand and harness for our reading–writing classrooms.

Finally, verbal imagery has been the one form of imagery that is considered a legitimate area of study for the reading–writing classroom. If there has been one face of imagery to pop up consistently in our classes, it has been verbal imagery in descriptive language, tropes, and concrete examples. We cannot talk about literature without talking about symbolism, and symbols are invariably image based. Jesus relied on verbal imagery in his parables to teach a moral lesson, as did Socrates and Plato. Epic poetry, dating from Gilgamesh, could not have existed without verbal imagery. We cannot talk about either literature or writing without also talking about the power of verbal imagery to move ourselves and our readers. Yet verbal imagery offers us more than just a framework for creating layers of meaning and more than just a starting gun for emotional response. Perhaps more than any other mode of imagery, verbal imagery offers us the hope for change—from self-transformation to world transformation. For example, metaphor, a linguistic form that relies on imagery for meaning, is the law of growth of every semantic, Langer (1962) pointed out, thus the law of change. Cornell (1991) went even further. Drawing on poststructuralist theories, Cornell argued that metaphor constitutes a trope merging the discursive with the nondiscursive. Because of this, a person or culture can never close down the meaning of a metaphor by restricting it to a single linguistic expression. Instead, the tension between the image and the word in metaphor opens up spaces within which meaning, and we along with it, can change and transform.

Common to each kind of image is its apparent transparency and universality. Everyone knows what images are because everyone evokes them. An image is something that we sense (see, feel, hear, taste, smell, etc.), either mentally in the absence of stimuli or physiologically in response to stimuli. The problem with this practical knowledge, however, is that it treats an image as a thing, one outside of us, in our environment, like a painting by O'Keeffe, or one in our heads, like a seating chart. We have photos filed in our family albums and in our memories. But images—graphic, mental, and verbal—are not things. Instead, they are relationships that we create. To understand this, we need to look at meaning itself, of which imagery is a founding part.

The Definition of an Image

According to G. Bateson (1972/1987, 1980, 1991), all meaning, which includes all communication, all thought, and all biological life, exists within the interface between the disorder of reality and the ordering of pattern. Life and meaning come to be when the barrage of material stimuli and the organization of some pattern, such as language, DNA codes, art, and ritual, overlap. Information becomes meaningful through relationships. A filtering process takes place, and what gets "through" the filters are relationships crafted from the enfolding of pattern and confusion. For instance, a stone lies along a path in the woods. But we do not perceive the stone. Rather, we perceive the stone in relationship to the ground, the grass, or our toes. We perceive the differences between stone and ground, stone and grass, or stone and toe. Perception, Bateson explained, requires a relationship between one stimulus (the stone) and another stimulus (the path) or between the same stimulus at a different time (the stone today and yesterday). In addition to this relationship, however, we need another: We need a "someone" for whom the relationship between stone and path matters. We can blithely walk down a path without "seeing" a stone—unless we stub a toe on it. The stone is not perceptible until it comes into focus, into significance. In a continuous stream of potentially perceptible stimuli, perception occurs when information emerges as "a difference that makes a difference" (G. Bateson, 1972/1987, p. 457). When that happens, we mark or punctuate that stream so that it yields a particular meaning: a stone to be collected, kicked away, or used to crack a nut. The stone exists not as a stone, but as an array of relationships, a way of organizing chaotic reality. It is never a thing in and of itself. We do not store physical stones in our heads, regardless of the number of times people tell us we have rocks in our heads; we store connections that include the label *stones*.

This idea of relationships is much more accessible if we think of it first in terms of language. After all, the whole concept of the definition of a word depending on the context in which it appears—its connection to other words in a sentence—is an integral part of our language teaching. Traditional grammar that many of us memorized as students—noun, pronoun, verb, and so on—undermines our recognition of the relationships necessary for meaning because parts of speech are treated as "discrete" things: A noun is a person, place, thing, or idea. More progressive approaches to a grammar of languages, such as Fillmore's (1968) case grammars, highlight that a noun exists as a noun only because of a particular relationship it holds with other words in a sentence (and with an individual's actions in the world). Halliday and Hasan's (1976) concept of cohesion in a text—that is, the "stickiness" of a text that transforms a jumble of words into a cogent structure that holds together as a single unit—also relies on relationships. One example of cohesion, called *pro-forms,* occurs when and where we use pronouns. To understand any pronoun, we have to connect it to its antecedent, which requires us to tie one portion of the text to another. This is only one sticky strand in the web of textual relationships that ensure a sense of unified meaning. Beaugrande and Dressler (1981) extended this idea of relationships to argue that, although *cohesion* sets up a network of textual relationships, to be *coherent* cohesion must be supported by another array of relationships, extratextual relationships among reader/writer/text/occasion. To make sense out of a string of sentences or a string of words, we must create connections between words and sentences, between writers (intent) and readers (desire), and between text and situation. Because of these multiple layers of relationships in language, we all possess a tacit awareness that what exists in language is not the thing; it is the idea of the thing. Thus, we rarely attempt to pick up the phrase "cup of coffee" and drink it.

More startling is the concept that an image also consists of a set of relationships. After all, although most of us would not try to drink a phrase, most of us have at one time in our lives confused the image with the thing, moments when we have reached for an image only to be surprised (and disappointed) by its illusiveness. Regardless of its "thinginess," imagery, like language, is a pattern of relationships. Aylwin (1985) called imagery a temporal pattern created by our attention shifting along particular pathways. "In the process of making sense of a stimulus, people . . . move their attention around it in a particular way, and this leads to the different constructions of meaning," she explained (p. 44). An image is evoked by this movement of our attention. For instance, a visual image is created when our attention flits between whole–part relationships, object–attribute relationships, and object–environment relationships. So if we attend to the play of feather, color, and tree branch in a set of stimuli, we create a visual image. If we attend to the play of aerial acrobatics, marveling at and wishing we could participate in the avian performance, we create an enactive image—an image in which we role-play and participate in an action. If we look at that same stimuli and think "parakeet," we are taxonomizing and crafting the hierarchical relationship undergirding language. An image, like a word, is not a thing; it is a pattern created as our attention organizes stimuli into particular relationships.

Complicating this already bewildering idea is the fact that these relationships—for both language and image—exist along three axes that are related. Envision the pathways crafting an image (or a word) as moving within a three-dimensional space. The horizontal dimension of relationships plots the shift of attention along structuring pathways: categorizing stimuli into hierarchical relationships (a cat is a feline, a cat is not a dog), into part–whole relationships (a wing is part of a bird), into cause–effect relationships (the bird performs to attract the attention of a mate), and so on. This axis highlights the mental moves that "punctuate" stimuli in particular ways, yielding a particular kind of representation of reality: a word, a visual image, an embodied image.

The vertical dimension of this three-dimensional schema can be marked *physiology* and represents the neural relationships that enable and constrain our shifting attention. We cannot see/imagine all things, nor can we see/imagine in all ways. We might be able to use our imagination to place a human torso on a horse's body, but we cannot replace either part with the color pink or the smell of roses (Aylwin, 1985). Our perceptions and imaginations are tied to the parameters dictated by our physiology. Differences in physiology mean different ways of seeing, thus different ways of organizing meaning. For instance, because of our ability to detect objects in steady motion and at rest, we are able to conceive of Newton's first law of motion, or inertia: Objects at rest stay at rest unless a force is exerted on them; objects in motion stay in motion unless a force is exerted on them. However, frogs cannot perceive objects at rest. They are physiologically constructed to detect objects—such as flies—in erratic motion. Therefore, even if cognitively capable (and predisposed to do so), frogs could not evolve the idea of inertia. So what are the limits of human perception? One thing we cannot perceive is slow change—we cannot "see" a flower open unless we use time-lapse photography (G. Bateson, 1980). Nor can we perceive holes in our visual field. All of us possess a *blind spot* in our visual field—the point in our brain where the optic nerves meet. Yet we are never conscious of that blind spot. Instead, we compensate, we fill in. Also, when we see a rabbit through a picket fence, we see a rabbit, not a head severed from a tail by a fence slat. We automatically and unconsciously fill in the portions of the rabbit we cannot see. Our physiology thus offers us the parameters within which we create our reality (Ramachandran & Blakeslee, 1998). (See Yates, 1966, for a fourth dimension—that of situational and historical time.)

Implications of this tripartite constitution are threefold. First, because we all possess the same neurophysiology, there are similarities in the ways we pattern reality. Second, that neurophysiology is differentiated from individual to individual because of our unique experiences in life: Therefore, there are always differences in the ways we pattern reality. Third, where we imagine is important to what we imagine. Carey and Harste (1987), working from Rosenblatt's (1978) concept of transactional reading, highlighted the role of material position in what they called *print setting*. The place where we read has a direct impact on the meaning we construct from that reading. Asking our students to read a story and enjoy that story in the classroom disregards the influence of that classroom—a context imbued with assessment, not pleasure. Regardless of seemingly shared stimuli (the word on the page, the stone on the path, the cup of coffee), we do not always construct the same image or the same meaning because we are all creating relationships out of individual physiology from a specific material position. Thus, we cannot expect that our students (or our colleagues) will construct the same relationships as we do, although we can expect them to construct relationships. Differences in physiology and physical placement always result in differences in relationships.

Finally, where, how, and when we evoke images, as well as what those images mean, are tied to what Jay (1994) called our *scopic regimes,* the cultures in which we were raised, which is plotted along the third, diagonal axis. First, the physical environment we are raised in trains vision. All people are subject to optical illusions, but not all people are subject to the same optical illusions. For example, according to the work of Rivers (Bolles, 1991) in the early 1900s, New Guinea tribesmen of the Torres Strait area did not perceive optical illusions that afflicted Westerners. In the Müller-Lyer illusion (see Fig. 1.1), tribesmen readily perceived that the lines marked A were equal—something people in the West have difficulty identifying (Bolles, 1991). The hypothesis offered for this phenomenon was that individuals raised in *carpentered worlds,* where buildings and furniture display straight lines and intersections form right angles, interpret the open angles of the Müller-Lyer effect as longer lines. Environment trained perception. In contrast, individuals raised in an environment of broad vistas, where horizontal lines dominated, would be less likely to be

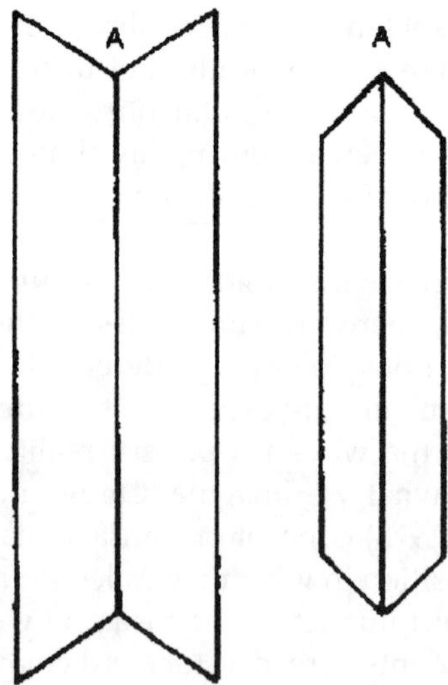

FIG. 1.1. Müller-Lyer illusion.

fooled by the illusion. Empirical testing confirmed this hypothesis. The physical environment and the cultural artifacts that punctuate an environment train vision.

Second, not only do the material artifacts of our culture—such as our architecture, photography, and urban planning—impinge on imagery, but abstract cultural rules also influence how and what we see. For instance, Malinowski (Bolles, 1991) noted that the Trobiand Islanders of New Guinea failed to perceive resemblances between child and mother or between siblings. Children could resemble their father, but they could not resemble either each other or their mother. Similarly, Berger (1972) argued that women's self-perceptions are influenced by the visual emphasis placed on them in the West, particularly in graphic imagery. Women do not see themselves, Berger said: they see themselves being seen by others, and they then use that self-vision to police themselves by regulating behavior, feelings, and thought.

Third, just as our placement within a specific material environment—a print setting—affects what and how we see, so does our placement in a particular social environment. Said (1978) maintained that one of the most invidious results of colonialism is that the colonized people begin to see themselves through the eyes and expectations of their oppressors. To counteract colonial influences, they have to resee themselves through different eyes from a different social position. McLeod (1997) applied a similar concept to the classroom in her Pygmalion/golem effect. Although layered in complexity and rarely directly causal, a teacher's expectations can adversely or positively affect students' performance and self-perceptions. In a round-robin of reinforcement, students perceived as bright by a teacher are evaluated accordingly, leading to the students' corresponding self-evaluation and self-perception. Students perceived as slower or less capable experience a similar construction of assessment and identity, only it yields a negative evaluation and self-image. Seeing, then, is not just attentional or physiological. It is also cultural. Students in the same writing class, but from different economic and ethnic backgrounds, construct different images and meanings in response to the verbal imagery in the same poem (see Hull & Rose, 1990).

The Play of Image and Language in Meaning

Given the definition of imagery and language as an array of relationships, it might be easy to conclude that language and imagery are essentially the same. After all, we map both image and word within the same three-dimensional space. Pylyshyn (1981) argued something along these lines. Because all knowledge, including imagery, is crafted out of abstract, amodal propositions, the abstract propositions are important, not any *dress* they happen to wear, either of words or imagery. Thus, the images (and words) that flit through our minds are epiphenomenal, outside of or irrelevant to the creation of knowledge. Imagery is rather like the flashing lights on a computer: interesting to see, but contributing absolutely nothing to the functioning of the computer. Sadoski and Paivio (1994) argued that schema theory, the dominant theory of knowledge construction in reading, is marred by a similar assumption. Because all knowledge is created out of abstract frameworks (schemas), both imagery and language are just different labels for the same thing. Such, however, is not the case. We construct and experience the relationships of language and imagery differently according to two different logics: metaphoric *is* logic in imagery and discursive *as-if* logic in language.

Imagistic relationships dance to the tune of a metaphoric, or *is,* logic—one that functions according to identification: An image for us is the "thing," which is why it is so counterintuitive to think of it as a set of relationships. Unless directed to do so by language, we do not discriminate or separate image from the relationships that create it or from our experience of those relationships. Metaphoric logic functions according to the logic found in the following syllogism: Grass dies. Men die. Men are grass (G. Bateson, 1991; G. Bateson & M. C. Bateson, 1987). This syllogism in grass, as G. Bateson (1991) called it, captures the metaphoric turn in imagery. The truth that "men are grass" is based not on the logic of predicates, which presumes or builds on the existence of a subject (we cannot have a predicate unless we have a subject). Instead, the truth that "men are grass" is built on the equality of subjects, the equality of "is," which underlies the truth of metaphors. If we look at the verbal form of metaphor—such as Juliet is the sun—we can better see this logic at work. A metaphor unlike a simile carries no linguistic markers to signal its status as an analogy. Instead, in the absence of these markers, it requires from us a leap across the "is" from Juliet is *like* the sun to Juliet *is* the sun. Drawn from the realm of the unconscious and the world of dreams, metaphoric logic is bereft of such linguistic pointers as verb tenses, modals, and negatives. We cannot say "not" with an image, we can only say "is." For a dog to communicate with another dog that it does not want to fight, it must go through all the motions of fighting, but without fighting. We cannot signal an absence with metaphoric logic as we can with language (the phrase "a cup of coffee" is not a cup of coffee). As a result, metaphor logic weaves us into the relationships we create, enfolding self and other, self and environment, self and self (Bateson, 1972/1987). It ties us to the realm of emotions, reactions, pleasure, and pain because we cannot separate ourselves out of the image we create. Evoking an image means experiencing an image, living an image.

If images flow according to *is* logic, then language functions according to *as-if* logic, the logic of substitution, not of identity. In language, relationships are formed according to a discursive logic in which the word names the relationships. Thus, a word is treated as if it were real in full knowledge that it is not real. It functions as a kind of digital code that allows us to parse our reality into an infinite number of facets that we can then treat as a substitution for that reality. Language endows us with the power of absence, the power of not. With it we can create the categories and differences necessary to communicate. "Not" gives us a portable reality—one that we can take away from our experience of stimuli and re-create in new combinations. With an image, we are tied to the experience, a participant carried along on and by the stream flowing through our heads and around us. Yet, with language, we can be the observer of our own participation, dipping into that stream of experience at will and reflecting on that stream. Except in the uncommon instances of a magical use of the language, such as when we curse or write love letters, we rarely confuse the word with the thing.

Let me summarize where we are. Imagery consists of relationships created by our attention shifting along certain pathways. It is a spontaneous, quasi-automatic process tied tightly to the unconscious, over which we have little control (and less understanding). Our material grounding in a particular body, place, and culture impinges on what images we create, why and when we create them, and what they mean. Because imagery resonates to the *is* logic of identification, it nests us within the images we create and experience, tying us to feelings, to the immediacy of the moment, and to the physical reality of place. Imagery is what we know of reality and serves as the core to our consciousness (Damasio, 1999). Although an image is not reality—it is a way of punctuating reality—it anchors us to our identity and our being in reality.

Because of the strictures of language (which by its nature separates and categorizes), I have written as if language and image were different domains. Yet image and word can exist apart only in language at the descriptive level. We might be able to disconnect image from language. We do this every night in our dreams. However, without language, we cannot do anything with that image except experience it. Imagery lives in the moment and ties us to that moment. To be tugged out of that moment, to be known as anything other than life as it is lived, we need language. Similarly, the process of naming, the meaningfulness of language, is predicated on the existence of imagery. Language that is disconnected from imagery loses its meaning. DNA offers a perfect example of this.

Currently, in scientific communities, DNA is treated as a language or code, and its grammar is being mapped systematically in the human genome project. Yet that DNA means nothing outside of the chemical context of the cell that calls that genetic language into play. Likewise, dead languages, languages that no human community speaks, can be mapped onto a grammar, but they exist with no meaning because there is no living imagery flowing through them, no human being evoking them. Without the *is* logic of imagery, language is inert. In life and in meaning, language and imagery enfold each other, creating each other as they do. We can no more separate language from imagery than we can tease out the individual folds of the *Black Iris* or point to the brush stroke that turns violet into black. We might use language to define imagery, but that language is born in imagery, catching us in a round-robin of image and word creating each other as they enfold each other. We cannot speak the world without also imagining the world.

GIVING VISION: THE GIFTS IMAGERY CARRIES WITH IT

We are currently experiencing a renaissance of interest in imagery across the disciplines: in philosophy, cognitive science, neuroscience, anthropology, feminist studies, and media studies. These myriad approaches to imagery and its many facets have yielded an array of riches. We have discovered that when we let imagery into our classroom, delightful gifts follow along. I focus on three such gifts: the gift of emotional engagement and response, the gift of forming, and the gift of transformation.

An outgrowth of the rebirth of interest in imagery has been the validation of an intuition that many of us have had: Imagery and emotion are connected. Emotion, a thread in meaning just as outlawed from the composition classroom as imagery, is inextricably intertwined with imagery (see Brand, 1989; McLeod, 1997, on emotion in writing). G. Bateson (1991) explained that the metaphoric *is* logic weaving throughout imagery is tied to what he called *algorithms of the heart,* echoing Pascal's famous observation: The heart has its reasons that reason knows not of. A variety of empirical research has also linked imagery with emotion. For instance, Paivio (1986) tied mental imagery to emotion and language through his dual-coding theory of thought—the theory that we represent reality imagistically and linguistically. Emotions and motivations are embodied in images, he argued; images can take on "symbolic significance as the conceptual peg for the predominant passion," a term Paivio (1983) borrowed from Coleridge to describe the role of emotion in the creative process (p. 12). Mental imagery also serves as a bridge between emotion and cognition, Paivio said. Whereas Paivio saw imagery as a bridge, Aylwin (1985) saw emotion and cognition as part of the same embodiment. We can no more evoke an image without an emotion than we can strip warm-bloodedness from mammals; it is part of an image's identifying characteristic. Many scholars confirm such an integration. Lyman (1984) defined emotion via imagery: An emotion is a "conscious experience characterized by a dynamic pattern of imagery and accompanying affect and particular experiential themes" (p. 78). After a series of free-association studies, Suler (1985) concluded that imagery abilities are related to an individual's ability to experience emotional ideation. The shifting attention that crafts our visual, verbal, and enactive thoughts automatically interweaves emotional tonality. Finally, Plutchik (1984) considered images to be part of the "mental 'maps' that organisms make of their environments, and are capable of serving as internal triggers of emotional behavior" (p. 105).

This brief overview of diverse scholarship indicates that imagery and emotion do-si-do into our classrooms linked at the elbow. When they do, they offer us a rich pedagogical boon, opening our classrooms to new possibilities for both our reading and our writing. The most obvious bonus is literature, for without emotion there is no literature. Rosenblatt (1978) put the matter quite plainly. Only by attending to the play of emotions can we *evoke* a work of literature from words on a page. Reading *aesthetically*, as Rosenblatt called reading literature, demands that we experience literature, that we live it viscerally. Doing otherwise yields not literature, but a text from which we attempt to carry away meaning rather than be absorbed in meaning. Without mental imagery, we cannot create a world in which to live. Echoing Rosenblatt, Britton (1984) argued that we can live more than one life allotted to us through literature because it requires of us a global rather than a piecemeal contextualization. To evoke literature (and not just information), we have to represent a poem as a whole instead of a series of sequentially connected parts. However, global contextualization relies on imagery. Only an image, Langer (1942) pointed out, can provide a "world image" (p. 128), a whole kind of actual happening; only an image "can hold us to a conception of a total phenomenon" (p. xviii). Imagery connects, nesting layers of emotion, sound, feeling, and meaning, rather than stringing them out like links in a chain. Without imagery, we would have no literature to enjoy, no worlds to create, no other lives to live. We would have only information to be digested in discrete chunks. Thus, with imagery we can craft a pedagogy that invites our students to experience what Rorty (1996) called the *shudders of awe* that great literature elicits. By focusing initial responses on images, we can invite our students to fall in love with literature.

Mental imagery and emotion not only open the way to an enriched teaching of literature. They also open the way to an enriched teaching of writing. "Pure meaning," Brand (1989) argued, "is so richly endowed with imagery and connotation that it is saturated with emotion" (p. 28), and that emotion weaves the writer into her or his evolving text. This is an essential point to keep in mind, even for the writing that students are usually required to produce in classrooms, because it can save us from eliciting what Britton et al. (1975) called *pseudotransactions*: writing that lacks life, purpose, and engagement. With no encouragement to relate to what they are writing, students will rarely "appropriate" writing assignments and make them their own (Mayher, Lester, & Pradl, 1983, p. 116). Instead, they craft the kind of motivation that Flower and Hayes (1980) described as writing to get a grade out of a class. As teachers, we indeed want our students to write so that they can get a good grade, but we want more for them than just a good grade. We want them to invest themselves in their writing—to see themselves as writers. Otherwise, will they be able to write when a grade for a class is no longer required? To encourage our students to both love and value writing, we need to introduce the power of imagery. By adding an imagistic layer to their writing, they can weave self and other, self and environment, self and self into their evolving essays. Regardless of the very real intellectual contribution that images offer us in terms of plumbing an idea, planning an essay, and grounding a point, imagery opens the door to caring about an idea, caring about a reader, because imagery nests all of us within the same dynamic.

Imagery also plays a direct role in our teaching especially as it applies to empathy. McLeod (1997) wrote of the importance of empathy in teaching: "It is empathy that we recognize in some of the best teachers in our discipline, teachers who work not only to understand their students but who also actively try to appreciate their perspective, who try to feel and think along with their students" (p. 114). Through empathy, McLeod argued, we can better encourage the Pygmalion effect and prevent the golem effect, using our expectations to draw the best from our students. Although McLeod did not tie imagery to empathy (she did tie imagery to intuition), mental imagery is an essential part of empathy. Empathy is an emotional orientation enabled by imagery. Hoffman (1984) explicitly tied imagery to empathy. Empathy, especially empathy mediated by language, relies on two processes: imagining oneself in the position of the other (called a *self-focus*) or imaging the situation of the other and responding to that situation (called an *other-focus*). Both processes rely on a particular kind of imagery Aylwin (1985) called enactive imagery. Enactive imagery is crafted when an individual's attention focuses on agency, action, and the act of doing something. It manifests itself consciously as a kind of ongoing movie in which one is a participant or an observer of the action. Such imagery emotionally connects the self and the other, investing the self in the world of the other. Tied to motivations, consequences, and agency, enactive imagery leads to empathy and the ethical behavior implicit with empathy. Thus, to teach empathically, as McLeod urged, we have to first imagine our students' worlds by focusing on those worlds as if we were either participants or observers committed emotionally to the participants. Either stance depends on the evocation of enactive imagery.

Beyond the largesse of emotional resonance, imagery also carries with it the power to structure our worlds and position ourselves in those worlds. Berthoff (1988) underlined this power. Imagery as a medium for representing the world need not be limited to mental representation. It also extends to graphic illustrations. Smagorinski and O'Donnell-Allen (1998) offered an example of the power of graphic imagery to shapes students' understanding of a text. Arguing that people rely on different means to express and represent meaning, Smagorinski and O'Donnell-Allen described the results of a study in which a small group of high school seniors studied the character of Laertes in Shakespeare's *Hamlet* by collaboratively creating a body biography—a life-size outline of a classmate's body that the group filled in with images and words that represented their understanding of the character. Through this multimedia technique, the authors concluded, students were able to evoke images of meaning, design and share literary understanding, and shift back and forth between graphic exposition of the interpreted text and that text itself. The body biography grounded them in kinesthetic aspects of meaning, provided them with a visual anchor for their discussions, and offered an alternative mode of meaning making. Although the authors did not specifically mention *felt sense,* a term Perl (1984) used to describe the body-based feel of an idea, body biographies also provided an imagistic outlet to the felt sense of students' literary experiences. Felt sense, is "the soft underbelly of thought . . . a kind of bodily awareness that . . . can be used as a tool . . . a kind of bodily awareness that . . . encompasses everything you feel and know about a given subject at a given time. . . . It is felt in the body, yet it has meaning. It is body and mind before they split apart" (Gendlin; cited in Perl, p. 306). So then, felt sense is an integral part of our first response to the evocation of a story world. Yet it is a kind of thinking-feeling-being that resists linguistic expression. Body biographies and other modes of multimedia representation offer our students a bridge between the lived experience of a story and critical writing in response to literature. Drawing and mapping bodies help students position themselves in between felt sense and language.

Images, especially those captured on film, can also be invaluable in helping our students shape their world as writers. One of the nagging problems we confront in our classrooms is helping our students conceive of their essays as active. They have difficulty thinking of a linguistic argument as requiring momentum or forward movement (which it does possess, at least in Western discourse). One way to help them perceive the activity weaving throughout an abstract argument is to introduce them to that phenomenon in film and analyze the techniques by which a director makes that forward moving argument via the images he or she constructs. Film is particularly apt because it is a medium with which the majority of our students are familiar and comfortable. Students will stand around in the halls between classes talking about the movies they watched over the weekend, whereas they will rarely stand around talking about the essays they read (or wrote) over the weekend. Because film is a graphic medium that is already part of their repertoire, they have little difficulty engaging with it. They respond positively to opportunities to watch films even if they have to analyze what they watch. Once engaged, they talk more easily about the techniques a director uses to advance the progress in the movie or the failure of those techniques, pointing to slow points or static moments that contributed nothing to the film's argument. With this conversation as a foundation, we can then ask them to construct visual storyboards to their own arguments, seizing on the places in their arguments where they merely tread water or backtrack to the reader's confusion. By juxtaposing film to exposition, they can develop a better sense of the techniques they need to become effective directors of their own texts.

In addition to shaping the world, imagery can enable us to change the world. In fact, it may be a necessary part of changing the world. As Anzaldúa (1987) pointed out, we cannot change the world until we change our image of it. Nor is the longing for change new to our profession. The entire concept of teaching for change, of education as a vehicle for change, is what drew many of us into teaching in the first place. Most of us are in this profession because we believe in the power of learning to transform us, to heal us, to guide us. Bridwell-Bowles (1995) stated this explicitly in her 1994 4Cs address: "I want to bring the passions and the dreams of transformation to our classrooms" (p. 47). Dreaming of transformation, however, requires that we attend to imagery as well as to language. Change is not an easy process to effect as most of us have discovered. After all, imagery and language cohere to craft for us a consistent representation of the world in which we act. Yet imagery and language can also contend, and it is within the sites of contention, the spaces where language and imagery do not match, that we find the hope of transformation. Reality is not seamless. Because imagery and language mark reality differently, resonating to different logics, there is no one-to-one relationship between the experience of the one and the articulation of the other. Aporias always exist between imagery and language. Le Dœuff (1984) pointed out that there is never any closure in discourse, never any one meaning, because imagery is "always seeking utterance" (p. 12). It is something cherished, but something that cannot be expressed precisely in language. Therefore, meaning is always a "compromise—or bricolage" (p. 19) between what we can say and what we want to say. Poetry lives within these gaps between language and image; because it does, understanding meaning requires of us a poetics (Le Dœuff, 1984). Transformation—small or large—is born at the site between image and word where objective, singular meaning unravels, where it shimmers simultaneously into myriad forms.

One of the manifestations of the transformation that can be effected by this tension occurs locally in our classrooms. Our students, because of their educational training and human predispositions, see meaning as lodged in the text, just as reality is something *out there.* Although they might acknowledge different interpretations of meaning, there is still just one right meaning, one right reality. It is this attitude that causes them such bewilderment when we as teachers cannot see the same meaning in their evolving papers that they see. "After all," they tell us, "it is right here," and they point. Introducing poetics into writing and reading shakes this certainty and helps our students see how they construct that right meaning. It is neither in the text nor in them. It is, in Rosenblatt's (1978) words, in the transaction between the two, in the space between the two. By focusing on what Le Dœuff (1984) called the *marginalized elements of a text*—its evasions and images—students can experience the compromises that constitute the meanings we all create.

Many feminists working in literature have successfully employed this technique. For instance, Schweickart (1986) identified one such point of transformation in readers. She offered as an illustration a verbal description of a young girl from Joyce's *Portrait of the Artist as a Young Man.* The description, Schweickart wrote, as we can see, tenderly renders the vision of a girl wading on a beach and teetering on the edge of sexuality. However, Schweickart asked, what happens when we interpret this image? To respond to this vision in a way congruent with the activity in the story, a reader must construct this vision from the point of view of a young man, a point of view that female readers are automatically required to assume. A woman's gendered identity must be submerged as she assumes this masculine perspective or stance. By focusing on the image as it is tied to language (and language to image), Schweickart emphasized the inseparability of gender and reading, leading students to an assessment of the gender woven into the majority of canonical literature, perhaps even into an assessment of the process by which a field determines which stories should be canonized.

Change can be similarly approached in a composition classroom that places the dialectic between image and word at the heart of its instruction. A focus on metaphors illustrates the possibility for such change. Within linguistic metaphors, we are required to leap between the *as-if* discursive logic of words and the *is* logic of the image expressed in words. The "is" in all metaphors negates the as-if separation between reality and language, tying us to contradictions. After all, how can Juliet be Juliet *and* the sun?

As Britton (1989) explained it, in metaphors we are always shuttling between meanings, unable to settle on one, a process that traps us in an enigma: Juliet is Juliet and the sun. The sun is the sun and Juliet. In computer programs, such a loop leads to a breakdown. Yet in humans, such a paradox can lead to transformation. Drawing on Frost, Smith (1986) argued that all linguistic metaphors break down—that that is the beauty of them. The breakdown in meaning is not a tragedy of failed meaning, but an opportunity for new meaning. The cracking of a linguistic metaphor becomes the site of what Smith called its "writability," the site of new insight, of transformation (p. 165). Thus, pushing the implications of the metaphors that undergird human thinking and weave throughout our writing can open up opportunities in our classrooms for change, both large and small. A practical illustration of this is fairy tales. Fairy tales offer children metaphoric lessons in socialization (Bettelheim, 1975). Therefore, inviting our students to push the metaphor of popular fairy tales, such as Cinderella with her Fairy Godmother and Prince Charming, provides a way for us to engage them in an examination of contradictions of gendered identity, class, and materialism. Through the metaphor of verbal imagery, we can teach writing in such a way that we foster growth and change.

Double Vision: Imagery in Our Classrooms

Traditional pedagogy in highly literate societies has been based on a linguistic model of forming (as well as a linguistic model of assessment) in large part because intelligence has been defined in linguistic terms and determined through standardized testing since the work of Alfred Binet in the early 1900s. The underlying assumption has been that we represent and navigate the world through language. Acknowledging the power of imagery, in all its myriad forms, to connect, shape, and change us requires that we see meaning as multimodal. Gardner (1983, 1993) emphasized the multimodality of meaning. Linguistic intelligence is only one of seven ways that we pattern our universe, but it, along with logical-mathematical reasoning, has been placed on a pedestal in our culture, Gardner (1993) argued. Important as well are spatial intelligence, musical intelligence, bodily kinesthetic intelligence, interpersonal intelligence (a kind of emotional intelligence tied to one's ability to relate to others), and intrapersonal intelligence (the ability to create a sense of self and function in the world according to that image). Five of the seven ways in which we form the world are lodged in some form of imagery: spatial, auditory, kinesthetic, emotional, and enactive. Hence, opening the door to imagery allows us to tap the multiple ways of knowing that our students carry with them into our classrooms rather than privileging a mode that only a few may excel at using. It also requires that we self-assess, looking at our own multimodality and our own preferred style to see the ways in which we unconsciously emphasize one to the detriment of the others. Aylwin's (1985) work with the relationship of thought and feeling also testifies to the multiplicity of forms. Drawing on Brunner's theory of iconic, verbal, and enactive ways of learning, Aylwin suggested three modes of representation: visual, verbal, and enactive. She contended that the three modes function together with visual imagery serving as the matrix from which verbal and enactive modes evolve. Although each individual taps one mode more frequently than the others, depending on what Aylwin termed their *preferred cognitive style,* we all depend on the three modes given the demands of a particular task and context. In addition, Aylwin argued that reliance on a preferred mode yields a personality style as well as a cognitive style, something that we need to be particularly sensitive to in the classroom. People who rely on a verbal mode of shaping the world tend to be interpersonally adroit; people who rely on a visual mode are characterized by what Aylwin called a *romantic subjectivity of receptivity;* and finally people who rely on an enactive imagery tend to be motivated by a desire for self-efficacy. Thus, we need to be sensitive to the layered relationships of emotion, personality, and cognitive style in our teaching.

Because of the multiplicity of intelligences of our students, Gardner (1993) said, education can no longer conduct business as usual. It must be business as unusual. One step in that direction is acknowledging the play of imagery in forming our representations of the world, our sense of living in the world. Such a move provides us with a framework that we can use to shift our methodologies and attend to the different intelligences our students bring with them into their classrooms. Our classrooms become marked by opportunities not just for imagistic learning, but for the integration of imagistic and linguistic learning. Harding (1987) said that the *woman* problem in science—that is, the absence of women and their gifts in the hard sciences—cannot be solved by the simple recipe of "add women and stir" (p. 4). Instead, the woman problem requires a transformation of the relationships by which science defines itself and its practices. The *imagery* problem in language arts requires a similar transformation. I do not believe that we can simply add imagery to our pedagogy and stir vigorously, although that may be a starting point. I believe that inviting imagery into our classroom will demand from us a sea change, one that redraws meaning as the nexus between language and image, transforming us, our students, and our classrooms.

REFERENCES

Anzaldúa, G. (1987). *Borderlands/la frontera: The new mestiza.* San Francisco: Aunt Lute Books.
Aylwin, S. (1985). *Structure in thought and feeling.* London: Methuen.

Bateson, G. (1980). *Mind and nature: A necessary unity*. Toronto: Bantam.

Bateson, G. (1987). *Steps to an ecology of the mind: Collected essays in anthropology, psychiatry, evolution, and epistemology*. Northvale, NJ: Aronson. (Original work published 1972)

Bateson, G. (1991). *A sacred unity: Further steps to an ecology of the mind* (R. E. Donaldson, Ed.). New York: HarperCollins.

Bateson, G., & Bateson, M. C. (1987). *Angels fear: Toward an epistemology of the sacred*. New York: Macmillan.

Beaugrande, R. de, & Dressler, W. (1981). *Introduction to text linguistics*. New York: Longman.

Berger, J. (1972). *Ways of seeing*. London: British Broadcasting Company.

Berthoff, A. E. (1988). *Forming/thinking/writing*. Portsmouth, NH: Boynton/Cook.

Bettelheim, B. (1975). *The uses of enchantment: The meaning and importance of fairy tales*. New York: Vintage Books.

Bolles, E. B. (1991). *A second way of knowing: The riddle of human perception*. New York: Prentice-Hall.

Brand, A. G. (1989). *The psychology of writing: The affective experience*. New York: Greenwood.

Bridwell-Bowles, L. (1995). Freedom, form, and function: Varieties of academic discourse. *College Composition and Communication, 46,* 46–61.

Britton, J. (1984). Viewpoints: The distinction between participant and spectator role language in research and practice. *Research in the Teaching of English, 18,* 320–331.

Britton, J. (1989). The spectator as theorist: A reply. *English Education, 21,* 53–60.

Britton, J., Burgess, T., Martin, N., McLeod, A., & Rosen, H. (1975). *The development of writing abilities*. London: Macmillan.

Carey, R. F., & Harste, J. (1987). Comprehension as context: Toward reconsideration of a transactional theory of reading. In R. J. Tierney, P. L Anders, & J. Nichols Mitchell (Eds.), *Understanding readers' understanding: Theory and practice* (pp. 189–204). Hillsdale, NJ: Lawrence Erlbaum Associates.

Cornell, D. (1991). *Beyond accommodation: Ethical feminism, deconstruction, and the law*. New York: Routledge.

Damasio, A. (1999). *The feeling of what happens: Body and emotion in the making of consciousness*. New York: Harcourt.

Diamond, J. (1998). *Guns, germs, and steel: The fates of human societies*. New York: Norton.

Fillmore, C. J. (1968). The case for case. In E. Bach & R. Harms (Eds.), *Universals in linguistic theory* (pp. 1–88). New York: Holt, Rinehart & Winston.

Flower, L., & Hayes, J. R. (1980). The cognition of discovery: Defining a rhetorical problem. *College Composition and Communication, 31,* 21–32.

Gardner, H. (1983). *Frames of mind: The theory of multiple intelligences*. New York: Basic Books.

Gardner, H. (1993). *Multiple intelligences: The theory in practice*. New York: Basic Books.

Goldhill, S. (1996). Refracting classical vision: Changing cultures of viewing. In T. Brennan & J. Martin (Eds.), *Vision in context: Historical and contemporary perspectives on sight* (pp. 15–28). New York: Routledge.

Halliday, M. A. K., & Hasan, R. (1976). *Cohesion in English*. London: Longman.

Harding, S. (1987). Introduction: Is there a feminist method? In S. Harding (Ed.), *Feminism and methodology: Social science issues* (pp. 1–14). Bloomington: Indiana University Press.

Hoffman, M. (1984). Interaction of affect and cognition in empathy. In C. E. Izard, J. Kagan, & R. B. Zajonc (Eds.), *Emotions, cognition, and behavior* (pp. 103–131). Cambridge, England: Cambridge University Press.

Hull, G., & Rose, M. (1990). This wooden shack: The logic of unconventional reading. *College Composition and Communication, 41,* 287–298.

International Reading Association and National Council of Teachers of English. (1996). *Standards for English language arts*. Newark, DE: Author.

Jay, M. (1994). *Downcast eyes: The denigration of vision in twentieth century French thought*. Berkeley: University of California Press.

Kucer, S. B. (1987). The cognitive base of reading and writing. In J. R. Squire (Ed.), *The dynamics of language learning: Research in reading and English* (pp. 27–51). Urbana: Educational Resources Information Center.

Langer, S. K. (1942). *Philosophy in a new key*. Cambridge, MA: Harvard University Press.

Langer, S. K. (1962). Speculations on the origins of speech and its communicative function. In *Philosophical sketches: A study of the human mind in relation to feeling, explored through art, language, and symbol* (pp. 30–52). Baltimore: Johns Hopkins University Press.

Le Dœuff, M. (1989). *Philosophical imaginary* (C. Gordon, Trans.). Stanford, CA: Stanford University Press.

Levi-Strauss, C. (1966). *The savage mind*. Chicago: University of Chicago Press.

Lyman, B. (1984). An experimental theory of emotion. *Journal of Mental Imagery, 8,* 77–86.

Mayher, J. S., Lester, N., & Pradl, G. M. (1983). *Learning to writing/writing to learn*. Upper Montclair, NJ: Boynton/Cook.

McLeod, S. (1997). *Notes on the heart: Affective issues in the writing classroom*. Carbondale: Southern Illinois University Press.

Mitchell, W. T. J. (1986). *Iconology: Image, text, ideology*. Chicago: University of Chicago Press.

Ong, W. J. (1982). *Orality and literacy: The technologizing of the word*. London: Routledge.

Paivio, A. (1983). The mind's eye in arts and science. *Poetics, 12,* 1–18.

Paivio, A. (1986). *Mental representations: A dual coding approach*. Oxford, England: Oxford University Press.

Perl, S. (1984). Understanding composing. In R. L. Graves (Ed.), *Rhetoric and composition: A sourcebook for teachers and writers* (pp. 304–310). Upper Montclair, NJ: Boynton/Cook.

Plutchik, R. (1984). Emotions and imagery. *Journal of Mental Imagery, 18,* 105–112.

Pylyshyn, Z. W. (1981). What the mind's eye tells the mind's brain: A critique of mental imagery. *Psychological Review, 87,* 16–45.

Ramachandran, V. S., & Blakeslee, S. (1998). *Phantoms in the brain: Probing the mystery of the human mind*. New York: Morrow.

Rorty, R. (1996). The inspirational value of great works of literature. *Raritan, 16,* 8–17.

Rose, M. (1989). *Lives on the boundary*. New York: Penguin.

Rosenblatt, L. (1978). *The reader, the text, the poem*. Carbondale: Southern Illinois University Press.

Sadoski, M., & Paivio, A. (1994). A dual coding view of imagery and verbal processing in reading comprehension. In R. B. Ruddell, M. R. Ruddell, & H. Singer (Eds.), *Theoretical models and processes of reading* (pp. 582–601). Newark, DE: International Reading Association.

Said, E. (1978). *Orientalism*. London: Routledge.

Schweickart, P. P. (1986). Reading ourselves: Toward a feminist theory of reading. In P. P. Schweickart & E. A. Flynn (Eds.), *Gender and reading: Essays on readers, texts, and contexts* (pp. 31–62). Baltimore: Johns Hopkins University Press.

Smagorinsky, P., & O'Donnell-Allen, C. (1998). Reading as mediated and mediating action: Composing meaning for literature through multimedia interpretive texts. *Reading Research Quarterly, 33,* 198–227.

Smith, L. Z. (1986). Enigma variations: Reading and writing through metaphor. In T. Newkirk (Ed.), *Only connect: Uniting reading and writing* (pp. 158–173). Upper Montclair, NJ: Boynton/Cook.

Suler, J. (1985). Imagery ability and the experience of affect by free associative imagery. *Journal of Mental Imagery, 9,* 101–110.

Tannen, D. (1989). *Talking voices: Repetition, dialogue, and imagery in conversational discourse*. Cambridge, England: Cambridge University Press.

Tierney, R., & Pearson, P. D. (1983). Toward a composing model of reading. *Language Arts, 60,* 568–580.

Vygotsky, L. (1962). *Thought and language* (E. Hanfmann & G. Vakar, Eds. & Trans.). Cambridge, MA: MIT Press.

Yates, F. A. (1966). *The art of memory.* Chicago: University of Chicago Press.

2

Learning From the Past: Verbal and Visual Literacy in Early Modern Rhetoric and Writing Pedagogy

Catherine L. Hobbs
University of Oklahoma

> *The history of culture is in part the story of a protracted struggle for dominance between pictorial and linguistic signs, each claiming for itself certain proprietary rights on a "nature" to which only it has access. . . . Among the most interesting and complex versions of this struggle is what might be called the relationship of subversion, in which language or imagery looks into its own heart and finds lurking there its opposite number.*
>
> —Mitchell (1986, p. 43)

> *Print-imprinted intellectuals, including professors, must relearn the world of the graphic, a word which derives from the Greek graphe and refers both to the written and the pictorial. The humanities/posthumanities/literacies must relinquish semiconscious resistance to pictorial communication and its technologies.*
>
> —Welch (1999, p. 208)

Writing teachers today are living through a revolution in literacy brought about by the capability of computers to combine blocks of text—or verbal *lexias*—with graphic images, sounds, video, and other multimedia (see Landow, 1992, on *lexias*). We are forced—at times by our failures—to grapple with the potential relationships between the ubiquitous and chaotic new visual and the comfortingly familiar, more linear verbal. Awash in both good and bad examples—on the Web, but also on TV and, lest we not forget, still in traditional print—we are discovering that it is no longer enough to fragment our concepts of literacy, bracket off our traditional blocks of text, and just stick to what we know. To condone and contribute to visual illiteracy contradicts our purpose of teaching effective and ethical written communication. Yet as we often tell ourselves, we are still trying to figure out how to teach just our traditional, single piece of the puzzle—nothing to sneeze at in its full complexity.

This chapter starts from the premise that our project of rethinking literacy in light of new technological capabilities might be done more easily with some historical context. This is because the translation of visual images into verbal text—and vice versa—has always been a part of writing and speaking instruction. Furthermore, as Mitchell (1986) noted in the epigraph, there have always been conflicts between the two media, as well as subversion of the one by the other. Why does the verbal find the visual lurking and vice versa? Perhaps this is because of the long history of translation of one into the other and the presumed convertibility of one to the other. Yet as with two circles overlapping, not quite congruent, there is, nonetheless, a *wild zone* each has to itself that has nothing to do with the other.

What interests me in this cultural history is how shifts in this long conflict/subversion affect writing instruction. For example, breakthroughs in the science of optics and vision occurred in the same time frame as interest in the image and imagination intensified in language pedagogy. This was before and during the 17th and 18th centuries, just as modernity coalesced and the Scientific Revolution occurred. Ideas developed at that time provided some of the historical foundation for our 20th-century values, beliefs, and practices in writing instruction. This chapter attempts to show that language arts teachers have always incorporated visual theory of one kind or another in their teaching. Yet verbal-visual relationships keep transforming as technologies change and our understanding of vision grows (see Faigley, 1999, for more on these changes). In the next section, I show that rhetorical arts always incorporated practice in translation from the visual to the verbal. Then, I present some significant developments in optics and vision science, followed by a discussion of how rhetoricians and writers responded to these developments in their pedagogical values and practices.

VISUALS IN ANCIENT ARTS

The Greeks systematized the art of rhetoric or public persuasive speaking over the same long historical period as the alphabet and writing developed (8th century B.C.E. for the alphabet). Genres developed linked with the sites of the speaking—the public forum, the courts, the legislatures—and by Plato and Aristotle's days (at least by 450 B.C.E.), schools were in operation to teach boys (almost always boys) first grammar and literary studies beginning to involve instruction in writing (see Welch, 1990). Boys worked on language arts until they reached the pinnacle of learning—rhetoric, or the public, persuasive oration. From the beginning, vision and description were important to persuasion and were overtly taught, as is made clear in the term from the art of style, *ecphrasis*—delineation, or description used in teaching. There had always been descriptions in Homer and the poets, and later in the early Sophists and pre-Socratics, who attempted to use language to put a magical spell on listeners to transport them and used vivid descriptions in the process.

Aristotle said little about description in the *Rhetoric,* although his emphasis on metaphor and visualization linked to poetics and description. The more poetic Plato, who banned poets from his *Republic,* placed a great deal of emphasis on light, vision, and knowledge, first in the realm beyond the sensory and in this world. His banning of the poets from the *Republic* gives us a glimpse of how powerful the poets were in Greek society. Indeed, in Greek society, poetry vied with rhetoric for pride of place in education, with rhetoric and prose composition building on and growing out of earlier studies of Homer and the poets led by the *grammatikos* or grammar instructor. Greek writers whose texts reveal the teaching of description include Theon, Hermogenes, Aphthonius, and Libanius, who discussed "bringing before the eyes what is to be shown" in a clear and vivid manner or, in the generic term, *enargia* (Lanham, 1991, pp. 64–65).

In his encyclopedic rendering of Roman education, based on the Greeks they emulated, Quintilian mentioned student writing of descriptions only to try to diminish the activity, which must have grown to elaborate proportions. By this time, the teaching of writing and rhetoric had become completely intertwined. In Roman education, the first century before Christ saw a shift to a systematic rhetorical program of (like the Greeks) male education. Quintilian, a master teacher, published the most extensive description of this system in 95 C.E. (see Kennedy, 1980).

Quintilian, who summarized the Greek and Roman arts of rhetoric, believed emotional appeals to be perhaps the most powerful arguments to sway an audience. Visualization is the key to the most powerful means of arousing emotion. "A powerful effect may be created if to the actual facts of the [legal] case we add a plausible picture of what occurred, such as will make our audience feel as if they were actual eyewitnesses to the scene," he explained (1921, p. 117).

Tracing the experience back to the Greeks, he discussed daydreamlike visions, hallucinations, in which absent experiences are revived in the imagination, a phenomenon common to all. He cited Cicero on the use of this as a rhetorical art. This involves not only a translation from visual scenes to verbal, but also a transformation to visual body language as the orator becomes actor moving the audience with physical depictions of the emotion his words attempt to arouse:

> [For,] if we wish to give our words the appearance of sincerity, we must assimilate ourselves to the emotions of those who are genuinely so affected, and our eloquence must spring from the same feeling that we desire to produce in the mind of the judge. Will he grieve who can find no trace of grief in the words with which I seek to move him to grief? Will he be angry, if the orator who seeks to kindle his anger shows no sign of labouring under the motion which he demands from his audience? Will he shed tears if the pleader's eyes are dry? It is utterly impossible. (Quintilian, 1921, p. 433)

The words are never separate from the performance of them in the rhetorical arts. Quintilian (1921) believed this power of vivid imagination is natural and can be cultivated, although some are more sensitive and can produce emotion to great persuasive effect. The method is "not so much to narrate as to exhibit the actual scene, while our emotions will be no less actively stirred than if we were present at the actual occurrence" (pp. 436–437). We must cultivate this power of daydreaming and also identify ourselves with those for whom we are pleading, to "for a brief space feel their suffering as though it were our own, while our words must be such as we should use if we stood in their shoes" (p. 437). Quintilian advised that a student declaiming in school "be moved by his theme, and should imagine it to be true" when "impersonating an orphan, a shipwrecked man, or one in grave peril. What profit is there in assuming such a role unless we also assume the emotions which it involves?" (p. 439).

In addition to the words and images, Greco-Roman judicial cases (as do ours today—remember O.J.'s glove?) made heavy use of actual visual presentations—the showing of a scar, a wound, a bloody weapon, or a toga. The audience's senses were all called on in this oratorical culture, rather than being fragmented and addressed in a single focus, the pictorial eye for seeing art, the ear for hearing music, the eye and intellect for reading, the nose for food and perfume.

Although the parts of Quintilian's educational system were Greek, the systematization was Roman. Roman education also emphasized a set of graded composition exercises called the *progymnasmata,* not treated in detail by Quintilian. These exercises, which began with the retelling of fables (such as Aesop's) and other tales, worked up to declamation of fictitious speeches (see Friend, 1999).

An advanced exercise was description as a self-contained unit that could be dropped into place in a discourse *(ecphrasis).* Quintilian (1921) discussed this in Book VIII as *enargeia* or vivid illustration. Of course, during this time of systematization, Roman education became based on translation and transliteration. These exercises in particular depended on translation of the Greek poets and writers and subsequent paraphrase or other transformation of those texts by students. For example, students would read a fable, for instance, as in Theon, "the fable of the dog and his reflection," and, as historian of Roman education Bonner (1977) explained, would subsequently paraphrase it or transform it in other ways:

> [C]arrying a piece of meat, the dog was walking beside a river, when he thought he saw another dog beside him, also carrying a piece of meat; the temptation was too great, and in attempting to acquire two pieces of meat, he lost what he had, or in Theon's version, was drowned. Here was an opportunity to describe the placid stream, the brightness of a sunny day, and the clarity of reflection in the water. All this encouraged the young to use their imaginations and at the same time developed their powers of expression. (p. 255)

Bonner also told us that poetry and history provided a broader scope for description than rhetoric, especially in the declamations in which descriptions became a stock theme. These later influenced the taste for what Horace called *purple patches* and were linked with transformations of Virgil and Ovid.

MEDIEVAL AND RENAISSANCE IMAGES

In his book on literature in the Latin Middle Ages, Curtius (1973) told how *ecphrasis,* popular in late antiquity under the Roman empire, became important in medieval times. The genre of rhetoric called *epideictic*—ceremonial speeches of praise and blame—became more important than deliberative, legislative rhetoric under tyrannical Roman emperors who were often praised. Thus, the Latin curriculum abounded in elaborate delineation of people, places, monuments and buildings, as well as sculpture and painting. From this great archive of descriptions, French writers later developed the romance, whose interest in nature and its creations created a cliche based on word–picture translation: "Nature created a beautiful being as a picture" (Curtius, 1973, pp. 181–182). Descriptions of beautiful men and women in courtly poetry were turned out in accordance with *recipes,* as Curtius wrote.

Landscape description was always important, but became especially so after Virgil had transformed Greek poetry in his Arcadian eclogues. The emphasis on pastoral landscape grew out of the epideictic praise of landscape and the rhetorical topics of *place* and *time.* For example, this pastoral description of Arcadia is filled with description of pleasurable topography *(topoi)* such as springs, hills, and animals:

> Springs bubble out, brook joined with brook runs streaming,
> Already gorge and slope and mead are green.

Where the plain heaves into a hundred hillocks,
The woolly sheep in scattered flocks are seen.

Beyond, with step as careful as 's certain,
The horn-browed herds toward the cliffside graze;
There could they shelter every one, for there
The stone is hollowed in a hundred caves.

There Pan protects, there vivifying nymphs
Dwell in the dripping, green-clad crevices—
And there aspire to higher airs forever
The intertangled ranks of branchy trees. (Curtius, 1973, p. 188)

Yet landscape descriptions in genres such as the medieval epic linked with pastoral poetry were soon challenged by the courtly romance, which appears in about 1150. Atmospheric scenery—in particular, the wild forest of chivalric romance–called forth new efforts in the classical *topos* of "situation" or "description of a place" (Curtius, 1973).

Notions of image and place were central in another medieval art drawn from rhetoric—the art of memory. Yates (1966) first elaborated on this art, pointing out that ancient memory systems were based on the principle that memory could be strengthened by linking it to the emotions through striking images. Architectural "places" in particular became imaginary sites for storing images to remind one of facts or, harder yet, the words of a poem or speech. This is the source of our locution, "in the first place."

This art of memory, first described in the pedagogical text *Ad Herennium* (long mistakenly attributed to Cicero), was a standard part of ancient rhetoric. The Sophists may have invented memory arts, and these were easily linked to the occult because they could produce such amazing feats of memory. Plato objected to artificial memory arts, but based his philosophy on vision and memory—knowledge became a remembering of archetypal forms visually glimpsed in the realm before birth and innately present in human minds. Overall, in the medieval period, memory arts from classical texts were progressively complicated and made into elaborate puzzles or games. These elaborate, visually based memory arts in the Renaissance became linked with Platonism; for example, Camillo's Memory Theatre tried to organize memory according to universal archetypes of reality, not trivial memory of speeches and facts. This helped incorporate classical arts of memory into the Hermetic–Cabalist tradition (see Calendrillo, 1995–1996).

In the Renaissance, memory arts became marginalized as they linked with occult thought, although they still had a place in pedagogy. The images produced by the memory systems were more likely to be expressed in print in illustrated emblem books. Here one can see images from classical fables and myths as well as spiritual or pedagogical reminders. The familiar assignment to tell a story from a picture is one that links us closely to writing teachers from the earliest times. More often, however, the process was reversed—illustrations and actual images (e.g., in emblem books)—were fashioned from oral and textual descriptions. For example, an early textbook on the liberal arts, the 3rd- to 4th-century allegory of *The Marriage of Philology and Mercury* by Capella, spawned many popular emblems (see Moseley, 1989). In the book, seven elaborately described bridesmaids give summaries of their liberal arts to the guests at the wedding. This book also spurred early scientific illustration, such as drawings of the textually described motion of Venus and Mercury centered on the sun—a motion Copernicus cited 1,100 years later to support his own system.

Emblem books were used for entertainment, education, spiritual instruction, and memory aids. Words and pictures worked together as equals in many of these books, although they center on the elaborate narrative-bearing emblems. Many editions of Ripa's *Iconologia* (1611/1976) appeared or were imitated on the Continent or in Britain in the 16th and 17th centuries. Ripa included the goddess Eloquence, helmeted and in armor, holding thunderbolts in her right hand and a book in her left. A word picture follows—an explanation that the end of eloquence is persuasion and that her arts, youth, and beauty contribute to that end.

Bacon's (1970) texts are a significant site on which to examine the various threads of imagery from memory arts to textual imagery because they come together to reveal a fault line—a point of slippage in how images and texts were transforming. Bacon, who knew and used arts of memory well, wanted to reform the art so it would better function for investigation or for ordering and classifying knowledge. Subverting the distinction and calling images *emblems,* he fully accepted the principle that images were more memorable than words:

> Emblems bring down intellectual to sensible things; for what is sensible always strikes the memory stronger, and sooner impresses itself than the intellectual . . . And therefore it is easier to retain the image of a sportsman hunting the hare, of an apothecary ranging his boxes, an orator making a speech, a boy repeating verses, or a player acting his part, than the corresponding notions of invention, disposition, elocution, memory, action. (cited in Yates, 1966, p. 371)

Bacon (1970) also relied on a system of faculties for the mind, originally from Plato's division of the mind and body into the reason (head), the passions (heart), and the appetites (liver). Bacon's faculties include: (a) understanding and reason; (b) the will, appetite, and affection; and (c) the imagination, which gets messages from the sense and reason and shuttles them as a messenger among faculties. Because of his emphasis on sense imagery and the central role of the imagination, his definition and goals for rhetoric shift: Rhetoric's end becomes to "fill the imagination with observations and images, to second reason, and not to oppress it" (Book IV, p. 456). Rhetoric for Bacon is visually insinuative; thus, he wrote of "coloring" an argument, piling together illustrations and observations that support a chosen aspect of the subject under consideration (Book VII, p. 77). His definition of *rhetoric* sets up a cognitive chain depending on imagery: "Rhetoric is subservient to the imagination as Logic is to the understanding; and the Duty and Office of Rhetoric, if it be deeply looked into, is no other than to apply and recommend the dictates of reason to imagination in order to excite the appetite and will" (Book IV, p. 455).

I focus on this shift because it is so key to the 17th and 18th centuries and their theories of rhetoric. The faculty of imagination, intertwined with memory, becomes central to the very definition of rhetoric, which carries with it a cognitive model. It forms the background of discoveries in vision and optics and is linked with the notion that we gain knowledge through observation. This centrality of vision and imagination is breathed in with the very air that formed the period its shapers called The Enlightenment.

Yet these themes of vision and imagination were transformations of the Renaissance preoccupation with emblems and pictorial representations. Vico (1668–1744) was on the cusp of the Enlightenment, but drew his intellectual energy from his forebears in the Renaissance. He named Bacon as one of his four major influences. Platonic in his orientation to vision and knowledge, Vico (1744/1984) believed that divine knowledge was like a sculpture, whereas human knowledge was flat like a picture. He traced the development of human culture from the image and imagination to rationality and the philosophical concept. A key turning point in his history—perhaps the beginning of a decline—is when the pictorial emblem failed to communicate to the culture as a whole and needed a written motto of explanation. Language originated with visuals—real things used as signs or visual gestures—a frog to signal place in the earth, a mouse to mean fertility, a sword to threaten violence. The very motive of language began when the beasts in the field after the flood heard a crash of thunder and *looked up* at what they took to be the thundering belly of Jove. Language, institutions such as religion and law, and society began with that act of fear and wonder involving vision (but also sound). Thus, language was metaphoric, imagistic, and poetic from its inception. Myths and fables with their magnificent images and figures were nothing more or less than true history.

Language for Vico traversed three stages—that of the gods, that of heroes, and finally that of men before decaying into barbarism, which returned humans to the age of gods. The languages of the first two stages were imaginative and full of symbolic imagery. In the age of heroes, thought was based on the imaginative universal (e.g., Ulysses, a figure who stood for a concept) (Verene, 1981). Each nation had its Ulysses, its heroic founder figure. The heroic age was the age of visuals, blazonry, crests, shields, images, rebus figures, and human symbols, such as Homer, a metaphor for collective poetry rather than a unique human being. With this elevation of symbolic language came the reverence for acute and witty sayings, language that could strike quickly and emulate the all-at-onceness of an instantaneous picture—what Vico (1996) called *sublime rhetoric* in his rhetoric manuals. That trend grew from the Renaissance into the eloquent salon language of the French Enlightenment and the wit and erudition of the English coffeehouses of the 18th century.

OCULARISM IN THE ENLIGHTENMENT

Vico sent an early version of his masterwork *New Science* based on his historical cultural cycle to Isaac Newton, but it is not known whether Newton ever received the book (see Dobbs & Jacob, 1995). Newton (1643–1727) is the figure most people think of when they think of the Enlightenment and the beginnings of modern science as well as the modern study of color and light. As Pope (1954) wrote in an epitaph intended for Newton:

> Nature and Nature's Laws lay hid in Night,
> God said, "*Let Newton be!*" and All was Light. (p. 317)

In 1666, when Newton started thinking about color and light, theories from Descartes described light as a pressure on the eyeball of the aether that filled the universe. Newton rejected this, working with a notion of light as a particle, thus having velocity. Hooke's *Micrographia* (1665), which was a collection of illustrations made under the microscope, at that time discussed color as pulses of light. Newton used a prism to determine that white light was a mixture of various colors that were refracted in different angles. This was not published until 1704, but was wildly popular. Later, the Italian professor, Bassi, who in the mid-18th century was the first woman to be offered an official university teaching position in Europe, taught the *Opticks* at Bologna (Dobbs & Jacob, 1995). Light became a key concept across fields; for example, architects tried to open up buildings to reveal the light of Newton's *Opticks*. Investigations into light and vision of all sorts multiplied in the Enlightenment period.

That "construction is the essence of vision" has long been known, Hoffman (1998) argued. The notion first appeared in Ptolemy in the 2nd century A.D., who wrote an *Optics*. Aristotle, Euclid, and Ptolemy all wrote on light and vision. The Islamic scholar Alhazen (Ibn al-Haytham, ca. 965–ca. 1040) wrote on the constructed nature of vision in his seven-volume *Optics.* His work, which refuted weaker Greek theories and synthesized stronger ones, was translated into Latin in the late 12th and early 13th centuries and became influential in vision theory (see Lindberg, 1992). Others mastered both the Greek and Islamic vision theory. The inferences from vision seemed so instantaneous that Malebranche (1638–1715) believed that God produces them (Hoffman, 1998). Molyneux (d. 1698) published the first English text on optics, *Dioptrika Nova,* and asked the famous question Locke repeated in his *Essay*: How would a man born blind see if he were suddenly given his sight? Would he recognize on sight the shapes he had heretofore felt? Many speculated on the answer, but Cheselden (1688–1752), the famous physician who cared for Newton in his last illness, published a famous case that began to answer the question. Having performed cataract surgery on a young man born blind, he discovered that the man had to learn to interpret what he saw at first only as colored patches. Berkeley (1685–1753) wrote about the ambiguity of vision and the need for interpretation. As the Cheselden case confirmed, he predicted that one born blind could not recognize shapes. The French encyclopedists led the Continental interest in vision, especially Locke's admirer Condillac and the better known Diderot, who wrote controversial treatises on the blind and deaf, which also argued that we actively construct what we see.

How does seeing work? Early thinkers based their new theories of vision on what they already knew—aesthetic theories of the imagination and natural philosophies like those of Epicurus. In 1604, Johannes Kepler had a theory of the retinal image that used the analogy of a camera—but the Kodak was as then unknown. However, philosophers played with the new pinpoint camera, like the ones we played with as children, which projected an image upside down. This was an exciting development, and they explained it by referring to the mind's eye and the imagination. The camera obscura image was found in Locke's *Essay* (1699–1705) as an explanation of how the mind took in images. The Greek atomists had a longstanding explanation that became deeply intertwined with rhetoric and the teaching of writing.

Kroll's (1991) history of language revisited the 17th century with its return to classical notions of the Epicureans and their visual theories of the image. During the Scientific Revolution, there was a "neo-Epicurean revival" centering on Lucretius' (1946) *De Rerum Natura (On the Nature of Things).* This amazing classical poem, which dramatically and abruptly ended in midstream just as the author visually described the sweep of the plague through Athens, was a staple of the educational canon and had particularly captured the imagination of Renaissance readers. Written in the 1st century before Christ, it is a verse explication for the Roman world of the Greek system of philosophy. It was popular in the early modern period despite its antireligious outlook based on a rationalist Epicurean theory of nature, optics, and vision.

Later blended with faculty psychology as in Bacon's rhetoric, Epicurean theory suggested that using language to present images to the intellect through the imagination *(phantasia)* is the way to arouse the passions and motivate the will. This is based on the theory of optics in the philosophy of Epicurus, as interpreted through Lucretius' poem: The atomic and dynamic constitution of bodies causes them continually to throw off microscopically thin representations of themselves *(eidola),* which almost instantaneously strike the eye or another sense organ, producing a presentation *(phantasia).* The mind can then take hold of the image by an act *(epibole).* Thus, the entire basis of Epicurus' mental economy presumes the mediating function of the *phantasia* as well as an active construction (Kroll, 1991).

Although the images that we see are true in that they exist, they are not presumed to match the actual nature of things. In the Lucretian version of Epicurean philosophy, mental images are in cognition the equivalent of the atom or minima in physics. They result from the things of the world's continual throwing off of images that strike our minds whether we are asleep or awake. This was called the *intromission theory,* in opposition to Plato's notion that the eyes shoot out rays to see—called the *extromission theory.* The intromission theory came to dominate in early modern science.

Epicureans believed that, in fact, the mind cannot think without images or ideas (significantly, the Greek word for "to see"). Images, the atoms of thought, were combined to make thoughts the way notes make up music or the alphabet makes up language. Lucretius' analogy between atoms and letters of the alphabet found its way into nearly every major consideration of natural science at the turn of the 17th-century, found in Bacon and Boyle and extended to rhetorical topics in Vico's use of topics in scientific inquiries. This image is a familiar one in Gassendi, an atomist whose language theory is Epicurean. For Gassendi, words are *ostensive* (Kroll, 1991), analogically pointing to things. Utterances partake of symbolic action, pointing to the cognitive image. Locke's language theory, in touch with Boyle, resonates with the spirit if not the letter of Epicurean thought, as he was steeped in French thought, especially Gassendi. In Locke's *Essay,* the notion of "idea" is central, which fed into the growing interest in the faculty of imagination. Locke's popular abbreviated logic and his educational advice for the son of a friend helped put these ideas into the mainstream of pedagogy.

In part, a return to Augustine (Kroll, 1991) was at the heart of this new emphasis on imagination, converging with notions of the Epicurean image. According to an Augustinian Biblical view, humans once were spiritual creatures, but since the Fall, they must live a predominantly physical existence. The imagination, the faculty of storing and reviving images, was often thought of as the intermediary between humans' physical and spiritual natures, between the senses and pure thought. It was, significantly, the faculty of representation. The centrality of the imagination as intermediary was held by many throughout the century, and it became key to rhetorical persuasion. It also became central to the rhetorical description, which is of so much value in the modern novel. As such, description became a key pedagogical tool in early modern writing instruction, which more and more exemplified French belles lettres rather than the classical rhetorical canon.

DESCRIPTION IN MODERNITY

During the 18th century, when it became clear that print and writing and associated book literacy were spreading, teachers worked to understand and teach how to translate visual scenes and images into text. One such teacher was a self-proclaimed follower of Locke, the French philosopher Condillac (1714–1799). His work influenced the Scottish Enlightenment rhetoricians, especially Smith, Blair, and Campbell. For many years, Condillac was tutor to the young Prince of Parma and associate of the French encyclopedist Diderot and Rousseau. In his pedagogy, Condillac liked to place his pupil before a window with shutters that were opened to give a brief view of the landscape. As Aarsleff (1982) summarized:

> In remembering and talking about this landscape, the young man was forced to analyze the instantaneous unitary tableau into elements he recalled as single units—trees, shrubbery, bushes, fences, groves, and the like. He was forced to think sequentially because discourse is linear. (p. 30)

Condillac explained the differences between the visual and verbal in this way: The visual world is holistic and is seen instantaneously as a picture. Verbal language is linear, occurring sequentially in units over time. Language decomposes holistic reality, allowing writers to convey what is really seen out there in the world into the mind, where we can once again recompose it to represent the holistic world. It also analyzes that reality by breaking it into bits. For Condillac and others in French belles lettres, the most expressive text is one that tries to re-create this all at onceness—this powerful tableau effect of prelinguistic, visual thought. This is because it hearkens back to the original language of gesture, a bodily visual art that was the first human communication. Gesture and body language were the first systems of human communication and analyzed or broke apart the holistic idea. Language, both gestural and verbal, were formed on the basis of analogy to earlier signs in a process of translation. Thus, the keys to the later process of translation from visual imagery to written text were memory and imagination, closely linked. They allowed the language user to recall and visualize past sights and experiences and link them to signs. This theory presumes a split between analytical and expressive language—a split that helps enact a separation of scientific from poetic text in the future. Like Vico's theories, the earliest language was more expressively poetic and imagistic, whereas language became more analytical, abstract, and philosophical over time.

Later in the 18th century, about the time of the American Declaration of Independence, French theory hybridized with earlier British thought in Scotland to produce what was called the *new rhetoric* of the Scottish Enlightenment. Key figures are the economist Smith, Blair (the first professor of English), Lord Kames, and Campbell (see Miller, 1997). The Baconian shift to make imagery and imagination central was apparent in the work of all these figures. To illustrate, we can examine Campbell's discussion of the ends of rhetoric as "to enlighten the understanding, to please the imagination, to move the passions, or to influence the will" (Golden & Corbett, 1968, p. 145). This was a classification system, but also an ascending progression: The intellect feeds the "fancy" or imagination, the fancy transforms and presents materials to affect the passions, then the passions spur the will to act (p. 146). Thereby, the imagination becomes the hinge, catalyst, or fulcrum for persuasion. For Campbell, the imagination is linked to painting:

> The imagination is addressed by exhibiting to it a lively and beautiful representation of a suitable object. As in this exhibition, the task of the oratory, in some sort, be said, like that of the painter, to consist in imitation, the merit of the work results entirely from these two sources; dignity, as well in the subject or thing imitated, as in the manner of imitation; and resemblance, in the portrait or performance. (p. 146)

Campbell linked the most perfect discourse to the sublime—"those great and noble images, which, when in suitable colouring presented to the mind, do, as it were, distend the imagination with some vast conception, and quite ravish the soul" (pp. 146–147).

Rhetoricians concerned with style and those building their rhetorics around models of texts also turned to the late Greek rhetorician pseudo-Longinus, whose *On the Sublime* was translated by into French by Boileau-Despreaux in the 17th century. These stylistic rhetorics also formed the backbone of the Continental belles lettres movement transformed by Scots such as Campbell over the century (see Howell's [1971] classifications).

The interest in vision and imagination formed the heart of the Enlightenment belles lettres movement, with its paradigm shift in language arts pedagogy to an aesthetics of taste (see Miller, 1997). This ultimately spread from France to Britain and, from both those countries, quite naturally to the United States. Belles lettres included written forms such as history, essays, and poetry, but also such visual arts as architecture and landscape gardening. The goal of *sublime rhetoric* (Vico's term) was often not to persuade as much as to transport an audience, and word painting of nature was a key method used. As a result, in British and American composition, textual description became an even more important mode, especially descriptions of landscapes. These were inevitably tied to moral values and were a continuation of the kind of oratory practiced at public ceremonials from classical times, epideictic rhetoric.

The development of the novel in the 18th century made use of these traditions of landscape description, as we can see in Austen's descriptions in *Pride and Prejudice* (1993) and again in *Emma* (2000). In the first book, when Elizabeth visits Darcy's Pemberley, Austen sets the reflective mode appropriate not only for landscape, but for consideration of values: "They gradually ascended for half a mile, and then found themselves at the top of a considerable eminence, where the wood ceased, and the eye was instantly caught by Pemberley House, situated on the opposite side of a valley into which the road with such abruptness wound" (p. 156). The passage not only reveals the imbrication of landscape design with its contrived views and picturesque writing, but also provides a tone that suits Elizabeth's full state of mind on entering the estate of the man whose hand she had rejected. Descriptions of Pemberley's buildings and grounds not only create a reflective tone, but also help support the ideals of reason, solidity, unity, and permanence of the structure: "It was a large, handsome, stone building, standing well on rising ground, and backed by a ridge of high woody hills; and in front, a stream of some natural importance was swelled into greater, but without any artificial appearance" (p. 156).

After describing Donwell Abbey and environs in a similar style in *Emma*, Austen revealed Emma's feelings on looking down on Abbey-Mill Farm, "with meadows in front, and the river making a close and handsome curve around it" (p. 236), all suffused with patriotic values and sentiments: "It was a sweet view—sweet to the eye and the mind. English verdure, English culture, English comfort, seen under a sun bright, without being Oppressive" (p. 236). The three-part (tricolon) structure harmoniously and reasonably emphasized the values Austen wanted to forward.

Although my analysis stops with the long 18th century in Great Britain, Clark and Halloran (1993) wrote about how such picturesque discourse in 19th-century American writing was a transformation of classical epideictic discourse, carrying the values of Romanticism and also its class hierarchy. In landscape description, harmonious composition makes the writing seem like a painting or actual landscape, but the language also increases adherence to certain values, Halloran explained, similar to what we see in the Austen passages. Such descriptive writing abounds in Emerson, Thoreau, Whittier, Longfellow, and J. Fenimore Cooper, helping form a sense of American identity. An overflow of "mass produced prints and boilerplate prose" poured over the nation as a result of this movement, and books such as *Picturesque America* (1874) combining engravings and essays became popular (Clark & Halloran, 1993, p. 245).

One significant element not examined in this chapter is the effect of technological advances on rendering visual images on writing. Yet it is clear that the invention of mechanical print—the book—and improvements such as the high-speed press in the 19th century all shaped the uses of graphics and affected how students were taught to write or interact with pictures in print. Although there were perhaps fewer pictures and graphic elements when they were more difficult and expensive to print, pictures, engravings, and even simple line drawings have always been cherished by readers to relieve the difficulty of reading.

Written language was always a chief way of translating the visual world. Yet in the 18th century, more and more literature in the vernacular was produced, and education began to shift to the vernacular. Translation as a central educational activity began a slow decline. That century saw the first literary criticism of literature in English and the appointment of the first professor of English literature in Scotland. In another shift involving the Scientific Revolution, some saw written language as a representation of the world rather than a translation into a different system of signs or a transformation of symbols serving as an interface to a mysterious reality. Thus, they feared metaphor and other rhetorical devices as distortions of the objective representation of a visual reality. They insisted on "clear and distinct" prose that would carry the writer's vision of reality into the reader's mental structure. This notion of prose as clear as a window that would allow a primarily visual reality to be seen became a dominant strand of writing instruction. It led to pedagogies encouraging good observational skills and clarity in style and structure. The scientific urge also led to the movement to classify and describe types of writing as if writing were a form of natural history.

This urge to taxonomize led to the pedagogy based on the "Four Horsemen," widely deplored when I was in graduate school, but tenaciously hanging on since. That form-based pedagogy evolved to present students with writing centered not on aims, but on genres or forms of exposition, argument, narrative, and, most important for this analysis, description. This pedagogy has been traced to figures like the 19th-century Scottish Bain's response to both the discourse of scientific classification, clarity, and belles lettres. The hybridizing of the old belles lettres theories with the newer scientific models produced the first modern rhetorics. Those first Scottish rhetorics were also part of the transformation that led to modern English literary studies (see Miller, 1997, for this history in detail).

How to understand and teach language and literature in an age of technical transformation that renews the age-old interest in the image is a significant issue that connects us to these rhetorical predecessors. We might also wonder how transformations currently taking place will change the current English studies model. We may not know how, but we can surmise that English studies in the new century will offer a very different product from traditional 20th-century print pedagogy (see Stroupe, 2000). The more we learn about both those elements, the more prepared we will be to teach our students how to make better meaning and communicate in the new era. The tension between graphic elements and text may not go away, but it can be a more creative and *interinanimating* tension if we know how to translate between modes (Richards, p. 47). We can do no better than emulate the Renaissance's da Vinci, who saw so much and wrote so well he could carelessly confuse the one with the other in his prolific notebooks during the Renaissance of learning. We might cajole our students as he prompted himself:

> Write [he reminded himself, for to him writing and drawing are all one], write the tongue of the woodpecker and the jaw of the crocodile. Write the flight of the fourth kind of chewing butterflies, and of the flying ants, and the three chief positions of the wings of birds in descent. . . . Write of the regions of the air and the formation of clouds, and the cause of snow and hail, and of the new shapes that snow forms in the air, and of the trees in cold countries with the new shape of the leaves. . . . Write whether the percussion made by water upon its object is equal in power to the whole mass of water supposed suspended in the air or no. (cited in de Santillana, 1956, pp. 67–70)

Such sublime vision as Leonardo's presents us with the gift of a moment in which scientific terminology and poetry are one and neither word nor image is valued as more sacred. If they once were divorced by print culture, the remarriage of word and image performed by digital technology signals the rebirth of literacy in the 21st century, a hybrid literacy in which we all may hope to share more of the potential of Leonardo.

REFERENCES

Aarsleff, H. (1982). *From Locke to Saussure: Essays on the study of language and intellectual history.* Minneapolis: University of Minnesota Press.

Austen, J. (1993). *Pride and prejudice* (D. Gray, Ed.). New York: Norton.

Austen, J. (2000). *Emma* (S. M. Parrish, Ed.). New York: Norton.

Bacon, F. (1970). *The philosophical works of Francis Bacon* (Reprinted from J. Spedding, R. L. Ellis, & J. M. Robertson, Eds.). Freeport, NY: Books for Libraries.

Bonner, S. F. (1977). *Education in ancient Rome: From the elder Cato to the younger Pliny*. Berkeley: University of California Press.

Calendrillo, L. (1995–1996). Mental imagery, psychology, and rhetoric: An examination of recurring problems. *JAEPL: The Journal of the Assembly for Expanded Perspectives on Learning, 3,* 74–79.

Clark, G., & Halloran, S. M. (1993). *Oratorical culture in nineteenth-century America: Transformations in the theory and practice of rhetoric*. Carbondale: Southern Illinois University Press.

Curtius, E. R. (1973). *European literature and the Latin middle ages* (W. R. Trask, Trans.) Princeton, NJ: Princeton/Bollingen Books.

de Santillana, G. (1956). *The age of adventure: The Renaissance philosophers*. New York: Mentor Books.

Dobbs, B. J. T., & Jacob, M. C. (1995). *Newton and the culture of Newtonianism*. Atlantic Highlands, NJ: Humanities Press.

Faigley, L. (1999). Material literacy and visual design. In J. Selzer & S. Crowley (Eds.), *Rhetorical bodies* (pp. 171–201). Madison: University of Wisconsin Press.

Friend, C. (1999). Pirates, seducers, wronged heirs, poison cups, cruel husbands, and other calamities: The Roman school declamations and critical pedagogy. *Rhetoric Review, 17,* 300–319.

Golden, J. L., & Corbett, E. P. J. (1968). *The rhetoric of Blair, Campbell, and Whately*. New York: Holt.

Hoffman, D. D. (1998). *Visual intelligence: How we create what we see*. New York: Norton.

Hooke, R. *Micrographia, or Some physiological descriptions of minute bodies made by magnifying glasses with observations and inquiries thereupon*. London: Printed for James Allestry, 1667.

Howell, W. S. (1971). *Eighteenth-century British logic and rhetoric*. Princeton, NJ: Princeton University Press.

Kennedy, G. A. (1980). *Classical rhetoric and its Christian and secular tradition from ancient to modern times*. Chapel Hill: University of North Carolina Press.

Kroll, R. W. (1991). *The material word: Literate culture in the Restoration and early eighteenth century*. Baltimore: Johns Hopkins University Press.

Landow, G. (1992). *Hypertext: The convergence of contemporary critical theory and technology*. Baltimore: Johns Hopkins University Press.

Lanham, R. A. (1991). *A handlist of rhetorical terms* (2nd ed.). Berkeley: University of California Press.

Lindberg, D. C. (1992). *The beginnings of Western science: The European scientific tradition in philosophical, religious, and institutional context, 600 B.C. to A.D. 1450*. Chicago: University of Chicago Press.

Lucretius. (1946). *On the nature of things* (C. E. Bennett, Trans.). Roslyn, NY: Walter J. Black.

Miller, T. P. (1997). *The formation of college English: Rhetoric and belles lettres in the British cultural provinces*. Pittsburgh, PA: University of Pittsburgh Press.

Mitchell, W. J. T. (1986). *Iconology: Image, text, ideology*. Chicago: University of Chicago Press.

Mitchell, W. J. T. (1994). *Picture theory: Essays on verbal and visual representation*. Chicago: University of Chicago Press.

Moseley, C. (1989). *A century of emblems: An introductory anthology*. Hants, England: Scolar Press.

Pope, A. (1954). *The Twickenham edition of the poems of Alexander Pope* (N. Ault, completed by J. Batt, Eds.). London: Methuen.

Quintilian. (1921). *The institutio oratoria of Quintilian II* (H. E. Butler, Trans.). Cambridge, MA: Harvard University Press.

Richards, I. A. (1936). *The philosophy of rhetoric*. New York: Oxford University Press.

Ripa, C. (1976). *Iconologia*. New York: Garland. (Original work published 1611)

Stroupe, C. (2000). Visualizing English: Recognizing the hybrid literacy of visual and verbal authorship on the Web. *College English, 62,* 607–632.

Verene, D. P. (1981). *Vico's science of imagination.* Ithaca: Cornell.

Verene, D. P. (1991). *The new art of autobiography: An essay on the* Life of Giambattista Vico Written by Himself. Oxford: Clarendon.

Vico, G. (1984). *The new science of Giambattista Vico* (T. G. Bergin & M. H. Fisch, Trans., abridged from 3rd ed.). Ithaca, NY: Cornell University Press. (Original work published 1744)

Vico, G. (1996). *The art of rhetoric (Institutiones Oratoriae, 1711–1741)* (G. A. Pinton & A. W. Shippee, Trans. & Eds.). Amsterdam: Rodopi.

Welch, K. E. (1990). Writing instruction in ancient Athens after 450 B.C. In J. J. Murphy (Ed.), *A short history of writing instruction: From ancient Greece to twentieth-century America* (pp. 1–18). Davis, CA: Hermagoras.

Welch, K. E. (1999). *Electric rhetoric: Classical rhetoric oralism, and a new literacy*. Cambridge, MA: MIT Press.

Yates, F. (1966). *The art of memory*. Chicago: University of Chicago Press.

II

MENTAL VISION

3

Mental Imagery and Literature: Centers and Vectors in Students' Visual and Verbal Responses

Terri Pullen Guezzar
American InterContinental University

> *Some revolutions occur quietly: no manifestoes, no marching and singing, no tumult in the streets; simply a shift in perspective, a new way of seeing what had always been there. New words enter the vocabulary, old words suddenly take on new meaning. Or they retain their meaning but their* position *changes: the peripheral becomes the central, the walk-on becomes the hero of the play.*
>
> —Suleiman (1980, p. 1)

Increasingly, educators demonstrate an awareness of visual studies and its potential for learning, marking the migration of a peripheral consideration toward a center: "The growth of scholarly interest in visuality marks a cultural reality: that images have become a predominant means of transmitting information in the 20th century and may be even more so in the 21st" (Heller, 1996, p. A8). This statement implies that our awareness of how important the visual has emerged in tandem with our advancing ability to encode and display images. However, certain theorists such as Rudolf Arnheim and W. J. T. Mitchell might characterize this shift as our finally recognizing divisive practices between visual and verbal modes in both theory and application. Mitchell (1994) describes the dichotomy between the image and word as representing underlying sociocultural power issues that are "linked to things like the difference between the (speaking) self and the (seen) other; between telling and showing; between 'hearsay' and 'eyewitness' testimony; between words (heard, quoted, inscribed) and objects or actions (seen, depicted, described); between sensory channels, traditions of representation, and modes of experience" (p. 5). Text culture resists the influx of a visual culture, fearing displacement in a media-oriented, image-driven world. To exert a degree of control, text styles of interpretation are often superimposed on discussions of imagery (Mitchell, 1986). The language used to describe images frequently carries a word-based agenda, thus giving us no way to describe the dynamic qualities inherent in visual thinking and mental imagery or in their external representations. Even the very word *language* implies a verbal system of symbols and not something pictorial or sensory in nature (Mitchell, 1986). Thus, any aspect of visual thinking and mental imagery must be accounted for through language-based frames in order to enjoy legitimacy; that is, the visual must operate according to the principles of *language*, although visuality is characteristically nonverbal.

Arnheim (1969) maintained that all perceptual activities suffer a "widespread unemployment of the senses in every field of academic study" (p. 3). Often relegated to second-class status as less reliable than the so-called *higher functions* of intellect, the senses are actually an integral part of concept formation: "Cognitive operations called thinking are not the privilege of mental processes above and beyond perception but the essential ingredients of perception itself" (Arnheim, 1969, p. 13). More recently, this stratification is characterized by what is cognitively penetrable, preserving the distinction Arnheim found so objectionable. For example, Pylyshyn (1999) separated perception in early vision from later cognitive intervention: "The early vision is encapsulated from cognition. It is cognitively impenetrable. Since vision as a whole is cognitively penetrable, this leaves open the question of where the cognitive penetration occurs" (p. 347). Arnheim (1969) argued that no such distinction occurs: "Visual perception is visual thinking" (p. 13).

Discussion of images and mental imagery frequently oscillates between internal mental imagery and external visual representations. Arnheim typically addressed both dynamics, whereas Mitchell focused primarily on the image as an external artifact. Cognitive science research focuses on internal imagery in three primary areas: picture or quasipictorial theory, description theory, and perceptual activity or situation cognition (Thomas, 1999). Picture theory suggests that we hold visual impressions in the mind that exist as copies or residual impressions from perceptual experiences (Thomas, 1999), whereas quasipictorial theory indicates a surface image that acts as a visual buffer that leads to deeper cognitive representations. Description theory and research, led by Pylyshyn, asserts that underlying propositions describing the perceptual construct support mental imagery. Perceptual activity or situated cognition critiques computational models developed for artificial intelligence, claiming that these representations are "inadequate for modeling active organisms or agents such as humans" as researchers address the relationship between cognition and context" (Pylyshyn, 2000, p. 197). Regardless of the particulars, all discussions recognize the dynamic role of imagery.

Can we develop pedagogical practices that invite both the visual and verbal as active, vital aspects of student engagement and learning? Can we recognize the visual response as well as develop an interpretive frame that respects its nonverbal characteristics? Mitchell (1994) stated that such an action must involve

> the realization that *spectatorship* (the look, the gaze, the glance, the practices of observation, surveillance, and visual pleasure) may be as deep a problem as various forms of *reading* (decipherment, decoding, interpretation, etc.) and that visual experience or "visual literacy" might not be fully explicable on the model of textuality. (p. 16)

One might expand the practices of observation to include self-awareness of one's own ability to generate and express mental imagery. If we define imagery as the "quasi-perceptual experience that significantly resembles [perception] (in any sense mode), [occurring] in the absence of appropriate external stimuli for the relevant perception" (Thomas, 1999, p. 6), and if we can experience imagery as "constructed inventively or retrieved from memory" (Thomas, 1999, p. 6), it follows that we can also expand our cognitive self-awareness, including our abilities to construct and expand visual thinking. How can we extend our current classroom practices to include mental imagery with greater integrity?

As we see later, mental imagery occurs in response to texts, particularly literary narratives. Past oversights in current practices pose new opportunities to solicit and understand students' visual thinking. Specifically, experiential or phenomenological theories of reader response offer a means of doing so as they address the "nature of readers' engagement or experiences with texts—the ways in which readers identify with characters, visualize images, relate personal experiences to the text" (Beach, 1993, p. 8). Wolfgang Iser (1978) and Louise Rosenblatt (1937, 1978) noted the existence of readers' mental imagery in response to literature. Unfortunately, neither actively solicited any representations or descriptions. Iser (1978) asserted that "we can only picture things that are not there; the written part of the text gives us the knowledge, but it is the unwritten part that gives us the opportunity to picture things" (p. 283). We can debate Iser's distinction as to when images are present. However, Iser did recognize the reader's ability to generate imagery.

Rosenblatt (1937) discussed the perceptual basis of the constructive imagination drawn on as the reader re-creates the text in "an attempt to grasp completely all of the sensations and concepts through which the author seeks to convey the quality of his [her] sense of life" (p. 133), which includes moving past "mere verbalization [to] get the full impact of the sensuous, emotional as well as intellectual (by which we mean here the perception of abstract relationships or patterns) force of the word" (p. 131). The *force of the word* varies between efferent and aesthetic reading events (Rosenblatt, 1978). In an efferent or

> nonaesthetic reading task, the reader's attention is focused primarily on what will remain as the residue *after* the reading—the information to be acquired, the logical solution to a problem, the actions to be carried out" whereas in an aesthetic reading "the reader must decipher the images or concepts or assertions that the words point to. 'Listening to' himself [herself], he [she] synthesizes these elements into a meaningful structure. (Rosenblatt 1978, p. 24)

Arnheim (1996b) emphasized the visual aspect of readers' responses, associating imagery with literary texts because description and metaphor preserve the initial perceptual impact of the visual sense: "Words gain their meaning only through the past experience of the reader. There are those who visualize the person and places of a novel with photographic exactness" (p. 277). Allen Paivio (1971a), author of the dual-coding theory for visual-verbal learning, concluded that language involves both coding systems: "We can think in terms of words and their interrelations and these implicit verbal processes can mediate our language behavior. The other code is nonverbal and is presumably tied closely to the private experience that we call imagery" (p. 7). Many researchers erroneously seek to separate language and imagery functions as two distinct, unrelated symbolic systems. However, the "aroused meaning process evoked by a word or other symbol is an organismic reaction with affective, or motor (including verbal) or imaginal components, or all of these at once" (Paivio, 1971a, p. 10). Like Arnheim, Paivio (1971b) asserted that more concrete and descriptive words have a higher imagery value than more abstract terms: "Concreteness and imagery are so highly correlated that they can be takes as defining essentially the same variable" (p. 210). Specifically,

> the major implication of the imagery approach for language acquisition is that linguistic competence and linguistic performance may be initially dependent on a substrate of imagery. Language builds upon this foundation and remains interlocked with it, although it also develops a partly autonomous structure of its own. (Paivio, 1971a, p. 29)

Given the high-imagery potential of concretely descriptive texts, the literature-based composition classroom offers a productive environment to explore students' representations of mental imagery. Here we can recognize both the perceptual and intellectual forces at play: "All cognitive exploration must rely on organized structures derived from sensory raw material. Both means [the perceptual and intellectual], the resources of direct experience and the instruments of concepts, are needed" (Arnheim, 1996a, p. 13).

So how do we expand our awareness of mental imagery and explore its role through pictorial representations in our classrooms? How do we do so without making the mistake of trying to understand the visual through frames of interpretation originally meant for language systems? Arnheim (1988) suggested that we address visual representations on the basis of their composition. The fundamental concerns of composition in the visual arts parallel those in writing: "the task in life of trying to find the proper ratio between the demands of self and the power and needs of outer entities" (Arnheim, 1988, p. ix). Visual representations, like any other symbolic form, are a part of the serious business of constructing meaning—that is, understanding the impact of our internal and external relationships:

> Far from being limited to playing with pleasant shapes, artistic form turned out to be as indispensable to human self-awareness as the subject matter of art and indeed as the intellectual investigations of philosophy and science. I deal with symbols only to the extent that the visual shapes reveal them through their dynamic behavior, in the conviction that these direct perceptual manifestations are among the most powerful conveyors of meaning available to the human spirit. (Arnheim, 1988, p. x)

When addressing students' pictorial representations of mental imagery, it is imperative that we recognize them as the act of composing knowledge depicting a relationship to the text from a perceptual rather than an intellectual impetus. These representations exist with an integrity equal to the written exploration. Compositional principles fundamental to all visual representations involve the presence of and tension between two spatial patterns of conceptual organization: centric and eccentric systems. Centricity is the tendency to remain organized primarily around an original center, whereas "the eccentric tendency stands for any action of the primary center directed toward an outer goal or several such goals or targets" (Arnheim, 1988, p. 2). These tendencies "are as basic to the physical as to the mental world, and they are easily represented through visual shapes" (Arnheim, 1988, p. 3). However, it is not the shapes that are of interest so much as the perceptual relationships between the shapes that create these vectors or lines of attention, "a force sent out like an arrow from a center of energy in a particular direction" (Arnheim, 1988, p. 4). The center of a composition can either emanate or attract vectors, and this attraction or repulsion is responsible for our sense of movement in our visual, perceptual energy. It is also this movement that conveys the meaning imbedded in the image. Thus, groups of static shapes transform into dynamic systems, demonstrating the essential tension between centric and eccentric tensions, and thus they visually capture the essence of human existence as we explore the relationship between self (centric) and other (eccentric).

When applied to students' pictorial representations, these principles allow us to understand how students are thinking visually. The following responses from a freshman-level, literature-based composition classroom represent part of the writing-to-learn activities in students' reading response journals. Students engage in two tasks when initially reading a work: drawing mental images envisioned while reading and reflecting verbally on what was depicted and why. Both actions contribute to a fuller sense of each student's developing relationship with the reading through visual and verbal means. Because the drawings are visual compositions, they demonstrate centric and eccentric systems. What is more, the two forms of articulation taken together depict an emerging visual-verbal relationship within each journal response.

Figure 3.1 is a student's response to Raymond Carver's "Cathedral," drawn in blue ink. This drawing renders a rather literal interpretation of

FIG. 3.1. Student response to Raymond Carver's "Cathedral."

text details, in which the student illustrates the description of the last and pivotal scene where the narrator and Robert, the bearded figure, draw a cathedral together. This student elaborates on the details of the scene by including the TV, glasses on the table, couch, well-stocked bar, and so forth. Although this drawing is centric as a whole, eccentricity exists on two levels between the figures. Robert, who enters the story as a close friend of the narrator's wife, connects with the resistant and jealous husband. By inviting the husband to draw the cathedral with him, Robert gives the husband a sense of vision in his own life. The student depicts this thematically significant moment, visually representing through spatial relationships the underlying tensions of the story. Robert and the husband form one primary center, whereas the wife forms a secondary center, creating a vector of perceptual attention toward the two figures on the floor. However, the wife's distance from the two men in the picture parallels the emotional distance in the story as she is no longer a key agent by this point in the narrative. Yet within the primary center, there is another division that creates an eccentric relationship. The husband and Robert are placed directly opposite each other, thus creating the eccentric or oppositional tension within the primary center. The hand of each figure meets at a third point in the primary center—the drawing of the cathedral on the floor. As a result, the centric–eccentric tension increases as a result of this two-way vector between the husband and Robert and by the point of union or centricity represented by the cathedral drawing. We have a visual representation of the two men and the action that brings them together. Drawing the cathedral resolves this tension between the characters, just as the cathedral drawing present in the picture resolves the perceptual tension between them.

Although the parallels in the story's actions and the drawing's vectors might seem coincidental at first, the student's verbal response reveals that he is often aware of the meaningful conceptual relationships both visually and verbally:

> This scene clearly stuck out in my mind. In the begin[n]ing of the story the husband displays resentment for the blind man coming to the house. As the two men talked during the evening we find both of them sitting on the sofa with the wife in between like a small link between their different worlds. After watching the documentary, Robert attempts to get the husband to see from his blind perspective and at the same time see a cathedral from the husband's perspective. This coming together of the two men's worlds is what I wanted to capture in the picture. The wife, the link, is now totally removed. It is just the two men communicating as best they can on their own.

This student notes the tensions captured visually using the centric and eccentric systems and the subsequent vectors creating perceptual direction and energy. This student demonstrates he understands, through both the perceptual (visual) and intellectual (verbal) means, as he renders a twofold articulation of the meaning he constructs from the text, with similar conceptual foundations expressed in each medium. The fact that this entry represents the student's first journal entry for the class might also indicate that this visual–verbal connection is immediately accessible for our students.

This relationship between the visual and verbal depiction remains consistent between students' responses. Figure 3.2 represents another student's response to Richard Wright's "The Man Who Was Almost a Man," rendered in pencil and placed vertically on the page. This drawing is an eccentric depiction in that the centers created by head and the gun are projecting outwardly, creating a sense of visual distance extending into the blank area of the page. This student takes a much less illustrative approach than we see in Fig. 3.1, thereby increasing the sense of weight given to the visual starkness beyond the large, heavy figures representing the firing gun and Dave's head. In this drawing, the viewer is in close

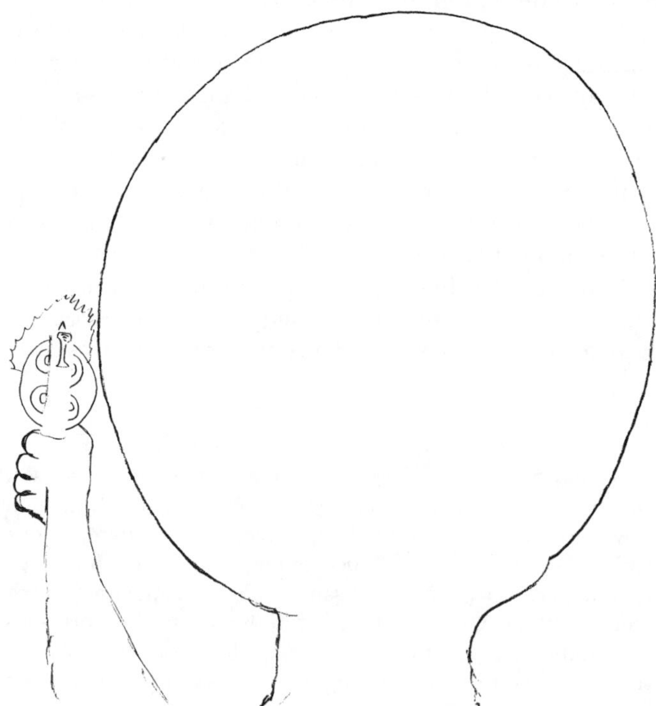

FIG. 3.2. Student response to Richard Wright's "The Man Who Was Almost a Man."

proximity to the figure, creating a greater affinity between the viewer and character than in Fig. 3.1. In this sense, the viewer is not given a bird's-eye view from the corner of a room, but an eye-level perspective from behind. There is tension between the viewer and figure because the viewer is placed in back of the figure and the action, simultaneously creating a sense of identification with and privacy for the center of the drawing from the viewer's perspective. Dave, the main character, is in his own world in this drawing, and blankness in front of the figure preserves this sense.

Once again the student is very aware of the perceptual relationships in the drawing, according to the verbal portion of the response:

> My picture is of the back of Dave as he shot his pistol for the second time. The reason I picked the second time was because it was more significant in his life. After his first firing, he was still a boy—a boy in serious trouble. After the second shot, the one he completed successfully, he was a man. Mentally, he no longer felt like a child although he still had a boy's thoughts. Also, after the second shot is when he made the decision to run away and in effect start his life. This is just a typical coming of age story in which the main character "grows up" before the readers' eyes.

The reader captures, both perceptually and intellectually, the thematic meaning developed during his initial transaction with the text. The visual represents Dave's turning point where he is able to focus his intention, aim the pistol, and fire. The blankness of the page in front of the figure represents the void ahead of Dave as he steps out into an unknown future.

Finally, Fig. 3.3 is a student's response to Alice Munro's "Boys and Girls." This drawing, rendered in color pencils, holds the two figures at the bottom as its primary center. Two vectors going out to the competing centers are represented by the horse and the figure of the main character, a young girl confronted with constraining, socially constructed gender roles. In this sense, the student is capturing the essential metaphorical implications of the story's pivotal action via the eccentric system she is creating through two competing centers. Thus, this student captures plot action, and subsequently, her thematic reading of the story:

> I struggled with this illustration just as the girl struggled to stay where she was. It is obvious that the horse and the girl are about to be shot by the same man, her father. The horse is being killed because he is old and is not good for anything but horsemeat for his foxes. The girl's life is over because she has become a girl. In reality the horse would still be shot but the girl would be spared even though she is useless to her father. On the farm she helped her dad everyday performing strong duties that most *boys* would perform. It seems today there is still that stereotype of women working in the house and men working "in the fields" where the real work is. At the end of the story

FIG. 3.3. Student response to Alice Munro's "Boys and Girls."

> when the girl performs a thoughtful task for a doomed horse, her actions were blamed on the fact that she was a girl. After that moment her whole life changed forever. Her gal was killed when her father made that hateful remark, "She's only a girl." She realized she could never go back to the faithful, hardworking *person* she was but become a woman of the house. The author makes the point of the separation of boys and girls, not by sex but by the qualities each must have to be titled a "boy" or "girl." There is no "person."

Like the first two figures, this response focuses on the interplay between action and theme. The dual eccentric tensions of the drawing parallel the tensions between the main character's choices. This student also noted that her struggle with representing her visual representation parallels the character's sense of struggle in the text, demonstrating a sense of the reader's identification with the character and struggle. Interestingly, the verbal discussion indicates that the visual representation is not a misreading of the text (the horse and not the girl is shot), but a strong, affective reading of the horse's role as a metaphor for the girl's situation as she is no longer of use in the "man's world." Of the three figures, this one represents the most symbolically interpretive pictorial rendering as the student visually captures the story's predominant metaphor relating to the theme.

The visual joined with the verbal in all three figures indicated a high degree of self-awareness in both modes during these aesthetic reading experiences. As we contemplate these drawings, it is important to realize that the verbal response does not explicate the visual composition. Instead, it is a mirror articulation, reflecting relationships in the more codified and external symbol system that language represents. The visual is a more private, open system, less willing to lull the spectator with the uniform predictability of language. Each medium embodies the recognition of centers and vectors, of the foundations of composing. Each exists independently while remaining capable of mutual enhancement. Together, the visual and verbal responses reinvigorate an aspect of established practice as we find a "new way of seeing what had always been there" (Suleiman, 1980, p. 1). We must concern ourselves with all facets of composing, and we must do so with a sense of integrity, operating with a greater understanding of the visual and verbal, and the centric and eccentric foundations of the energy that constructs our world: "At every level, it involves perception and conception, the concrete and the abstract. The schooling of the human mind must always employ an intimate union of both" (Arnheim, 1996c, p. 173).

REFERENCES

Arnheim, R. (1969). *Visual thinking*. Berkeley: University of California Press.

Arnheim, R. (1988). *The power of the center: A study in composition and the visual arts.* Berkeley: University of California Press.

Arnheim, R. (1996a). Lemonade and the perceiving mind. In *The split and the structure: Twenty-eight essays* (pp. 169–173). Berkeley: University of California Press.

Arnheim, R. (1996b). *Toward a psychology of art: Collected essays.* Berkeley: University of California Press.

Arnheim, R. (1996c). Two sources of cognition. In *The split and the structure: Twenty-eight essays* (pp. 17–23). Berkeley: University of California Press.

Beach, R. (1993). *A teacher's introduction to reader-response theories*. Urbana, IL: National Council of Teachers of English.

Heller, S. (1996, July 19). Visual images replace text as focal point for many scholars. *The Chronicle of Higher Education,* p. A8.

Iser, W. (1978). *The implied reader: Patterns of communication in prose fiction from Bunyan to Beckett.* Baltimore: Johns Hopkins University Press.

Mitchell, W. (1986). *Iconology: Image, text, and ideology*. Chicago: University of Chicago Press.

Mitchell, W. (1994). *Picture theory*. Chicago: University of Chicago Press.

Paivio, A. (1971a). Imagery and language. In S. J. Segel (Ed.), *Imagery: Current cognitive approaches* (pp. 7–23). New York: Academic Press.

Paivio, A. (1971b). *Imagery and verbal processes.* New York: Holt, Rinehart & Winston.

Pylyshyn, Z. (1999). Is vision continuous with cognition? The case for cognitive impenetrability of visual perception. *Brain Sciences, 22*(3) 341–423.

Pylyshyn, Z. (2000). Situation vision in the world: Opinion. *Trends in Cognitive Sciences, 4,* 197–207.

Rosenblatt, L. (1937). *Literature as exploration.* New York: Appleton-Century.

Rosenblatt, L. (1978). *The reader, the text, the poem: The transactional theory of the literary work.* Carbondale: Southern Illinois University Press.

Suleiman, S. (1980). Introduction: Varieties of audience-oriented criticism. In S. Suleiman & I. Crosman (Eds.), *The reader in the text: Essays on audience and interpretation* (pp. 1–3). Princeton, NJ: Princeton University Press.

Thomas, N. (1999). Are theories of imagery theories of imagination? An active perception approach to conscious mental content. *Cognitive Science, 23,* 207–245.

4

The Mind's Eye View: Teaching Students How to Sensualize Language

Debra Innocenti
St. Mary's University

The mind had to be first about the body, or it could not have been.
—Damasio (1994, p. xvi)

In Doré's drawing, "Don Quixote in His Library," Quixote wields his sword and book amid a room cluttered with visions. A dragon worms its way under his tall wooden chair. The fringe of the thick drapes swirls into the wild locks of an enormous head that watches two mice scurry across the floor, each mounted by an armored rider. A medieval damsel smiles coyly on the window sill, and behind Don Quixote's seated figure stampedes an army of knights on muscled, frenzied horses. Books, as master illustrator Doré understood so well, are no dull, intellectual pastime for Quixote. They transform his everyday existence to the fantastic. The boundary between reality and the dense, fierce world of his imagination dissolves.

Some students share Quixote's passion for reading and by the time they enter college have already devoured piles of books and filled composition notebooks with their own array of spectacular visions. Others have had and expect to continue having dull and even hurtful experiences with reading and writing. For these students, a good teacher's enthusiasm is not always a strong enough medicine to remedy the malaise. The aversion and fear are deeply rooted. Their previous schools may have had limited funds and therefore limited supplies, books, and opportunities for cultural events. They may have come from families in which education and a passion for learning were undervalued and even ridiculed. They may have had apathetic teachers as well—the ones who teach students—perhaps unknowingly—that they have nothing to offer the world. Reading and writing each become *a chore,* the popular vernacular of many students.

Apathetic attitudes, although daunting, are not unchangeable. One key to reaching a large percentage of students—from the brightest to the most detached—lies within a writing course design whose assignments facilitate a physical relationship with the words on the page—whose assignments, in other words, link the sensual experience of daily living with the texts students read and write. This is not to say, however, that sensual writing equals expressionist writing. Although physicalizing language does enable a student writer to paint her or his own experiences vividly enough to engage a reader (and him or herself), it also works the opposite way—enabling the student to imagine into and therefore understand a foreign subject before him or her, which may be as widely varied as paintings, historical events, explications of changing ideologies, and so forth.

I began researching the elusive notion of images and the imagination and how they applied to English course design after reading a revealing entry in a student journal. While reflecting on her experiences with reading, a student mused that there was a time when she hated to open a book. She would follow each sentence along, making her way through chapter after chapter with no enjoyment. When she complained to her middle school teacher, he responded that she had no imagination. The student went on to write that it was years and many experiences later that she finally realized what her teacher's assessment meant. She understood that *she,* too, had to participate in the text; it was not complete without her. Sensualizing the stories—making mental, personal movies—played an important part in involving her imagination. She finally *experienced* a story instead of picking through it for possible test questions.

Writers throughout the ages have had these same kinds of sensual experiences with words. Ackerman (1990) collected dozens of instances wherein professional writers describe heightened physical experiences with language. Included in her calvacade are Colette, Sand, Crane, Auden, and almost every name one could spot in a collegiate literary anthology. She reported that Rimbaud ascribed particular colors to each of the vowel sounds, including "the black hairy corset of loud flies," which was the letter *a* (cited in Ackerman, 1990, p. 291). Nabakov, too, associated colors and textures to the alphabet. In *Speak, Memory,* he explained a complicated system into which he categorized different letters from "the tint of weathered wood" of the long *a* to the "ivory-backed hand mirror" of the *o.* He had "black groups," "blue groups," groups for dipthongs, and so on (cited in Ackerman, 1990, p. 291). In an interview with Moyers, poet Kunitz (1995) recalled childhood retreats to the woods behind his house in

Worcester, Massachusetts, where he would "shout words, any words that came to me, preferably long ones, just because the sound of them excited me" (p. 239).

To begin writing, these sensually acute writers almost invariably engaged in some form of physical activity. The poet, Schiller, breathed in the scent of rotten apples (which he kept handy under his desk) to help him find the perfect word for his manuscript. Franklin and Rostand each wrote while his skin was soothed in a comfortably warm bath (Ackerman, 1990). Asberry, Oliver, Hall, Ackerman, Stafford, and numerous other writers begin their writing ritual by taking a long nature walk—an activity that steeps the participant in the motley soup of sensory input, smells, sounds, sights, touch, taste, plus the kinetic sensation of movement.

Poet R. Hass (1984), renowned for his study of the distilled image in haiku, wrote of the nature of epiphany: "In stories, in incidents that might be stories, I suppose there is a moment . . . when the image, the set of relationships that seem actually to reveal something about life, form" (p. 272). He meant that realizations, those kernels of wisdom, arrive as a picture or series of pictures in the mind. "Images haunt," he went on to say, and it is this haunting that spurs the writer to write and the reader to never quite forget (p. 275).

Sensualizing language in the imagination is a necessary skill for understanding it, producing it, remembering it, enjoying it, and even analyzing it. The need for the writer/reader to supply this sensualization is what makes written language so difficult. Vygotsky (1962/1984) wrote, "it is the abstract quality of written language that is the main stumbling block, not the underdevelopment of small muscles or other mechanical obstacles" (p. 372). Oral speech, he posited, is easier to learn than written discourse *because* of its "musical, expressive, intonational qualities" (p. 375). Fornes, an award-winning playwright, found drawing a valuable companion to writing because it evokes the physical life of the imagination. "If the imagination doesn't conceive matter," she wrote, "(the life, the physical life of the persons [that the students] are writing about, or the place, the physical life of the place, the air, the tone of light), if all that is not in the imagination, the writing is disembodied and quickly asphyxiates itself" (Coles, Fornes, Hyde, & Patton, 1994, p. 20).

This idea seems to be well supported by neuroscience, too. Our senses are the means through which we delight in and define the world. Even abstract concepts stem from sensory experience. Our understanding of *courage,* for instance, was probably formed through numerous, converging encounters: A man rushes into a burning building then carries out an injured child who clings to his neck, or a woman frightened by public speaking addresses a crowd of at-risk teenagers about how her son died of a drug overdose. We perceive these experiences (the man panting, his skin darkened by smoke, or the woman's voice trembling into the microphone)—or we endure them ourselves—and then form the concept. Even as we produce language, speaking, or writing, we undergo a microcosm of this same process. Damasio (1994) explained, "Most of the words we use in our inner speech, before speaking or writing a sentence, exist as auditory or visual images in our consciousness. If they did not become images, however fleetingly, they would not be anything we could know" (p. 106).

It is easiest to see how necessary images are to language comprehension when examining the autistic mind—a condition that makes imaging much more acute. In her book, aptly titled *Thinking in Pictures,* Grandin (1995), a renowned designer of livestock-handling facilities and an autistic woman, wrote of her difficulties with abstract concepts when learning to speak and write as a child. Concrete nouns were the easiest words for Grandin to understand as they could readily be associated with a mental picture of the person or object. Other parts of speech such as spatial prepositions were slowly assimilated into her vocabulary through representative images. "Even now," Grandin wrote, "when I hear the word 'under' by itself, I automatically picture myself getting under the cafeteria tables at school during an air-raid drill" (p. 30). Her capacity for language broadened as she learned to link new words and concepts with pictures. Grandin, for instance, would be particularly conscious of what image or experience formed her understanding of courage.

It is also noteworthy that Grandin (1995) spoke of books evoking mental movies. As an autistic, however, her experience with this kind of visualization is even more pronounced:

> When I read, I translate written words into color movies or I simply store a photo of the written page to be read later. When I retrieve the material, I see a photocopy of the page in my imagination. . . . To pull information out of my memory, I have to replay the video. Pulling facts up quickly is sometimes difficult, because I have to play bits of different videos until I find the right tape. This takes time. (p. 31)

Although this is the experience of someone in an exceptional situation, it does reveal, through its markedness, underlying patterns of thought in the rest of us, whom neurologists often refer to as *normals.* Consider the many mnemonic devices we have employed to retain large amounts of information: colored highlighters, flashcards, sketches, and so on. Consider as well how many instructors have made concepts from addition to DNA replication clear by doing some brief drawings on the blackboard. Images aid in both understanding and recall.

It is important to be aware that an image is not necessarily visual. Grandin (1995) also spoke of *sound images* in her book. Linguists tell us—

as does common sense—that language has an underlying onomatopoetic nature. We have mimicked our environments through gesture and sound to convey emotions and communicate information with each other and other species. What we now call *advanced languages* are simply modified and augmented appropriations (Abram, 1996). The resulting semantics are derived partly from the landscape of our brain's and body's electrochemical responses to the sounds. In fact, the more potent the response, the better we remember the sound. This is one of the reasons we tend to remember expletives in a foreign language more than other words: They often contain one strong syllable surrounded by fricatives, and, when said, breath is emitted in a forceful punch. No wonder their meanings are associated with strong emotions.

New findings about how image formation fits into the brain's dual hemispheres also shed some light on the connections among images, semantics, and reasoning. Although it was once believed that the modules for processing images were located in the nonverbal right hemisphere, scientists have recently been discovering that both hemispheres contribute to this function, particularly the left, which also processes logic, reasoning, and language. The right hemisphere simply generates a holistic, outline image, whereas the posterior lobe of the left hemisphere generates a more detailed image by parts. Corballis (1991) speculated, "It is, in a way, not surprising that the generation of images should be controlled by the side of the brain [the left hemisphere] responsible for language, since one of the functions of language is to evoke images. . . . We can talk about other places and other times precisely because our words are born of images and convey those images (or something like them) to others" (p. 129).

Damasio (1994) took this theory a step further. He suggested image creation and image manipulation are the very substrates of thinking. Images are not simple neural phenomena whose influence is limited to sensory input. They are actually generated by numerous, synchronous systems also responsible for perception, memory, and reasoning. For instance, we cannot physically see what our brains are not wired to understand and process. Patients with achromatopsia (damage in early visual cortices) not only lose the ability to *see* color, but also lose the ability to *imagine* or *conceive* color even if the damage occurs late in their lives. Restak (1994) agreed: "Vision . . . is not at all like a camera where the eye focuses light on the retina where a 'picture' is taken and conveyed along the visual pathways to the brain for interpretation. Rather, the brain actively constructs what we 'see,' and we are at once camera, film, photographer, and picture" (p. 31). Not only are the same neural systems involved in imaging and understanding, but the two processes are simultaneous.

It is this same neurobiology that seems to be the foundation of play—in humans and other species. Children create multisensory images, sometimes physically or imaginatively interacting with them, to understand and assimilate within themselves the adult roles they will later don. They do this in the same manner a cat will play by pouncing on a falling leaf or chasing a sibling's tail; it prepares the animal for the adult responsibility of hunting for and feeding itself.

Educator and psychologist Shuman (1989) might include this kind of instructional visualization in her concept of the *fictional self.* She credited this imagined self with cutting "through the limits of time and space in ways the physical self cannot" (p. 72). Is not this the basis for our love of reading and writing: imaging ourselves into fictional or hypothetical situations? It is what we experience through language early in childhood. Imagination allows us to transcend our lives' boundaries and understand concepts our immediate environment does not provide access to. Indeed, reasoning and problem solving may be said to involve *imaginative trial and error.*

In fact, one of the commonalities of great minds, according to Gardner in *Creating Minds,* is a childlike quality or having "the conceptual world of a child" (cited in Grandin, 1995, p. 180). Besides Grandin, other famous thinkers, including mathematician Mandelbrot, physicist Feynman, and Einstein, confessed to thinking predominantly (and consciously) in images, whether they be visual, auditory, or another sense. Einstein even admitted that after forming image-based concepts, "conventional words or other signs [had] to be sought for laboriously only in a secondary stage" (cited in Damasio, 1994, p. 107).

Rosenwasser and Stephen offered an even more compelling understanding of the importance of imagistic thinking. In *Writing Analytically* (1999), these writers described the first step toward good analysis as becoming aware of one's thinking processes and "eliminating habits that get in the way" (p. 2). One of the key roadblocks to analysis, said Rosenwasser and Stephen, is a too-immediate leap to the abstract—a knee-jerk response to judge before the subject is fully present in the mind's eye. "When people leap to judgment," argued the writers, "they usually land in the mental pathways they've grown accustomed to traveling, guided by family or friends or popular opinion" (p. 3).

What Rosenwasser and Stephen (1999) suggested is not merely that details can be used to engage the reader, but that details must be used to challenge and advance the thought of the writer. An awareness of one's thought processes requires the writer to rigorously focus on the mental movement from sensualization—suspending the subject in the mind—to making something of the subject with the mind. It is a circular process that must be replayed again and again when developing a composition. In other words, sensual detail is necessary not just for personal or expressive writing, but for most forms of analytical writing.

We may then reasonably conclude that images are indispensable to a person's understanding, reasoning, recall, and engagement. Yet how does an instructor effectively foster the production of images in a composition class especially when students may have had a privation of imagistic learning in their lives?

When designing composition classes, I have begun devoting the first few weeks of the semester to analysis work, wherein our first goal—with Rosenwasser and Stephen's (1999) text as a guide—is to explore a subject, initially suspending judgment that often comes in the guise of description (words like *beautiful, terrifying, good, convincing*) in order to get that subject, intact and specific, on the page.

We begin with paintings and other artwork. For the past year, I have used a couple of Tooker's lithographs—*The Voice* and *The Mirror*—which are both visually detailed and yield to dense interpretations. I tell the students to first describe each lithograph as concretely and objectively as possible, consciously suspending initial judgment that manifests itself in the form of abstractions. The descriptions are written outside of class and then shared aloud in class so that students as a group can identify what is vivid, concrete description and what is abstract. They are often surprised at how much of what they first write is judgment. Following is an early semester attempt written by a student, David:

> The subjects of the painting [*sic*] are two men who look to be in there [*sic*] mid-50s. They are both wearing a coat and tie and are separated by a wall or door. The man on the right seems to be very frightened and worried and looks as if he is trying to talk to the man on the left. The man on the left has his ear pressed up against the wall or door and is trying to listen to what the other man is saying. The man on the left has a very concerned look on his face and is probably a friend of the other man. An interesting aspect of this painting is that the man on the right, who seems to be in trouble, is in a very dark or shadowy room, which is probably representative of the predicament he is in. The man on the left is in a bright room, or outdoors, and has much more light shining on him, probably to represent him as a good person who is trying to help. Also, the hand of the man on the right is pressed up against the door, but it is not near the same spot where the other man's hand is, which is a little higher up. This might represent that the man on the right probably won't be able to help the other man. The collar and tie of the man on the right is a little messy compared to the man on the left, which probably serves to stress the trouble that he is in.

In many ways, David was successful in this writing application. He effectively described what the men wear, their positions (right and left), their gestures (an "ear pressed up against the wall or door" and the other man's hand "pressed up against the door . . . near the same spot where the other man's hand is"), and the location of light and dark. After discussion in class, we were able to pinpoint places where abstractions still managed to hide. Words like *frightened, worried, concerned,* and even *mid-50s* are, of course, initial judgments that could even hinder an accurate interpretation of the lithograph. By rewriting descriptions of the lithographs, eliminating all knee-jerk conclusions, students can then enter into a more reasonable analysis, being attentive to what thought processes lead them to certain conclusions and deciding whether these thought processes are logically valid. Was the man indeed worried? What facial expressions of his prompted this judgment? Does that expression only indicate worry?

As the semester progresses, we expand our subjects to advertisements, campaign speeches, and films. Students compose both in and out of the classroom and then share their results orally. Hearing these exercises aloud has proved an energetic way for students to be presented each other's work. A human voice is tagged to the words, and reader and listener can achieve a connectedness. Additionally, the writing classroom becomes a more physical place. Rather than just the teacher's voice, many voices fill the room. Students write hurriedly and loosely on plump composition books and usually settle into more relaxed postures. I have found it helpful to encourage them to buy journals that are pleasing to hold and look at, and to assure them that these physical pleasures are not a childish habit. Dumas, for instance, used special colored paper for each of his genres—blue for fiction, rose for nonfiction, and yellow for poetry (Ackerman, 1990). As the semester progresses, sketches and doodles, sometimes quite beautiful, begin to cohabit the prose in these notebooks.

Throughout the semester, we continue to flex our sensory muscles. I provide students with an opportunity to experiment with senses they do not often employ in their work. Visual images usually dominate essays, but senses such as sound can be notably absent, which becomes an important part of analyzing film or TV advertisements. To expand their repertoire of senses, I devote a few classes to vignette writing: They cluster and then freewrite different people and places from their memories based on a conceptual theme around which the class is organized. We again share the writings orally as a class and discuss which senses are predominant and where initial knee-jerk judgments might have entered the composition. I notice a number of students relax with these exercises. They get to know and feel comfortable with each other as a group—a valuable foundation for future, more thorough peer edits.

To prompt olfactory or tactile images, I bring in different objects for the class to describe. Frankincense, rubbing alcohol, or rose water can produce rich descriptions and associations. Other good objects include small- or medium-size sculptures; students can be asked to close their eyes and use their hands to obtain a sense of the piece. The resulting freewrite is focused solely on touch in this way.

Smell is a particularly useful sense to encourage students to write about in these vignettes. The part of the brain that processes smell is disconnected from the brain's language centers; we have no real vocabulary for smell. Most words are nondescriptive and, in fact, simply name our emotional response: *stench, rotten, appetizing,* or *delightful.* Other words, such as *sweet* or *fruity,* draw on synaesthesia. Every attempt to accurately describe smell becomes a creative attempt. Smell is also directly linked to the emotion and memory centers in the brain, which can make olfactory images an ardent, vivid encounter for both the writer and reader (Ackerman, 1990). Vignettes can be done for all five senses and can further aid students to associate writing and reading with reexperiencing or imagining physical experience.

An added bonus of this exercise is its brainstorming nature, enabling difficult to inspire students to find an explorable subject in which they are interested. Images foster associative thinking because of their fluidity. Unlike words or other signs, images do not have specific meanings. Therefore, they not only are open to interpretation, but can lead the mind on a journey by suggesting other images or patterns of images. Somewhere along the way, the mind unconsciously finds its gold.

In later essays, in which I asked my students to evaluate or interpret an incident, trend, or phenomenon that related to our theme, they had to remain vigilant in their quest for concrete detail. In many cases, students only were not recollecting their *own* experiences, but guiding a witness to recollect his or hers. One student, Edna, interviewed her brother about his experiences in Desert Storm and his resulting poor health, and she compared his story with the official government findings. She wrote:

> In the months following the war he [her brother, Cesar] would occasionally share some stories about his experiences in Desert Storm. In the last couple of years, his participation in the war faded in the background and as a family we have not really talked about it: no anecdotes, no complaints, not even a mention of what the weather was like.... We seem to have a secret agreement with each other not to talk about the war for the sake of everyone.... I was a little hesitant about calling him up to ask him about the war, but he offered the information quite easily with no objections. I know this is only because I explained to him the reason I was seeking this information.

Together, Edna and her brother re-create his experience in the Gulf using detailed images:

> The information that I got from Cesar was very different from the Defense Department report I had read. For example, the report did not mention that the water the troops used to shower was transported in gasoline tankers. When they would shower the water smelled of fumes and was a brown

> color. As Cesar put it, the water looked like iced tea. The large can-type containers that the water was stored in above the showers were not treated so consequently they were rusted. He mentioned that when showering he would feel little scraps of rust falling on him in the water. . . .
>
> But all of this was minimal compared to the last story he told me in our conversation. He recalls being outside his tent one night and hearing a loud explosion. As he and the other people with him looked up into the sky, about a mile away they saw a Patriot missile intercepting a Scud that was intending to attack. Immediately, Cesar said, there was a "funny odor" in the air that he could not describe. Then for a few moments, as seemingly harmless bits of debris were falling all around them, they felt what they thought to be little water drops, as if it were raining.

In her process evaluation, Edna noted, "I have had to replace myself, mentally, in the times and the places that I am writing about. . . . I had never written anything that accomplished this; not even essays that I had written about myself. Wow! I had not thought of that until just now."

The pages of many writers' memoirs and critical essays are peppered with references to the transcendent power of reflection and contemplation. We do not fully comprehend or appreciate an experience until it is reconstituted later in the mind. Wordsworth, in his Preface to *Lyrical Ballads,* coined his famous maxim, "Poetry is emotion recollected in tranquility." In our modern century, poet Forche (1995) credited reading and writing with slowing us down so we may "sustain and extend our capacity for contemplation," a skill that is constantly threatened by a fast-paced, sound-bite culture (p. 131). If Damasio (1994) was right, if thought *is* image formation and manipulation, then a writer slows her or his thought down and deepens it by seeing and focusing on images.

Our challenge in teaching, regardless of the subject, is to reinvigorate a student's imagination, her or his ability to sensualize language and learning, and integrate it as part of her or his physical, intimate world. When this happens, words become, as Fornes (Coles et al., 1994) demanded, embodied, breathing, and full of possibility. The world, in turn, becomes more interesting, more complex, and more important.

REFERENCES

Abram, D. (1996). *The spell of the sensuous: Perception and language in a more-than human world.* New York: Pantheon.

Ackerman, D. (1990). *A natural history of the senses.* New York: Vintage.

Coles, R., Fornes, M. I., Hyde, L., & Patton, J. (1994). Educating the imagination. In C. Edgar & R. Padgett (Eds.), *Educating the imagination: Essays and ideas for teachers and writers* (Vol. 1, pp. 1–24). New York: Teachers & Writers.

Corballis, M. C. (1991). *The lopsided ape: Evolution of the generative mind.* Oxford, England: Oxford University Press.

Damasio, A. R. (1994). *Descartes' error: Emotion and reason in the human brain.* New York: Grosset/Putnam.

Forche, C. (1995). Interview. In B. Moyers & J. Haba (Ed.), *The language of life: A festival of poets* (pp. 129–141). New York: Doubleday.

Grandin, T. (1995). *Thinking in pictures: And other reports from my life with autism.* New York: Doubleday.

Hass, R. (1984). *Twentieth century pleasures.* Hopewell, NJ: Ecco Press.

Kunitz, S. (1995). Interview. In B. Moyers & J. Haba (Eds.), *The language of life: A festival of poets* (pp. 239–255). New York: Doubleday.

Restak, R. (1994). *The modular brain: How new discoveries in neuroscience are answering age-old questions about memory, free will, consciousness, and personal identity.* New York: Touchstone.

Rosenwasser, D., & Stephen, J. (1999). *Writing analytically.* New York: Harcourt Brace.

Shuman, S. G. (1989). *Source imagery: Releasing the power of your creativity.* New York: Doubleday.

Vygotsky, L. S. (1984). Thought and language. In R. L. Graves (Ed.), *Rhetoric and composition: A sourcebook for teachers and writers* (pp. 371–376). Portsmouth, NH: Boynton/Cook. (Original work published 1962)

5

Sight and Insight: Mental Imagery and Visual Thinking in the Composition Classroom

Sheryl A. Mylan
Stephen F. Austin State University

Writing teachers often link writing and vision. We ask students their *views* on an issue, we ask them to *look* at each other's papers, we inquire if they *see* what we mean, and we call for *revisions*. Yet often their writing is not what we or they *envision*. I wonder if developing writers *review* their work in ways we know to be beneficial because they have never truly *viewed* it in the first place. By *view,* I mean using one of the most basic ways of knowing—the visual—as part of their writing processes. Visual knowledge, through mental imagery and visual thinking, has long been used in other disciplines. Yet it is often culturally devalued and frequently opposed to the verbal—a hierarchy that needs to be dismantled much as Derrida (1974) did with speech and writing when he showed that writing was not inferior to speech, but complicit with it. The same is true of the verbal and visual.

In this chapter, I would like to discuss strategies for using visualization first to help students see themselves as writers and then to assist them throughout their writing processes. To do so, I believe it is helpful to examine Western assumptions in which the visual is often regarded as an inferior venue to knowledge. Its use in the composition classroom is hindered by such devaluation, especially by academic views that privilege the verbal. Yet when we incorporate visualization into our repertoire of contemporary pedagogical approaches, such strategies can encourage us to reexamine the cultural assumptions about the ways of knowing, the apparent opposition between the image and the word, and the status of logic and reason.

Despite our image-saturated culture, contemporary positivist Western culture is at best ambivalent about or at worst biased against the visual. When we think of popular culture, the visual certainly is more pervasive than the verbal. For instance, popular music is often accompanied by music videos. With TVs in American homes turned on for an average of 7½ hours a day, this amount of viewing is almost equivalent to another full-time job for large numbers of people. We can hardly escape from the barrage of advertising, which, too, is largely visual. The visual is everywhere, but ubiquity does not necessarily denote high status. Although the print media are increasingly displaced by visual media, we still often associate the visual with the less sophisticated or less intellectually developed. When a child progresses from looking at pictures accompanied by little text to reading large amounts of text alone, we consider this movement a sign of greater cognitive complexity and comprehension. So, in many ways, the written word, although devalued in popular culture, actually maintains a higher prestige than the visual image, especially in academic and professional life.

When we consider the status of various kinds of vision—the physically observed and the mentally imaged—we see how the Western tendency to privilege one term over the other further devalues mental imagery. So it is not merely that the visual is less valued than the verbal, but that the visualized image is less valued than the ocular. To understand this, one need only consider how eyewitness testimony is supposed to be one of the most persuasive forms of testimony, acting as a substitute for actual presence, even though it is notoriously subject to distortion. In some senses, we see what we expect to see. Although eyewitness testimony is not unmediated reality, many people regard it as such, and thus superior to circumstantial proof, which may actually be stronger evidence. Suppose, for example, we wake up one morning, look outside, and see everything blanketed in snow. Because we have not actually seen the snow fall, the snow is only circumstantial evidence of such an event having taken place during the night. Who would deny that the snow actually fell, however? No one. Still, in the popular mind, there is a strong tendency to devalue the circumstantial. What can only be imagined seems to be valued less than what is physically seen. Yet whether we see an event or object with our physical eyes or visualize it in our mind's eye, we are always in the realm of interpretation—something that we who study texts and writing should use to our advantage in helping students become better writers.

When we really understand how the visual operates, we can see how the distinctions between physical sight and visualization collapse. To see something, to have visual perception, energized particles bounce off an object, striking rods and cones in the retina and releasing a chemical to start depolarization along the neural network in back of our eyes, which then travels along the optic nerve to the brain. The neurons recognize this signal pattern—what is perceived—as an object. This percept is a visual order or pattern that the brain imposes on the chaos of the signals. So, in effect, the brain "sees," not the eyes; the brain creates our visual reality. As Burke (1985) explained, culture has an important role in how we see. Culture reflects the contemporary model of reality. So when we see something, "the meaning of the experience is recognized by the observer according to a horizon of expectation within which the experience will be expected to fall" (p. 309). When we also consider that, because of binocular vision, each eye receives a slightly different image, we again see the role of the brain in fusing these images to get a three-dimensional representation of reality. It is an illusion, albeit an absolutely convincing one—so much so that we call it *reality* and set it in opposition to visualization, which we call *fantasy, illusion*, or *hallucination*.

If the products of physical vision and visualization are, in a sense, both illusions and mental constructions, why is there such a strong impulse to oppose the two rather than to acknowledge their similarities? Why is there such a distrust of visualization, not just in popular opinion, but in academia as well? Perhaps this is because Western culture privileges reason, logic, and order over what is perceived to be irrational, illogical, and uncontrollable. Visualization is associated with the latter, although it is actually more controllable than mere visual perception.

Our suspicion of the irrational has some of its roots in Greek culture, certainly from Plato. Although the Greeks valued reason and order, they also thought of understanding as a kind of seeing. Ong (1977) believed our contemporary society with its post-Cartesian outlook is even more visual than the Greeks were, although he considered this "hypervisualism to be fragmenting" (p. 138). Further, he said that to analogize knowledge and sight is to "rob knowledge of its interiority" (p. 122). To Ong, sight applies to surfaces; so whereas it can work as an analogy for explanation, it cannot get beneath the surface for deeper understanding. If we have as part of our legacy from the Greeks a fear of the irrational, we should not discount their estimation for sight, both physical and, more important, mental. Aristotle, a keen observer of the physical world, also said in *De Anima* that mental pictures are essential to thought. If visualization is necessary for thinking, then it is connected to reason and depth, not to irrationality and superficiality, as Ong maintained. Yet it must give us pause if so careful a thinker as Ong regarded the visual as deeply alienating, distancing us from both life and thought. Is it any wonder, then, that visualization is distrusted as a deeply harmonious and analytical way of thinking?

Visualization can and will be trusted as a mode of nonlinear thinking, not necessarily better or worse than linear, logic-based thinking, as more and more discourse communities regard it as a legitimate focus of inquiry.

As Foucault (1973) pointed out, what we learn, simply put, depends on what questions we allow. Knowledge is not a function of progress in the sense that we are more perceptive than previous generations. Rather, it is that those generations organized knowledge differently than we do because they viewed the world differently, asked different questions, and thus discovered different answers. So, for instance, chaos theory, in which the regularity of the irregular has been observed in sciences as disparate as meteorology and biology, was something scientists did not acknowledge only a few decades ago. Yet once the possibility was considered and the questions asked, these patterned irregularities, in weather systems, heartbeats, and other phenomena, are now regularly observed. One interesting, final point about chaos theory as it relates to the visual is that these patterns of nonlinear systems manifest only when the data are put into visual form.

Increasingly, researchers in a variety of disciplines find visualization a worthy field of study and validate it as a form of thinking rather than viewing it as a kind of hallucinatory state of nonthinking. Lindemann (1995) pointed out that sometimes we think in words and sometimes we think in images. She said that, "to separate cognition into seeing and thinking forces an artificial distinction between two processes that must work together" (p. 88). Sommer (1978) saw visual thinking as a kind of code switching and said that, "the goal of imagery training . . . should be the development of the capacity to switch back and forth between different modes of thinking as needed" (p. 149). In composition, we can readily compare this to linguistic code switching, in which one suits various types of discourse to the different communities to which one belongs.

Sommer (1978) also discussed the kind of linear thinking that has accorded the highest honor to abstraction. He stated that there is no sound basis for believing that pure abstraction is the highest form of reasoning: "Loss of contact with the tangible world and detachment from experience are not virtues" (p. 149). Imagery connects us with the world and a realm of thinking that is holistic and integrative. Berthoff (1996) also decried abstraction, particularly as it relates to writing. She stated that, "visualizing, making meaning by means of mental images, is the paradigm of all acts of the mind: imagining is forming par excellence, and it is therefore the emblem of the mind's power" (p. 42). In speaking of the ladder of abstraction that many teachers use, limiting the visual to descriptive writing and relegating it to the bottom rung, she cautioned, "it's that metaphoric ladder itself that's dangerous" (p. 43).

In many ways, visual thinking is off-putting to some writing instructors more so than to people in other disciplines. Visual thinking has and does lead to reasoned thoughts in many fields, as I show later. Yet as McKim (1980) pointed out, "not all visual thinking is language thinking:

visual thinking can utilize operations (such as the act of synthesis), can be represented by imagery (such as perceptual and mental imagery), and can occur at levels of consciousness outside the realm of language thinking" (p. 130). Perhaps the operation of visual thinking beyond language suggests to some writing teachers that it cannot then operate within language. However, such attitudes fall into an oppositional trap. Thinking can be translated into various forms. As Sommer (1978) pointed out, "visual material is not necessarily remembered or even conceived of in visual form" (p. 40). If this is true, cannot the reverse also be true—that language thinking or the verbal or analytical can be encoded in visual thinking?

Perhaps eventually writing instructors will look on visualization with more favor and reap the benefits that researchers in other fields of study and even people in ordinary pursuits have found. Visualization can be used in controlled ways like mental rehearsal, where one imagines improved motor skills such as better athletic performance. This visualization yields demonstrable results, is popularized in approaches like the "inner game of tennis," and is used by Olympic athletes and champions in many fields of sports. Physical practice, combined with visualization, yields performances superior to practice alone. So seeing in the mind's eye can lead to accomplishment, and this accomplishment need not be limited to physical activities and leisure pursuits.

Visualization, for instance, is used in scientific fields where spatial design is important. In classic studies on mental synthesis, people are shown parts of a pattern, and then they mentally assemble it. These mental transformations are not just static images like pictures, but are images that can move, change, and be mentally seen from different angles (Finke, Ward, & Smith, 1992). The brain perceives both in the same way, whether one is physically seeing the object as he or she actually manipulates it to observe the object more closely or whether the person is performing these actions mentally while seeing the object in his or her mind. In writing instruction, we are not really concerned with such spatial maneuverings. Yet, for my purposes in this chapter, what is important about these findings is the brain's identical response to the image, whether its origin is in the external world or in the mind. If the brain makes no distinction between a visual perception from the external world and a visualization or a mental image, then we miss a useful tool to improve creative cognition in writing if we dismiss visualization's importance in intellectual activities.

I want to focus for a moment on visual approaches to creative cognition that underlie many discoveries in science. I do so for the reason that, whereas many people grant that artists like painters or writers of fiction or poetry may begin with a visual image, they are less likely to concede that mental images can serve as a basis for analysis. Such reasoning leads to the conclusion that visual imagery would not help students deal with academic and professional writing. Yet visual imagery has been key to many researchers in both the social sciences and the so-called hard sciences; this demonstrates that visual thinking is not antithetical to the kinds of analysis that students are called on to do. For example, Feldman (1988) had been studying child prodigies and creative development when he began dreaming of an amusement park ride, the kind with spokes, each with a car at the end, emanating from a hub around which it spins. This image appeared in his dreams over a period of 2 years and eventually led him to a macromodel of the internal and external forces that result in prodigiousness. Faraday visualized lines of immaterial force that were the basis for the first truly modern field theory of electromagnetism. The German chemist, Kekule, often visualized atoms dancing before his eyes. Looking into a fire one day, in the flames he envisioned a ring of atoms that looked like a snake eating its tail; from this image came his discovery of the molecular structure of benzene. Physicist Feynman used visual images to think about particle interaction (see Sternberg, 1988, on Faraday, Kekule, & Feynman). Most famously among physicists is the story of Einstein's image of riding a beam of light, which led him to the idea of relativity. In fact, Einstein claimed that the visual was one of the main characteristics of his thought processes:

> The words of the language, as they are written or spoken, do not seem to play any role in my mechanism of thought. The psychical entities which seem to serve as elements in thought are certain signs or more or less clear images which can be "voluntarily" reproduced and combined. . . . From a psychological viewpoint this combinatory play seems to be the essential feature in productive thought. . . . The . . . elements are, in my case, of visual and some of muscular type. Conventional words or signs have to be sought for laboriously only in a secondary stage, when the associative play is sufficiently established and can be produced at will. (cited in Gardner, 1993, p. 105)

Einstein's views on the relation among visualization, his own creativity, and language are borne out by some recent studies on insight. Schooler and Melcher (1995) reported that, although solving an analytic problem is not hindered by verbalization, solving an insight problem is impeded. So metacognitions are needed instead of standard logic. The implications from this for writing instruction are, it seems to me, that if we see all writing as creative exploration, then we must explore the use of visualization as a way of encouraging insight, which will add depth to our students' work.

As the examples from scientific discovery show, visualization is not antithetical to thought. It is another type of thinking, both preverbal and averbal. It does not substitute for having students read widely on issues they wish to examine. As Ippolito and Tweney (1995) stressed in their work on the inception of insight and their analysis of "eurekaism versus accretionism," "perceptual rehearsal" is essential: That is, "the saturation of one or more of the senses with all aspects of the phenomenon of interest to the discoverer . . . [is] a means of defeating the inherent biases of our perceptual apparatus and increasing the impact of unexpected insights" (p. 435). So reading, research, analysis, or language thought are not replaced by the visual image. Rather, they work in conjunction with the visualization that can lead to an insight, which, in turn, spurs verbal, analytic thought.

In a composition classroom, under perceptual rehearsal fall all of the ways we engage students in writing as we help them understand their role as participants in knowledge-making communities. Visualization can fit well in such a social conception of learning and writing because creativity and insight are crucial if students are to be more than knowledge consumers or education technicians. Unfortunately, in our materialist, positivist culture, the major formative institutions of education overvalue left-brain learning, which excels at sequential processing, linear thinking, rule-dominated ideation, motor sequencing, and information sorting to the exclusion of other types of learning. In such a climate, the kinds of visualization that come so easily to children are discouraged as they grow older. By the time these students reach a college classroom, most of their capacities for visual thinking that would enhance their creative cognition lie dormant. Yet we can reawaken their possibilities by adapting visualization strategies to a writing course.

Presently, when applied to writing, the visual means many things, including visual perception and observation, visual memory, mental imagery, and visual thinking. Instructors often use visual perception, observation, and visual memory or recall already, usually when description or narration is involved, grafting them on to traditional approaches. Mental imagery and visual thinking, which are larger, transformative approaches to knowledge, are seldom used. Yet these strategies can become part of one's writing processes from the moment when a person struggles with the idea of seeing him or herself as a writer—often the first major obstacle a student writer faces—through the process of conceptualizing an issue, idea, or question, and the recursive acts of revising.

One of the most important visual images anyone trying to write needs seems almost too simple—that is, a person must see him or herself as a writer. Many people might be tempted to neglect this step because of its apparent simplicity. Yet often the greatest challenge many students face is seeing themselves as capable writers. Difficulty doing so leads to a blockage. As we all know, writers at every level suffer dry spells. As readers, we tend to understand those writers we admire when they suffer a creative drought; we never cease to call them writers. Students are often less forgiving of themselves when they encounter difficulty writing. They say, "I'm not a writer," even though they may be experienced graduate or undergraduate English majors with many successful writing projects to their credit. Sometimes these students are unable to see themselves writing a particular paper or project. To help them with these kinds of blockages, it is important to relax the student and have him or her imagine writing a paper, finishing it, or whatever image is most meaningful to the student in that particular situation. With English majors, we may look at Book I of *The Prelude* where Wordsworth (1995) saw himself as a poet before he even began writing:

> . . . while upon the fancied scene
> I gazed with growing love, a higher power
> Than Fancy gave assurance of some work
> Of glory there forthwith to be begun,
> Perhaps too there performed. Thus long I mused,
> Nor e'er lost sight of what I mused upon
> (ll. 76-81)

This passage is filled with visual language, and the sight he was musing on is a mental image of himself as a poet. Our students may be more concerned with finishing the next essay or taking an essay exam than with writing a poem, but, like Wordsworth, they need to imaginatively see themselves doing it. Such an image reverses the materialist assumptions that we are what we do into the assumption that we do what we are, or what we can see ourselves as.

Like most writing teachers, helping blocked English majors is far from the bulk of my work. Most of my composition work is with basic writers, a group that I admire for their persistence in the face of years of academic discouragement and neglect. We always begin with literacy narratives so they can see the visions they hold of themselves as writers and readers. Often we begin with a discussion, either in small groups or as a class about their views of themselves as writers. Many times they resist the term *writer* itself, and sometimes they even deny that they have ever written anything. Gradually, though, either by actually closing their eyes and recalling times when they wrote, brainstorming on paper or aloud, they bring to mind pictures of their past experiences with writing. I have even had students sketch pictures of some of the situations when they wrote. Eventually a pattern emerges of significant experiences that shaped a student's attitudes toward writing. These are mental snapshots, forming a collage, as it were, that students then use as the basis of a literacy narrative. This becomes a written portrait of each writer.

Unfortunately, the visions they uncover of themselves as writers are often quite negative. They frequently recount painful experiences with both reading and writing—being ridiculed in class for mistakes on an essay, being told they are stupid, incapable, or lazy, getting low grades after struggling hard over a paper, receiving an essay awash in red without any praise, encouragement, or assistance. These are the pictures that spring to these students' minds when they try to see themselves as writers. No wonder these writers are so often blocked, lacking confidence in their abilities. Despite these past experiences and views of themselves, often they are determined, if only they could conceive of a way to succeed. Yet they cannot, often saying, "I just can't see how I'll ever do this." The words may come out slightly different from student to student, but they are all variations on the same theme, and the students frequently use sight verbs to describe their blockage.

It is little wonder then that when we, as writing teachers, try to coach them, as the Nike ad says, to "just do it," whether that is freewriting, journaling, brainstorming, or some other technique, they just cannot do it. The old pictures—the experiences that have become the students' visions of themselves as writers—are too deeply internalized to vanish with the use of exercises that work on such a surface level.

One strategy I have tried recently serves as a companion piece to the literacy narrative. This time, however, I ask them to focus on what they do well, whatever that might be. Because the literacy narrative so often elicits students' recollections of painful experiences, I want to counterbalance this with writing that recalls successful moments and positive attitudes toward themselves. This piece serves several functions. Its foremost purpose is to bring to the surface an image of confidence, pleasure, and success that ultimately can help students change their views of themselves as writers.

I first attempted this with a student majoring in modern dance. She was frustrated with writing, angry at having to take basic writing for the fifth time, and near despair at the prospect of never finishing college because of her difficulties with writing. Almost totally blocked, she wanted a set pattern she could use to pass her writing requirements. Watching one of her performances, I saw the fluid precision and grace with which she interpreted the music into a seamless work of beauty. Later, I remember how often during our weekly tutorials, she spoke of dancing when we would reach an impasse on her writing. I understood then that dancing was her vision of success, her escape from the painful view of herself as an academic failure because of her poor writing. We began talking more about dancing during our writing conferences, about how she focused her thoughts and feelings as a dancer so that she could communicate them to her audience, how her movements flowed smoothly but not in a way she could rigidify into a formula. Eventually, I asked her to try to picture herself dancing just before she sat down to write, to feel as relaxed and free as she felt dancing, and to try to sustain those feelings as she wrote. Though I was trying to link her feelings of accomplishment in dancing to a new vision of herself as a writer to generate the same kinds of determination and sense of potential, I found that we were also developing a new language to talk about writing, an analogic mode that related dance and writing where we could both begin to better see what the other was saying.

The union of dance and writing worked for this student, but not just because both are arts, allowing the free play of expression. The key element was linking writing with what students can see themselves doing successfully, and it worked with a number of students, all with widely different interests. A math major, for instance, who loved the certainty of mathematical formulas and problem solving, which she excelled at, hated the vagueness of writing. She told me in great detail about her efforts to write for one teacher, only to be told by the next year's teacher that what she was doing was wrong. When she wrote her literacy narrative detailing all of these incidents, she concluded by saying, "What I've learned about myself as a writer from twelve years' of experience is that everything I do is wrong." It is rare to hear students say of their studies in any other field that the more exposure and training they had in it, the more they learned that they knew nothing about it and were incapable of improvement. But often students express these very sentiments. So totalizing are these experiences that a student like this who takes yet another writing course believes that what she learns in it too will be proved wrong. With this student, I used her view of herself as a successful student of mathematics to help her see writing as a problem to be solved, questions she could answer, sections of an essay like parts of an equation making up the solution. This gave her the basis for a new view of her abilities and gave us a shared language about writing.

This strategy has worked with others as well. A forestry student had no real problems with writer's block, but he did have difficulty collaborating on his work, which limited the effectiveness of his revisions. When we talked, he said he could not see why negotiation in a group was useful, and he could not see himself doing it. Because he was resistant to collaborate in our composition classroom, I needed to have him see how collaboration in another setting was valuable to him. From discussions we had had, I knew he donated his time to experimental forestry projects done jointly between the university and a local forest products corporation. I saw this as an opportunity for him to see how competing interests were negotiated. He was able to have some participation and to see how others bridged the gaps among industrial interests, environmental concerns, and community needs on issues like land use and reforestation. Because this work engaged his interests and fit in with his view of himself as an environmental negotiator, I could use this self-image in his composition class work as a peer reviewer to make him more skilled in receiving and giving suggestions about writing. In the process, he also began to see how no one writes in isolation and how important rhetorical considerations of audience and purpose are.

These techniques demand time and receptivity on the part of both student and teacher not just to the concept that thought and consequence, image and action are integrally related, but also to the need for exploration of the kinds of self-concept we hold. They also demand much intensive one-on-one work, but visualization can be used in other ways by the student alone as well. One type of visualization that I suggest to students is to brainstorm in a hypnagogic state, the dream state that occurs just before one falls asleep. During that time, alpha brain waves of 8–10 cycles/second are generated, and the stresses of the day fade. Many students report feeling stress in school, especially when they write and try to force ideas into some shape or to closure when these ideas are still in the incubation stage. So finding ways to deal with stress, especially over schoolwork like writing, has its appeal. Many students are familiar with the experience of having good ideas come to them just as they fall asleep or just as they wake up. So they have already experienced a hypnagogic state and need only to learn that they can mine it for help with their writing. When a person is in a hypnagogic state, sometimes an image will come, or perhaps even in a dream itself as it did for Feldman (1988) with the image of the amusement park ride or for Einstein (Gardner, 1993) with his trip on a light beam. This image may suggest a new view of an issue. Or if the student has begun gathering information and verbalizing the insights he or she already has, new patterns of arranging the material may suddenly emerge.

As more and more images come to the student, he or she may find it helpful to cluster. Rico's work (1983) on using right-brain techniques, especially clustering, is invaluable. At some point in the clustering—a highly visual approach that disrupts linear thinking—all of the random clusters suddenly make sense in the mind's eye; a pattern emerges, which Rico called the "trial-web shift," and one gets a sense of the whole. Some people might be misled by the book's subtitle, *Using Right-Brain Techniques to Release Your Expressive Power,* and believe that it is old-style Romantic expressivism. Although Rico's approach does develop an aesthetic sense, her techniques also work extremely well to help writers discover a nucleus of thought about an idea. They also work well in a collaborative, rhetorically based classroom. The book's visual approach to brainstorming can yield insights suited to academic writing, however that term is construed, as well as to so-called personal writing.

Once students have begun the recursive process of structuring their ideas, the visual can again be helpful. When students try to plan their papers, some try outlining, even though most of them find it useless and frustrating, but they often use it as a last resort because they cannot imagine a pattern other than a linear sequence. Lindemann (1995) suggested blocking, which asks students "to draw a picture of what they propose to write" (p. 133). Asking questions such as "what do my readers need to know here?" to help them decide what to put where and how big of a block it will take, they eventually fill in their drawing and their essay.

There are possibilities for using visualization at all stages of students' writing processes. Yet it is important to make sure that the mental imaging arises from the students rather than from the teacher's imposed vision, no matter how helpfully intended. A teacher taking ownership of a student's paper is a common danger; what is really being hijacked, of course, is the student's vision. This is particularly true of unconfident writers, who are often eager to relinquish ownership of their writing. They ask teachers or tutors to look at their papers to see what is wrong with them. It is all too easy to suggest places for more examples or detail, new ways to organize, and so on, and soon the piece is no longer the student's vision. So the teacher must take care to nurture the students' visions of themselves as writers and the development of their own work.

Another potential problem can arise when students are given examples, by either professional writers or students, to see how to write more effectively. Seeing how others write effectively can be disabling to some writers, for whom such models reconfirm the students' poor images of themselves as writers. What should be modeled are more effective writing processes based on students' individual needs, interests, and backgrounds, and it all begins in the vision they hold of themselves as writers and their work.

Helping students reenvision themselves as confident writers through strategies such as these will not completely erase the picture created by years of the institutional devaluing of visual thinking. But, although mental imagery and visual thinking have been culturally marginalized, being on the margins often gives the best perspective from which to view a culture and its practices. Perhaps, with a fresh perspective on visualization, we can put the vision back into writing so that our students' creative cognition and writing abilities develop into all that they and we envision.

REFERENCES

Berthoff, A. (1996). The intelligent eye and the thinking hand. In M. Wiley, B. Gleason, & L. W. Phelps (Eds.), *Composition in four keys* (pp. 40–44). Mountain View, CA: Mayfield.

Burke, J. (1985). *The day the universe changed.* Boston: Little, Brown.

Derrida, J. (1974). *Of grammatology* (G. Spivak, Trans.). Baltimore: Johns Hopkins University Press.

Feldman, D. H. (1988). Creativity: Dreams, insights, and transformations. In R. J. Sternberg (Ed.), *The nature of creativity: Contemporary psychological perspectives* (pp. 217–297). Cambridge, England: Cambridge University Press.

Finke, R., Ward, T. B., & Smith, S. M. (1992). *Creative cognition: Theory, research and applications.* Cambridge, MA: MIT Press.

Foucault, M. (1973). *The order of things: An archaeology of the human sciences.* New York: Random House.

Gardner, H. (1993). *Creating minds: An anatomy of creativity seen through the lives of Freud, Einstien, Picasso, Stravinsky, Eliot, Graham, and Gandhi.* New York: HarperCollins.

Ippolito, M. F., & Tweney, R. D. (1995). The inception of insight. In R. J. Sternberg & J. E. Davidson (Eds.), *The nature of insight* (pp. 433–462). Cambridge, MA: MIT Press.

Lindemann, E. (1995). *A rhetoric for writing teachers* (3rd ed.) New York: Oxford University Press.

McKim, R. H. (1980). *Experiences in visual thinking* (2nd ed.) Belmont, CA: Wadsworth.

Ong, W. J. (1977). *Interfaces of the word: Studies in the evolution of consciousness and culture.* Ithaca, NY: Cornell University Press.

Rico, G. L. (1983). *Writing the natural way: Using right-brain techniques to release your expressive powers.* Boston: J. P. Tarcher.

Schooler, J. W., & Melcher, J. (1995). The ineffability of insight. In S. M. Smith, T. B. Ward, & R. Finke (Eds.), *Creative cognition approach* (pp. 97–133). Cambridge, MA: MIT Press.

Sommer, R. (1978). *The mind's eye: Imagery in everyday life.* New York: Delacorte Press.

Sternberg, R. J. (Ed.). (1988). *The nature of creativity: Contemporary psychological perspectives.* Cambridge, England: Cambridge University Press.

Wordsworth, W. (1995). *The prelude: The four texts (1798, 1799, 1805, 1850)* (J. Wordsworth, Ed.). New York: Penguin.

6

The World Through Different Eyes: Mental Imagery, Writing, and the Reconceptualization of the Self and Other

Christopher Worthman
DePaul University

I am in a room full of teenagers. We are on the third floor of a park fieldhouse in a predominantly Latino neighborhood in Chicago. It is a Saturday afternoon in January, and outside the sun is shining, a harsh, almost blinding brightness, but it is cold, maybe 20°, and windy. The wind whistles through the crack under the door that leads out to the fire escape and rattles the glass in the windows. Only one of the black-painted radiators works, and it is too hot to touch. The room is a stage with a heavily lacquered and polished wooden floor. The teenagers are lying on their backs on the floor, their eyes closed. They are part of a group called TeenStreet, which is the youth outreach arm of a larger community-based theater arts program called Free Street.

It is a mixed group, three Whites, three Latinos, five African Americans, and one Asian, with most of them going to public schools, a few to private schools, and a few having graduated. Nearly all of them are from low-socioeconomic homes. They came together in November, chosen from the 100 or so who auditioned, to create, rehearse, and perform an ensemble production. The 6-month creative process includes 6 hours of rehearsal per week, 2 hours on Thursdays after school and 4 on Saturdays. Movement, writing, and improvisational workshops fill the first 3 months. From these workshops, an ensemble script is gleaned, made up entirely of the teenagers' writing and incorporating the movement and music of the rehearsals. The teenagers say it is a different way of writing than they are accustomed to. It is a writing process borne of imaginal interaction, where their real and imagined experiences are played out visually, improvisationally, and in writing, and allowed to interact with and be responded to by other teenagers. These images, both one's own and one's interpretation of others', fuel the writing, which is an interactive process including cooperative writing and peer review.

This chapter presents TeenStreet's writing process, including the use of visual and enactive imagery and their relationship to the writing, and the significance of these things for these teenagers. This chapter shows what is going on here as a way of understanding the nature of the writing process at TeenStreet; using multiple ways of representing oneself and the world. It is a dialogical process that moves from images of the self to interaction with others and then to writing. The process described is, as Heath (1996) wrote, a matter of putting a living being within a scenario and pondering the consequences of certain actions and processes. Such a matter is premised on a unique type of relationship between oneself and others that is marked by a confrontation of possible lives, the life of oneself, and the lives of others, all of which is at the heart of TeenStreet's educational life. The analysis of the process included in the description is embedded in the conceptualization of TeenStreet as a safe place for using alternative representations of the self and in reformulating the relationship of the self and others so that writing is contingent on both expression and communication. Movement and improvisation exercises precede the writing exercises, allowing the teenagers to write from the immediacy of their and others' emotions. The process offers them a new perspective on writing that differs from the one commonly provided by formal literacy instruction.

FROM MOVEMENT TO WRITING

Finding the Voice in the Body

Like all rehearsals, Saturday's begins with a 20-minute stretching warm-up that starts with the teenagers on their backs on the floor and moves slowly into extending different muscles and holding their bodies still at full extension. Ron, the director, talks quietly and slowly, giving instruction and working along with the teenagers, imploring them to focus on their bodies and feelings. Voice exercises are part of the warm-ups, beginning with listening to the sounds of one's breathing and evolving into exploring the pitches and rhythms of breathing and the changes in sound that result. The voice exercises stress the physicality of voice—that is, the voice being a product of air moving through the body and causing bodily vibrations, which underscores the fundamental need of a body, of *being,* to have voice, make sounds, and use language. A common utterance repeated during the voice exercises is "the breath is the voice," meaning voice is something a person creates from within. Today, like most days, the warm-ups end with the teenagers on their backs again, breathing easily, an introduction to the movement improvisation. Everyone's eyes are closed.

Momentarily, Ron instructs the teenagers to begin imagining the room as something other than a theater stage. He, in effect, is creating a scenario for human action and interaction that the teenagers will define based on their experiences. He says to give the room a color or an emotion, something like blue or anger, meaning to think what emotional effect a totally blue room would have or what a room filled with the energy and tension of anger would be like. Everyone is quiet. When you get that image in your head, he continues, let it wash over you and start shaping your movement.

The teenagers begin to move slowly, their legs and arms bending slightly, as if they are waking from a sleep. The movement is reflexive and repetitive, with bursts of energy mixed with slow, elongated extensions of arms and legs. Everyone remains quiet, appearing to be fully focused on their own movement. After a few minutes, some of the teenagers begin rolling onto their knees and feet, with some going back to the floor again. There are moments of stillness, where the energy of a body appears to be pulled inward and, from my perspective as observer, will burst outward at any moment. I participated in the movement and improvisation exercises in rehearsals prior to this one; now as an observer, I am able to imagine the playfulness taking over the body and to know how easy it is to forget anybody is in the room with you. Yet, in moving, people come in contact, and the contact is a stimulus from outside the body. In response, the teenagers linger in the contact or pull away as if they had touched the hot radiator. Ten minutes into the exercise, all eyes are still closed even as the movement carries the teenagers across the room and into contact with others.

Ron opens his eyes and looks around. He moves from Charles to Karen to Nick, whispering something to each of them. They stop, listen, and then continue the movement exercise until they are off stage, where they unpack their instruments. Charles sets his bass by the fire escape door and begins to play, creating a thumping rhythm of low notes, with each individual note fading slowly away and the next one exploding as the previous one dies. Karen and Nick join him. Nick sets up his drums as Karen begins playing her violin, settling in between the hard notes of the bass. Nick begins a soft rhythm on the snare drum.

All of the others are now on their feet. Some have their eyes open; others do not, but everyone is still quiet. It took most of them about 2 months to get comfortable with the movement exercises, with moving freely by responding first to how they felt and then to others around them. They learned first to focus on their bodies, their emotions, or, what Ron calls, the *little mind* and to suspend thoughts of what is going on around them. Theoretically, by beginning with complete focus on the body, when it is time to interact, one's response is borne of the body and wholly from one's own particular place and time. Ron tells them to use geometric shapes—circles, lines, triangles, figure-eights, and so forth—to define the movement because they are the most natural types of movement. The teenagers are to be as nonjudgmental and uninhibited as possible in their movement, trying to suspend their learned sociocultural and societal perceptions of themselves and others as much as possible. When they do arise, they are to respond to them as if they are intrusions on who they are. Hence, the closing of eyes and the admonishment not to perform or act are ways of getting over inhibitions. Yet the inhibitions are much of what defines us as members of a community, as social beings. The inhibitions are often a result of how we see ourselves in the world or how we imagine others see us.

Redefining the Self Through Visual Representation

According to Aylwin (1985), such seeing of oneself, or one's conception of oneself in a particular context, is one's visual imagery, which is at the center of the three-pronged imaginal lives we live, with verbal imagery on one side and enactive imagery on the other. At TeenStreet, there is a recognition of the significance of all three ways of representing oneself. All the exercises are designed to access or highlight one type of imaginal representation as a way of developing not only that particular representation, but the others, too. For example, often visual imagery evolves into enactive imagery, which evolves into verbal imagery and vice versa.

Aylwin (1985) classified *verbal imagery* as language—both spoken and unspoken—which is different from the mental images—the visual and enactive imagery—that are constantly a part of our thoughts. Based on her empirical research, verbal imagery is hierarchical and oppositional, ideal for creating binary classifications and taxonomies that evaluatively compare objects and people. The effect of such imaging is that experience becomes subordinate to language, with the *word* taking precedence over *experience*. The movement exercises are designed to bypass initially such verbal representations and to allow the teenagers to figuratively re-create language as borne of themselves by using their visual imagery to represent themselves.

However, in the visual imaging at TeenStreet, the environment in which one places oneself is not the sociocultural context of daily existence, à la Aylwin, but one of the teenagers' own creation. The environment, in fact, is the physical body, the self, where the responsiveness of the self is not directed toward others, but toward one's own body. One figuratively turns inward, allowing one's imagination to propel the body forward. Thus, visual imagery takes on a meditative quality. Yet it is a meditative quality that is played out in movement and not in the contemplation of self, which Aylwin (1985) suggested is the root of our visual imaginings. Although this visual representation does not align with the environmentally dependent representation defined by Aylwin, it is a peculiarly similar concept in that the self is still a body of attributes that it evaluates and tends to in order to define itself. At TeenStreet, the focus is on those attributes and their place within the body. Within the context of the theater group, such images are the stuff of warm-ups and preinteractive movement, or the little-mind activities, wherein Ron exhorts the teenagers to concentrate on their bodies and how they feel.

In *An Experiment in Leisure*, Field (1937) described the significance of such visual images as she recounted her lifelong exploration of self, including her efforts to excavate the images of her life that continually recur regardless of how old or out of place they are. She came to call these images "inner facts," which are marked by "a warmth and certainty" (p. 53) in the body of the experiencer. She wrote, "the imagination uses mental images in two ways: it uses them as 'wish fulfillments,' as a means of evading hard facts; but it also uses them as a way of thinking about hard facts, as an instrument, not for evading the truth, but for reaching it" (p. 50). Although she described her journey as a purely meditative one, a contemplation on those images that come to mind when least expected or desired, she wrote of the effect these images have on her body, including the feeling they create within her body as if she were experiencing these images for the first time deep within her. She described the feeling she gets from turning inward as a "goodness" like "a cat lying in the sun" (p. 53), although most of her meditations were on what she considered to be "bad" thoughts and "rebellious" or "utterly fantastic" ideas (p. 52). These thoughts are labeled such because they are conceived as socially unacceptable—against the norms of society. Yet, Fields wrote, in exploring these thoughts, in facing that within her that is "other" than who she appears to be, she felt good. She described her exploration of these "inner facts" as making "direct contact, facing 'something,' which is I think inside me, without words or purposes or protection, a direct touching of something which feels like a raw experience of being alive—coming face to face with something inside you, something intensely living—but it's certainly not 'thinking about' something inside you" (p. 53). Such inner facts, when juxtaposed against the seemingly "outer facts" of the world, lay one open, and, as Fields noted, one reaches the truth of who one is. Such an exploration is suited for providing "reflective intervention" (Bruner, 1986) of the knowledge one encounters in the world. It prepares one for meeting the world. The little-mind activities of TeenStreet succinctly help in this preparation by turning one inward, bypassing the use of language. As Field wrote of her own exploration, it requires one "to sink down, out of my head, and into a deeper part of my body" to where language can be reborn (p. 53). Only at this point can one authentically interact with others because it is here that one becomes embedded in one's own singular time and place as who one is and not as who one is expected to be or classified as.

This notion of visual representation does not misconstrue Aylwin's (1985) definition of *visual representation* as one of constructing a social persona. Its inward turning allows one to redefine a social persona from one's own time and place in the world, and not as established and impressed on oneself by outside. The visual imagery of TeenStreet is a starting point for entering into the third of the image-creating structures described by Aylwin—that is, *enactive imagery,* a place where the snapshots of one's life, those visual images, can begin flowing forward into the future.

Listening to a Cacophony of Voices

As the movement of this Saturday's rehearsal continues and people come into contact, the focus is enlarged to include responding to those around you. The movement is transformed into enactive representations or a "big mind" activity and everyone's eyes are open. In a big-mind activity, the individual is aware of her environment and responds to it, doing so, however, by acting from her body, from her emotional state, which the little-mind activity has made her aware of. Big-mind activities necessitate a response to others. Thus, in a sense, they foster an awareness of others in space and time. One is not only an actor in the movement, but also an experiencer of the actions of others.

Indeed, enactive imagery are those images that make us actors in our own imaginings and that propel the body of visual imagery into the world of others. They are the playing out of our emotional existence where our actions have consequences and are done for a purpose. Simply put, they are visual images made live, making us agents, as well as experiencers of others' actions. These images are the stuff of movement and improvisation exercises, where the teenagers do act and experience others' actions.

Ron rejoins the movement and says, "Whatever you're working on, flavor it with blue. Explore blue. What does blue look like, feel like?" Suddenly the nature of the activity becomes improvisational, a sort of role playing, where the role one takes on is an emotional, conditional state. The music settles into a softer, looser rhythm, less pulsating, and the movement becomes muted, almost stilted, as if boundaries had been put on the extension of the bodies. When people come in contact, it is often marked by quick bursts, as if they are drawn to but immediately repelled by others and move away, surprised by the contact. Ron often describes the big-mind activities as focusing on the entire room. "Imagine what's going on all around you," he says. It is hard for me to tell what blue connotes, but it is obvious it means different things to different people.

Some of the teenagers nearly stop moving, appearing to withdraw into themselves. Tonya and Terri try to turn away from everyone, with Tonya running from one side of the stage to the other as other teenagers approach her. She moves quickly, making sudden stops. Yusuf spins around as if he is trying to see if anyone is behind him and acting as if lost. Whenever anyone comes near him, he becomes calm, almost secretive. Denise gets up off the floor and twists along the wall, then settles back on the floor again, pulling her body across the surface with outstretched legs and arms as others stop to watch or jump over her.

After a few minutes, Ron steps off to the side and watches. Over the past month or so, as the teenagers became less conscious of how they may look to others and the movement activities took on a quality of play, Ron became more of an observer. He lets the teenagers interact, only reminding them once in a while to respond to or be aware of what is going on around them.

Creating a safe place for the exploration of mental images is fundamental to TeenStreet's success and is probably what makes the movement and improvisation activities possible. The teenagers, through the use of movement and improvisation, are creating "untrue" situations—situations that, although imbued with real-life concerns, are still distinguishable from their lives outside TeenStreet. It is as if they came to TeenStreet to reflect on their lives, but once there are not faced with the concerns they face every day in their homes, communities, and schools beyond reflecting on them. The nature of TeenStreet activity, I suggest, is different from any other activity the teenagers may experience in that, while participating at TeenStreet, lived experience is honored and is the basis for expression.

Movement and improvisation arise from the teenagers' lives and, thus, what happens in the workshops is art effused with life. Although they carry with them similar risks and fears as life, such activities are supported and understood seldom as life is. How their representations of self are responded to is different from real life because the significance and importance of those representations are always responded to aesthetically, with a focus on interpretation. This rule, along with others, was established during the first rehearsal.

During that first rehearsal, Ron stressed that the success of an ensemble rests in its ability to have everyone working together, especially where physical interaction is involved. Although it is imperative to learn to depend on others, one is also responsible for oneself. Part of being responsible is knowing how to present oneself so that one does not lead another astray or into danger. The little-mind activities help the teenagers get ready to interact by focusing consciousness on the self. In this sense, effort was made to exclude how one thinks others might see oneself, to exclude the public self.

Ron expressed the concept of responsibility within the context of physical interaction; however, Bryn, the ensemble writing instructor, tacitly made the same correlation when discussing writing: A person is responsible for listening closely and trying to understand what others not only do but also write and say. The same could be said about the small-mind activities and writing. The nature of a safe space is not only respecting others' rights of expression, but being responsible for one's own expression so that others can understand or seek common ground for coming to an understanding.

"When you find a place that seems appropriate," Ron says, "start talking to yourself, start your character and interact. Create relationships with others." The characters he refers to are people the teenagers have been working on in the movement and writing of past rehearsals. They are characters they would like to play in the performance and can be themselves acting a certain way, someone they know, or a compilation of people they know. Always it is someone each of them created through movement and writing and now put into improvisational situations.

Some of the teenagers begin talking, mostly to themselves; others begin responding to what they heard, sometimes verbally, sometimes gesturally. Ron moves across the front of the stage. "When the music stops," he says, "the room will change from blue to anger." Charles nods, taking his cue, and continues to play. Karen and Nick look at him. They continue for another minute, then stop. The room explodes with accusations almost immediately as if the anger has been dying to get out. People start confronting each other. Yusuf places his hands over his ears and shakes his head, turning away from anyone who comes near him. Anthony points at others and laughs. Noticing him, Tonya stands alongside him and looks at where he is pointing his finger. When Anthony laughs, she laughs too. Sharon tries to run away from others, catching Anthony and Tonya's attention. They start following her, always staying back just enough that she does not notice. Everyone appears to be blaming someone else for something. After a minute or so, Ron pulls Elena, Donna, Terri, Yusuf, and Mona off stage, leaving Anthony, Chau, Denise, Sharon, and Tonya to continue the activity.

Beginning with Denise, the women begin to circle Anthony and Tonya, pointing fingers at them and talking. Anthony moves backwards in little circles. He runs into Chau, who pushes him toward the others. He is still in character. He is Pip, a New York Italian he created in a past writing activity. Pip is obnoxious and loud, a joker who exhibits a lot of body movement and physical gestures but says little, as if too cool to speak. Anthony tries to push his way out of the center of the group but is pushed back inside. Suddenly, Tonya appears to turn on him, too. She steps away from him and laughs heartily. She then steps toward him and waves her finger in his face. Anthony grimaces and turns away, faking a laugh once she is behind him. Sharon, who has been behind Tonya, turns away from her in the opposite direction that Anthony is going. Chau and Denise stay by Tonya's side, following Anthony across the stage. Finally, the women move away and, just as it looks Anthony is free of them, Denise and Tonya confront him again, slipping back in front of him. They bombard him with a flurry of words. Anthony responds, yelling back and waving his hands in their faces as if to say "get out of here." When they do not respond, he smiles and shrugs his shoulders, then walks away, waving his hand over his shoulder as he goes, indicating to them to stay away. Reaching Sharon and Chau, who have moved across the stage where they continue the movement by themselves, he tries to engage them in conversation. They act like little girls, jumping around like frogs and giggling. Anthony imitates them. Sharon rolls her eyes and turns away, pulling Chau with her.

Ron yells for the music to become a part of what is going on, and the musicians begin playing loudly. Denise and Tonya yell over the sound, but I cannot understand what they are saying. There is no rhythm to the music. The sounds are harsh, a cacophony of noises of which the women are one part. It reminds me of watching an altercation from afar, in the streets perhaps, wondering what brought the people involved in the encounter together and what, if anything, I should do. It is unsettling for me, even as I know it is improvisation. Anthony acts unfazed, infuriating Denise and Tonya even more. Chau and Sharon again separate themselves from the group. They step back into a corner, becoming observers, more privy, however, to what is going on than I am.

The others return to the activity and the room changes from anger to indecision, then to white. "How does a white room make you feel," Ron says. Finally, the room becomes one of bending fingers, where the teenagers focus on each other's fingers. Sharon stands at center stage and holds her hands in front of her. I am reminded of arthritic fingers and how their movements can feel as if fingers are digging into my skin. Yusuf recoils from Sharon's gesturing, and I wonder if his impressions are the same as mine. The teenagers stay in character as they are thrust into each new scenario, adapting to where they are and responding to others.

"How does bending fingers relate to the rest of your body, to your character, to what you're saying?" Ron yells. He reminds them to use geometrical shapes in their movement and not to act cute. "Don't act," he says, "react." They have been on the floor for 40 minutes, and their exhaustion shows. Next is the room of comfort. Comfort appears to mean rest and compassion, and many of the teenagers slump against each other, any animosity displayed during the room of anger gone. The drums soften and the bass drops behind the violin. Ron tells everyone to find an ending. Within a minute everyone has stopped.

When the activity is over, everyone meets in a circle on the floor. Ron asks what they thought. Yusuf says he experienced things he had not before. His character is a man from his neighborhood who fronts as someone of great knowledge, but whom Yusuf sees as weak and unsure of himself, someone relying on others for reinforcement. His characterization of this man is of a person who hears voices in his head that mimic the voice he uses in interacting with others. Everyone is quiet, and I am not sure if Yusuf means he knows more about his character now or that the movement is different than before.

Anthony says it took him a while "to lose himself," to get into the movement and then his character. Others agree, insinuating that there is a process whereby your thinking changes and you actually feel comfortable doing the activity.

Imaginal Interaction and Writing

Later, Bryn uses the movement and improvisation activities to structure and define the writing activity. He told me the year before that he looks for ways to tie writing in with the movement because he feels a lot of what goes on in the movement activities—the imagery and emotions—is lost by the time the teenagers write. Over the course of the workshops, he tries such things as having teenagers write in the middle of movement and improvisation activities; turn to writing or moving whenever they wish; write immediately after an activity; and write in response to others' movement. Bryn's reasoning is pragmatic: The ensemble is creating a performance out of teenager writing, a performance that combines that writing with music, dance, and movement; thus, the best performance grows out of the interaction of these elements, all supporting one another.

This day, the image of the room—maybe as it was during the movement activity, maybe a room from one's past, or maybe as it was when they are writing—is the context for what is written. Bryn instructs the teenagers to imagine themselves going into a room and observing. "Get a sense of the room and compose a sentence in your mind that captures that sense, and then start writing." This sentence could be a snapshot of sorts, an image of an environment or context that one puts one's character in, or another scenario, so to speak, that the teenagers will subsequently write about.

During the first part of the activity, the teenagers write about the room they are entering—what it looks like, what is in it, and how they feel in the room. Sheila poetically describes the room that she imagines like this:

Time, moving, and stillness . . . violence
Rums Swiss Almond Trolls
that danced across the table
Honey marinated sperm
that awakened his sleeping sex
Ransacking the house
which held the clock set at midnight
Spotlights of lust
and beds full of pain
Pulse barely moving
and windows kidnapping rain
Cheddar cheese and buttered popcorn
Sourpatch kids and friendship bracelets
Kids begging for macaroni
And rats nibbling on old pieces of bologna
Old mops full of dust
and pissy underwear under the table
Four kids to a bed and roaches as pets
Three shards of families
And one dying generation
Twelve locks on the door
And three knives under your mattress
Twenty-four kids shot in drivebys
And two minds full of dreams.

Sheila writes this in about 15 minutes. The last two thirds find its way into the script for that year's ensemble. In the script, it describes a young woman torn between love and sexual desire, between a boyfriend pressuring her and what awaits her at home, as described by Sheila.

After describing the room, the teenagers pair up and share their writing with each other. Sheila and Denise read theirs and talk about the imagery created. They turn to the second part of the activity, taking what they wrote and finding a phrase in it that caught their attention, then writing a stream of consciousness piece that reflects how they felt in the room.

Denise, who chased Anthony around the stage bent on confronting him, writes for her second part:

> No one needs to come up to my face talking about revolution. I am a child of change, born of evolution, raised through hardship, surrounded by tall broken down struggles with busted windows and stairs that creak. When I cry I tell stories, each drop gives life to the oceans and puddles for others to drink from.
>
> My unimportance keeps the earth from falling off its axis and rolling down the alley to the gutter. Me and my ghetto keep the rest of the earth's assholes from suffering. We pay society's debt all on our own. No wonder we're always on food stamps—they owe us.

Significant here, I think, is not only the semblance to Sheila's room, tweaked by Denise to capture her own perspective, but the similar evolution of Denise's piece to Sheila's, going from room description to individual concerns to community issues. Here also, Denise notes the significance of her stories as ways of both representing her community and keeping the world from going askew.

The power of written storytelling was something Denise was coming to terms with at TeenStreet. Much of her early writing reflected her unwillingness to write. Her excuse was that she was a dancer and never wrote well before. In fact, during the first rehearsal of that year's ensemble, she wrote in a freewrite:

> Nothing Nothing It was like nothing likes ok but I don't wanna talk about it why cause cause cause why did I write that I feel really dumb just in case you thought I was a writer I'm not I'm a dreamer that's my profession this has nothing to do with shut up I'm a dreamer full time I go places you can't meet people you don't feel things unfelt because you're not courageous enough to step out of yourself and be a genuine person get rid of the fronts and let yourself shrink into sincerity that's what life's about?

Much of what shows up later in her writing, the poignant descriptions and succinct analysis of herself, her community, and how others see her, is hidden in this choppy rambling text about herself as a dreamer, which she juxtaposes with what she implicitly thinks a writer is. Early on, Denise rejected the ability of language to define who she is. In time, she appeared to come to understand writing as a means of expressing who she is and not as something definitive of who she is not. As rehearsals went by, Denise became more adamant in writing about how she saw the world.

During the last part of the writing activity, where the teenagers are to describe themselves alone in the room, Denise continues her reflections, writing:

> I can't sleep 'cause I'm too tired. Can't cry 'cause I'm too sad. Quenching my thirst for culture by cramming tamales down my throat and bowing to the white Jesus with a mother named Guadalupe. I guess my only hope lies in men in coffins with hopes in their heads and names banished from history books, because not enough teachers knew how to roll their *R*s. Salsa and stereotypes make my Mexicanness seem like a fad, a habit to grow out of, maybe even just a bad memory that a dangling pocket watch can fix.

Again, Denise addresses her own life and makes sense of how she is seen by others.

Using multiple ways of approaching a writing task and having others respond to what you wrote is a common practice at TeenStreet, as is writing about the movement and improvisation activities. This is imaginal interaction. The language used to describe the writing, although shrouded in words such as self-expression and emotional connection, always wound its way back to communication of one's emotions and thoughts to others. It was about defining one's world and one's place in it for others by ferreting out the experience behind the expression. Allowing others to respond was paramount.

The focus placed on the body and experience while doing the movement and improvisation activities readied the teenagers to write from their experiences, both past and present. Ultimately, the teenagers came to rely on their understanding of the world as a source for meaning making because it was these experiences that guided their movment and improvisations. Their lives were the text for everything that was done. The language that arose from the activities was expressive of experience and understanding. As such, it was the voice of the teenagers, borne of their perspectives. Because each teenager inhabits a unique time and place in the world, her voice is uniquely hers and thus offers new understanding to others.

Because of one's unique perspective of the world and potentially unique voice, it is only through interaction that one's experiences can be more fully excavated and understood. Experiences become more meaningful in interaction, in our coming together to "hear" each of us "speak" of our experiences, even when language is not a part of that dialogue. In interaction, voice is fully developed, given its communicative capacity in that we hear and see how others respond or address us and our existence, and, thus, are in a better position to make sense of our own and others' experiences.

INTERACTION AND THE POSSIBILITIES OF SELF AND OTHERS

Fleckenstein (1996) noted that enactive images are sensitive to the idiosyncratic individual experience, reflecting less interference from socially constructed reality. Yet it is this reality that one is responding to, that one cannot but respond to. It seems that when the enactive images arise from visual imagery, as defined in this chapter, this is even more the case because it arises from a reality grounded in one's own time and place, one of which the teenagers have conjured up and focused on. The focus of such images is on doing, on action, on expressing intent and motivation. Enactive imagery allows us to reconceptualize binary thinking—the thinking associated with verbal representations—by giving it a fluid sense of realities. Thinking becomes process, grounded in the body as it moves forward in time. Such imagery represents reality relationally and not oppositionally. Thus, how the self is related to the other is not a matter of either/or or hierarchical or comparative evaluations of seeing someone and identifying differences and similarities but an evolution, a relationship that is additive in nature. I posit this as an and/but relationship of self and other, where in interaction I know you as this but also as that, but because of my singularity, I also know there is always that that I do not know (and therefore any classification of you is tenuous at best).

In the theory of writing conceptualized at TeenStreet, this and/but conception is what transforms writing from its solely verbal framework to a bodily response, one grounded in the participants' own space and time, yet answerable to others. As such, writing is a communication precipitated by a necessity, or a responsibility, to respond to others, the same type of need to communicate that will be expressed by many of the teenagers when they discuss their writing. Aylwin's (1985) and Fleckenstein's (1996) descriptions of enactive imagery make light of the nature of this self–other relationship, and although they both noted the significance of the other or the experiencer in enactive imagery, neither fully defined the nature of the relationship.

Aylwin (1985) noted the cathartic potential of enactive imagery in many therapeutic exercises. The goal of such exercises is to get people to act, to become agents. The movement exercises at TeenStreet create similar opportunities of heightened experiences as those created in the therapeutic exercises described by her. However, whereas the cathartic potential of enactive imagery is the pursuit of psychoanalysts and therapists, for Ron and Bryn, and ultimately the teenagers, the search at TeenStreet is an aesthetic one. Here, the concept of a self–other relationship is prioritized and a potential context for living in the world is created. Here, also, literacy takes on the hue of communication because the purpose is not only to heal the self but to transform and be transformed by the self and others.

The interaction of the self and other in enactive imagery can be conceptualized as one of possibilities. To borrow a phrase from Levinas (1991), this interaction is a "face-to-face" encounter with the other. It is a pure, conceptless experience similar in many respects to Bakhtin's (1990) conception of the self–other relationship, wherein we all maintain a unique position in time and space and, as such, are dependent on others for making our limited perspective of the world more whole. Because others have unique perspectives, they offer the self ways of looking at the world that the self cannot experience or imagine without the other.

Levinas (1991) and Bakhtin (1990) posited the self's position in time and space as unique and as a prerequisite for interaction with the other. For Levinas, however, the other is unconsummated, presenting to the self excess, or possibilities. In effect, Levinas suggested that we cannot author others. To do so, would, at best, limit the self's understanding of the other and, at worst, lead to oppression of others. In this sense, the world is not a text, and others, like the self, move within an environment—a socio-political context—and, although the self responds to the other within the context, the context itself is unfolding in the interactions of self and other, and, in that, the other, who is face-to-face with the self, is full of possibilities, dynamic and yet to be finalized. The improvisation and movement exercises fully exemplify this dynamic and fluctuating state of existence.

Beginning with a grounding of the self in visual representations, teenagers interact imaginally, bringing their experiences—hopes, aspirations, fears, and understanding—to the fore, telling their stories, which present alternative possibilities for others. In the movement exercises, the self can see the other as unconsummated, as declassified, moving into the future. Because it is a safe space, TeenStreet fosters an interaction that honors the idiosyncrasies of individual members by foregrounding the body as actor and experiencer and not as something to be subsumed or consumed by outside stimuli or the effects of language itself. Yet, the notion of responding is important to the creative process because it is in response to others that the body moves forward and into the future, takes on different forms, explores possibilities, and rewrites its stories. Much of that response, I suggest, is contingent on honoring the unfinalizability, or possibilities, of others.

The theory underlying the creative process at TeenStreet is basically one of representation, starting with visual imagery, which Purves (1994) argued is the essential representation of youth today; moving to enactive imagery; and then to verbal imagining, or narration. This is a wholly different process than the teenagers are accustomed to at school. Moving from these images to writing, to verbal imagery, foregrounds the experience and emotions of the writer, but it does so within the context of interacting with others. The effect of beginning with the body in movement and improvisation and concentrating on interaction within a safe space is peculiarly emancipating in the same way that therapeutic exercises that are enactive representations are cathartic. The movement and improvisations free up the body for interaction. They also contextualize language within the body, where it is one's own, arising from the body as a product of physical action. The movement from visual to enactive to verbal representations precipitates a need to harness one's understanding of one's place and time in the world and to get one's words "out there" for others to hear. It becomes imperative that one communicate one's stories.

LOOKING AT THE WORLD THROUGH DIFFERENT EYES

During an earlier rehearsal, Bryn concluded a writing exercise and discussion by summarizing the conversation about voice that was woven throughout the entire discussion. He asked what voice is. The teenagers

offered ideas wholly grounded in the self, such as "thought," "experience," "attitude," and "emotion." Voice, Bryn agreed, is something of one's own, yet voice, he made clear and all the writing exercises demonstrated, is something one must nurture. It includes "mood, rhythm, and a sense of self. It's like shifting out of yourself," Bryn said. This hearkened back to the voice exercises, the notion of "the breath is the voice," and hearing the sounds others make, and placing one's voice against and with others. The way someone hears something is his perspective of it, Bryn said. What he hears, however, is another's voice emanating from a body, from a being.

The teenagers' notions of writing—ones that they have developed from school experience—are challenged by the structure of TeenStreet described in this article. Also, notions about artistry and creativity, about human interaction, and the relationship of the self and others, are being reconceptualized in the movement, improvisation, and writing exercises. Things they never would have considered doing when interacting or writing become habitual, with many of the teenagers saying they are transferring these newfound notions and conceptions to their lives outside the walls of TeenStreet. After only 2 weeks of rehearsals, most of the teenagers were making distinctions between the writing they do in school and in the workshops, noting how the emotions that seem to guide the movement and improvisations also guide their writing, making them feel for the first time that they are expressing who they are in their writing. Yusuf noted that most of the writing he did before TeenStreet "didn't have any type of emotional connection. It was more appearance, how your paper looked and how good it sounded, instead of . . . is there any depth to it." In an interview, Denise concurred, saying she had never "written from emotion" until joining TeenStreet. She joined the ensemble during one of its summer workshops and was returning after being away for a year. She told me how the process of "letting go," of allowing her experiences to enter into the writing, took time:

> [E]ven after that first summer I felt like I really hadn't let go. I felt like there was a lot of stuff I was holding back. I was writing something from honesty but there was still things I wasn't. I mean, you'd go back to school and you'd go back to the same way, writing things in the same pattern, bullshitting through papers.

She described the exercises at TeenStreet as "writing from sincere emotion." "School," she said, "somehow takes it and makes it clinical."

Chau said that before joining TeenStreet she was never really interested in writing. "School (writing) is hard because of the correct grammar." Although English is her second language, having emigrated to the United

States from Cambodia when she was 5, Chau's writing is both descriptive and reflective, with her problems of grammar being minor, and as Bryn suggested to her, maybe requiring her only to relook at what she writes to ferret out the meaning of some of her unique phrasings. Tonya said she now goes further with her writing, using metaphors to find connections with how she feels. Sheila said she, like others, has tried to transfer what she has learned at TeenStreet to her writing for school and has found that her English teacher is more interested in understanding what she is writing about and why. "He tells me this [her writing] really tells a story, then he asks me to explain it to him [to tell him how she came to her ideas]."

Nick noted that he had a good opportunity to learn how to write in school, but that he "kind of blew it off" because "it didn't seem important at the time because it wasn't what my life was about." The writing, he said, was heavily structured, "like 1, 2, 3, . . ." Now, however, he said, there are so many things he can do creatively that he had never even considered before. He watched the first rehearsal from the chairs, saying later that he was "freaked" by what was going on although he felt he understood the purpose of the exercises. "I just couldn't see myself doing it," he said in reference to the movement exercises. Now he is looking for ways to incorporate the same level of expressiveness—the experimentation and expression—that he experiences during rehearsals into his artistic projects outside TeenStreet, which includes playing in two bands he has founded with some friends. Yusuf, too, sees what is happening at TeenStreet as an awakening to possibilities. "This [the creative process of TeenStreet] is another option," he said. "It affects the way I look at the world." Of the effect of the movement and improvisation activities on her writing, Denise later told me, as she pointed her index finger outward away from her eyes: "TeenStreet has not changed what's on that side of my eyes. It's changed what's behind them. It's changed the way I want to look at things. It's changed the way I want to see life. I'm just looking at it through different eyes."

REFERENCES

Aylwin, S. (1985). *Structure in thought and feeling.* London: Methuen.

Bakhtin, M. M. (1990). *Art and answerability: Early philosophical essays.* Austin: University of Texas Press.

Bruner, J. (1986). *Actual minds, possible worlds.* Cambridge, MA: Harvard University Press.

Field, J. (Milner, M.). (1937). *An experiment in leisure.* London: Virago.

Fleckenstein, K. S. (1996). Images, words, and narrative epistemology. *College English, 58,* 914–933.

Heath, S. B. (1996). Good science or good art? or both. In D. Baker, J. Clay, & C. Fox (Eds.), *Challenging ways of knowing in English, math, and science* (pp. 13–18). London: Falmer.

Levinas, E. (1991). *Otherwise than being, or beyond essence.* London: Kluwer Academic.

Purves, A. C. (1994). People prose. In R. Fox (Ed.), *Images in language, media, and mind* (pp. 21–28). Urbana, IL: National Council of Teachers of English.

III

GRAPHIC VISION

7

Teaching the Language I/My Students See

Eric H. Hobson
Albany College of Pharmacy

> *Since children are both visual and verbal learners, and since both images and words are effective and compatible tools for communication, it seems obvious that the two should never be separated. Unfortunately, the traditional understanding of the visual image has been far too narrow and greatly misunderstood by most language-arts teachers.*
>
> —Olson (1992, p. 45)

Writing centers are dynamic environments, educational spaces that encourage continual reflection and reassessment. Working in writing centers and within their one-to-one and small-group writing tutorials forces writing center staff to revisit previously accepted ideas as part of the process of dealing with the fluid and shifting situations encountered within writing tutorials. Writing centers provide an unending chain of "ah-ha" moments—encounters and realizations that shape one's educational theory and practice. For example, one such catalyst for change occurred when I worked as a consultant during graduate school.

My fellow writing center staffers were aware of my undergraduate training in the visual arts, and they frequently manipulated the appointment book so that I worked with clients from the university's art program. They assumed that my art and composition training prepared me to work effectively with art students and their writing. They also believed that most (English-based) writing consultants would find it difficult working with these writers. Among other shortcomings, this sorting reveals the extent to which compositionists are unaware of the composition processes that drive other arts. To their credit, however, these colleagues were consistent with their biases: They routed all engineering students to the one consultant with corporate technical writing experience.

Students who gravitate to the mechanical and visual arts frequently carry emotional baggage about writing. Often writing is not a preferred or comfortable realm of action for them; rather, they use images, tools, lines, mathematical formulae, and so on to solve problems and communicate the results of their investigations. To develop an effective, low-risk bridge into writing, I worked with these reluctant writers by moving as much talk about writing away from the alien territory of writing terminology and abstract concepts to the more concrete, visual, and kinesthetic domains familiar to these students. These writers used sketches and diagrams—visual media with which they were comfortable—to discover composing strategies that increased their written competence and confidence by allowing them to produce written texts from a position of strength and control. The art students sketched paper plans and explored and assessed ideas through drawing (see Childers, E. Hobson, & Mullin, 1998; E. H. Hobson, 1990). Similarly, the engineers hunched over writing center tables, mechanical pencils, and plastic templates in hand-planning and revising written documents—frequently highly complex arguments—that the authors would translate from images to words, shifting from a rarely acknowledged academic text form to the preferred academic form of written texts. For the most part, these documents-in-process more closely resembled flowcharts and relationship-based diagrams than linear, worded texts (see Zimmerman & Marsh, 1989, on storyboarding).

Although the educational redlining illustrated by the manipulation of the tutoring schedule is philosophically disconcerting, the results were rewarding. Working with arts and engineering students established a set of assumptions about teaching writing that continue to influence my practice:

- Many visual artists are skilled compositionists whose design talents can transfer to writing.
- Taking chances is risky, and it is no surprise that visually dominant students may not achieve the same success in the writing classroom as do their verbally dominant classmates, or that they are anxious when they write.
- Drawing offers tools for helping students work through writer's block.
- Drawings offer powerful invention heuristics, problem-solving tools, and planning, drafting, and revising activities.
- Visual learners enter many writing classes with the deck stacked against them.

Much postsecondary writing instruction assumes that students learn alike, particularly through reading and writing. Yet as educational leaders across all levels of education have long noted, no single learning style allows all people to succeed equally (Fleming & Mills, 1992; Myers, 1990). However, acknowledging learning style differences and creating multimodal learning environments are very different. More often than not, when it comes to common models for teaching writing, visual learners get the short end of the stick, a reality that led Olson (1992) to note, "Visual learners know from an early age that it is verbal proficiency that really counts in school!" (p. 75).

FIGHTING THE CURRENT: VISUAL LEARNERS IN A VERBAL STREAM

The extensive research on the topics of personality and learning styles demonstrates that students excel in different learning domains, in part, because they prefer to interact with the surrounding world in different ways (Gardner, 1983; Jensen & DiTiberio, 1989; Lawrence, 1993; Myers, 1990). Such variety leads to many educational mismatches. For example, most secondary and postsecondary composition teachers are verbal learners who, among other traits, are comfortable with abstraction, whereas most of their students are not (Hurd & E. H. Hobson, 1999; Jensen & DiTiberio, 1989). When not acknowledged and acted on, this mismatch of student and teacher preferred learning styles can result in classroom-based writing instruction comprised of layers of abstraction: spoken instructions; words about words; references to such abstract ideas as pacing, form, audience, and thesis; and reading assignments of exemplary written texts. The writing assignments that accompany these discussions are often quite abstract, too. Students who are primarily concrete thinkers, visual learners, or multimodal learners with some combination of learning styles that do not include reading/writing as primary tools find writing within this instructional framework frustrating. Ongoing research using the VARK Learning Styles Inventory (Fleming & Mills, 1992) supports studies (e.g., Lawrence, 1993) that show the difference between the perceptual modalities that students use to interact productively with new information and those modalities that their teachers prefer. Bonwell (1998) and Hurd and E. H. Hobson (1998) found that college faculty are predominantly verbal learners—they prefer to interact with new information as printed words. Their students, however, are predominantly kinesthetic learners who prefer to interact with new information via concrete examples, real-life application, practice, and, if possible, hands-on exploration. To learn effectively, they need to see concretely how to do these tasks, often through frequent modeling and individualized instruction (Fleming & Mills, 1992; Jensen & DiTiberio, 1989).

Mismatches between learning and teaching styles contribute to students' frustrations with writing. Many students who come to the writing center looking bewildered and lost are neither lazy nor trying to buffalo tutors into doing their work for them. They are truly bewildered by their writing classes, teachers, and their assignments. Without frequent and specific examples of assigned tasks and the use of concrete practice activities, many students, particularly those who are largely visual or kinesthetic learners, genuinely find much of the in-class discussion about such writing issues as revision or closure unfathomable. In the face of such abstractions, visual and kinesthetic learners often resort to the learning algorithms—effective or not—that have served them best in the past and that allow them to work from a position of personal strength (Fleming & Mills, 1992). Many students whose observable writing process does not fit the mold of *good* writers (e.g., their pens may create pictures, not words) can use drawing as a productive prewriting process (Childers et al., 1998; Ernst, 1994; E. H. Hobson, 1990; Olson, 1992).

Whereas image preference fits the learning styles profile of visual and kinesthetic learners (Fleming & Mills, 1992; Gardner, 1983), mounting evidence from cognitive research is suggesting provocative linking of visual and verbal sensory data processing. This evidence bolsters anecdotal claims that visually based activity offers all students opportunities to make their writing processes more efficient and flexible. The strength of using images early in the writing process lies in the fact that much of human cognition is imagistic and impressionistic, more linked to general gestalts than to specific words. Recent neurobiological research by Sereno (Gutin, 1996) at University of California-San Diego suggests that visual image lies at the root of human thought and subsequent communication. Sereno's primary research area is the neurological architecture of vision in primates and rodents, and he has developed an interdisciplinary, complex theory about brain evolution and the origins of human language:

> Reduced to almost haiku proportions, Sereno's idea is this: language ability arose in the human brain not through the development of a new, uniquely human language organ, as most accounts have it, but by "a relatively minor rewiring" of a neural system that was already there. And that neural writing belonged largely to the visual system, a part of the brain that recent research—including Sereno's own—has shown to be almost unimaginably complex. (Gutin, 1996, p. 84)

Intuitively, this model makes sense because images would seem to be much more compact and efficient storage units than are words. Supporting this intuitive leap, Sereno's research into the origin of human language use suggests that visual images serve as the basis of language for a logical reason: The wiring in the brain that produces language is built on long-standing visual processing systems put to new use (Gutin, 1996).

CONFESSIONS

I have no notebooks squirreled away from any point in my education, a situation I now realize is quite atypical every time colleagues move and I heft their moving boxes filled with their notebooks. Their notebooks are considered priceless. My wife, for instance, still rues the fact that I persuaded her to throw away several undergraduate notebooks in a move years ago.

Notebooks were rare in my postsecondary education. Early notebooks duly bore a course title that would be crossed out and replaced by new course titles as they accompanied my progress through more than one degree program without getting filled with copious notes, neatly transcribed condensations of professor's lectures. By late in my doctoral work, these traveled notebooks were finally thrown into the recycling box. I do have sketchbooks from these periods, in which I recorded pertinent course information. Figure 7.1 came from a semester's study of Shakespeare. Although it presents no standard, recognized markers of the genre *class notes,* this page and others provide the prompts that my classmates' notebooks did. Whereas a rough transcription of a professor's lecture or a topic-based outline of important points raised in a seminar discussion help another student recall the texture of a particular moment, visual images have always provided me with more powerful mnemonic tools.

My watercolor instructor Bruce Bobick's advice about how to paint still serves me well although I rarely paint anymore. Unlike many of his colleagues, Bobick continually stressed that the sketchbook was an artist's most valuable resource: It provides a safe place to explore ideas in private, to record observations and assorted images that might (or might not) come in handy later; it allows the time and distance needed to let an image or idea lie dormant while the subconscious mind continues to explore the possibilities it contains, and then to return to play with these ideas and images; it provides a convenient place to think. My sketchbooks continue to validate this claim.

Bobick is responsible for my questions about how visual and verbal communication systems interact, in large part, because he made writing a central element of the watercolor studio. Although his painting students did not like it much and tended to write off as eccentricity his emphasis on writing, Bobick demanded that students use their sketchbooks as multimediated surfaces, with images sharing space with words. As a model, he shared his sketchbook with the class. Page after page of notes and

FIG. 7.1. Shakespeare seminar "notes."

sketches were interspersed with miniessays whose sole purpose was to record thoughts, ideas, impressions, feelings, choices, and experiments as he tested them before setting the outlines of an image down lightly in pencil on watercolor paper. If students asked which were more important for him as an artist—the sketches or words—he would attempt to show that such a hierarchy created a false dichotomy between two forms of thinking that he considered inextricable. He always pointed out that each sketchbook kept him from reinventing the wheel every time he started to tackle a new idea or take on a new project. These books provided him a detailed database of how he had explored other ideas and engaged other projects.

Like Bobick, I believe that sketching and doodling images—at times incorporating words—sharpens my awareness and encourages me to see and listen more acutely than when I take notes. Because the resulting *texts* are richly layered and deeply embedded with relevant, related images, working from them, I often remember directly linked and associated events accurately and clearly. Even more than a decade removed from the events recorded in these sketchbooks, I can use these sketches and doodles to re-create the actions and conversations of that course. It has been nearly 15 years since I was last in an art studio as a student. However, many lessons learned there about getting ideas to paper still serve as composition tools. Sketching can be an activity analogous to freewriting, offering students the same types of opportunities to learn from the activity in insightful and unique ways.

DRAWING TO WRITE

An effective way to show correlations between the composing process(es) of writing and the composing process(es) used by many visual artists is to use a discipline far removed from writing. Architecture is an apt example because in the minds of most writing teachers architecture is about as visual a discipline as one gets: The end products are such visual documents as site drawings, models, blueprints, and completed structures.

Graves (1977) argued that drawing is as an essential part of an architect's discovery and creation process. As such, it should be presented to students as an essential part of their education and training. Graves' argument is similar to many arguments made about writing in that it offers a familiar starting point for exploring the similarities between writing and drawing. Graves wrote:

> In exploring a thought through drawing, the aspect which is so intriguing to our minds, I suspect, is what might be regarded as the speculative act. Because the drawing as an artifact is generally thought of as somewhat more tentative than other representational devices, it is perhaps a more fragmentary or open notation. It is this very lack of completion or finality which contributes to its speculative nature.
>
> There are of course several types of architectural drawing. By clarifying the dominant nature of each type according to the intention the architect assumes for his drawing, we find three primary categories: 1 the referential sketch, 2 the preparatory study, and 3 the definitive drawing. (p. 384)

The three stages Graves (1977) mentioned—referential sketch, preparatory study, and definitive drawing—bear striking resemblances in their process and purpose to the writing process stages of invention, revision, and publication.

Graves (1977) used examples from one of his own projects—the Crooks house—around which to focus his discussion of the need for using drawings and the drawing process as a problem-solving tool. Referring to the difficult task of placing the building on its site, he identified as the source of the difficulty the task's "extreme level of geometric abstraction" (p. 390). As a strategy for working through this dilemma, Graves returned to his sketchbook. He wrote, "For me, the idea that seems to distinguish the general themes from others is that I not only admired them intellectually, but had also made a visual record of them. Because of the act of drawing they were made more accessible to me, for by reinterpretation I was not only understanding the physical phenomenon but also seeing it in my own personal vision" (p. 390).

For artist and writer, invention is essential activity. Just as verbal texts do not spring fully formed into the world, neither do pictures and other types of visual texts. Rather, a time and place for exploration, play and invention help verbal and visual artists alike discover what they are trying to say and explore what options exist for best making this statement. Sketching, the visual artist's primary medium for participating in a wide variety of invention heuristics, is necessary for playing with initial ideas, discovering what a person knows, identifying gaps in knowledge, developing solutions to problems, and retaining and retrieving images. For highly visual learners like myself, sketching and doodling is often a more productive prewriting, problem-solving activity than many invention heuristics presented in composition textbooks. The following activity is one that I use in a range of writing courses, including first-year and advanced composition, business, professional, and technical writing. Building on description (of events, places, people, processes) as a common rhetorical feature in texts composed for various purposes and audiences, I encourage all of my students (regardless of their dominant/preferred learning styles) to draw before committing themselves and their subjects to writing. A sample assignment follows:

Sketch your subject

Directions: On an unlined piece of paper, draw the person/place/item/process about which you are thinking of writing.

Time: 10 minutes

Tips: 1. Sketch quickly. Complete accuracy is not essential yet. 2. Don't worry about how the drawing looks. You aren't creating art, so it doesn't have to look "good"—however you wish to define that term.

The resulting drawings are rarely beautiful. Instead, they are functional tools, images that record important data in a tangible way that memory or

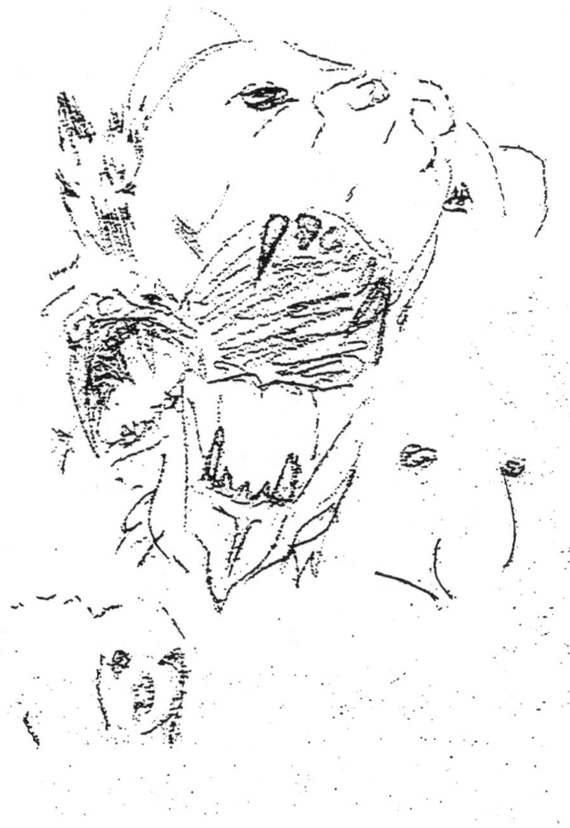

FIG. 7.2. Discovery sketches for essay.

reflection simply cannot (see Fig. 7.2 for one of many example sketches I provide students who request a model). Once this information is committed to paper, writers can begin to reflect on it and begin to plan how they might need to manipulate and revise it to achieve a specific communicative goal.

Taking the invention process into the visual rather than verbal realm helps to reveal the similarities between the way in which visual artists conceive of and discuss this exploratory part of their drawing process. Graves (1977) linked the *referential sketch* to invention within written composition by defining it in the following terms:

> *The Referential Sketch.* This kind of drawing may be thought of as the architect's diary or record of discovery. It is a shorthand reference which is generally fragmentary in nature, and yet which has the power to develop into a more fully elaborated composition when remembered and combined with

> other themes. Like the physical artifact collected or admired as a model holding some symbolic importance, the referential sketch is a metaphorical base which may be used, transformed, or otherwise engaged in a later composition. (p. 384)

The following two drawing activities build on the activity outlined previously and allow writers to explore their topic without having to add the often frustrating additional burden of wrestling with appropriate wording:

Zoom In/Out Task

Directions:

1. Divide a clean sheet of unlined paper in half along its horizon.
2. Focus on one specific area or detail within your exploratory drawing of your subject that you think might be most/least important or significant. In the top half of the page, draw this limited area again, focusing on including as much specific detail as you can.
3. On the bottom half of the page sketch a quick reproduction of the original drawing you made; however, this sketch should only fill the center of the available space. Then, fill in the surrounding blank space with the details that would exist around the outside of that first picture.

Time: 20 minutes total (10 minutes per drawing)

Working with images of the proposed subject matter from two divergent perspectives—up-close and at a distance—provides writers with concrete strategies for achieving two goals considered essential for effective expository writing: (a) Including specific details that support or illustrate general statements or specific claims made in the text, and (b) situating central concepts and claims within a larger context of people, events, ideas, and processes.

The following drawing activity was designed originally for out-of-class use in a technical report–writing course to help writers plan both an effective organizational structure and logical yet engaging, reading options for their World Wide Web home pages. Modified to reflect the context of other types of writing tasks, it has proven itself effective in helping reluctant writers plan (and, used later in the process, to critique) the overall structure of their writing projects.

Document Architecture Activity

Directions: On a blank sheet of unlined paper, complete the following task. Using a system of your choosing, draw the structure of your WWW home page so that another classmate can see (and understand) the following:

- what information you plan to include; topics you plan to cover

- the order in which that information will be made available to the reader
- what navigation routes you win provide the reader within your website
- how sections of your website relate/build on other sections of the site
- what links to other websites you plan to provide and at what places within your home page

The process of taking an idea through the stages of exploration and refinement that lead to a completed product transcends genre and media. Planning for and executing the revision of ideas are central activities for visual artists as well as for writers. Within the discipline of architecture, the activity—mental and physical—that provides a corollary to written composition's planning and revision stages is that of the preparatory study, which Graves (1977) described as follows:

> ***The preparatory study***. This type of drawing documents the process of inquiry, examining questions raised by a given intention in a manner which provides the basis for later, more defined work. These drawings are by nature deliberately experimental. They produce variations on themes, and are clearly exercises toward more concrete architectural ends. As such they are generally developed in series, a process which is not wholly linear but which involves the reexamination of given questions. (p. 384)

Three points in Graves' description of this activity merit further discussion: Graves (1977) focused on the systematic nature of drawings undertaken at this point in the architect's composing process—the fact that the drawings are "by nature deliberately experimental." Unlike the referential sketch, which is often attempted quickly and records fleeting ideas for later consideration, the preparatory study is more a conscious, less fortuitous process. As is also the case with writing, planning and revision involve a critically aware series of choices, not dependence on happenstance.

Graves (1977) noted the cyclical nature of the preparatory study—the exploration of "variations on themes." As in teaching writing, one of the most difficult activities that introductory drawing teachers face is convincing students that a first pass at an idea or image rarely produces results that translate completely to finished product. In only rare instances are images and ideas not tweaked, manipulated, altered, excised, and otherwise transformed. Students want their creation processes to travel in neat, linear trajectories; they want their papers and pictures to emerge fully formed. Their instructors face the task of revealing the naivety of this desire.

Particularly salient is Graves' point that this process of revising and extending initial ideas and images works to make the abstract concrete. By working more than once and from more than one angle, through nascent and usually abstract visual or verbal ideas, artists make their ideas more tangible and more likely to achieve communicative success.

Students, however, find it difficult to plan for and carry out revisions especially if their level of maturation and cognitive development limits their perception of the world to a largely egocentric perspective. As a result, many novice writers and artists assume that because they know what they are trying to say, everyone else should, too. Experienced visual and verbal artists recognize the naivety of this assumption and know that revision helps make their ideas more accessible to a wider audience than themselves. As Graves (1977) commented about the results of his own revisioning of the Crooks house project, "the preparatory studies for the Crooks house led me to see the relation between building and landscape as less abstract and more figurative" (p. 390).

IN CLOSING

Although I teach writing, not painting, Bobick's belief in the usefulness of writing to lead to drawing influences my teaching and writing. My first drafts of essays, chapters, articles, and letters can look more like cartoon-infected flowcharts than ideas fleshed out in words. This composing pattern gets me over the first-draft hump without staring at a blank piece of paper or computer screen. Once I sketch the images and ideas I am aiming for, I can begin to effectively shape them for my reader. I translate my initial image/text from one communicative medium to another, making my thoughts and intentions accessible for the verbally dependent audiences to whom I usually write. Moving from a drawing to a worded manuscript is a process of reforming the text to meet a specific audience constraint.

As a teacher in a college of pharmacy where few students see themselves as strong writers, I offer alternative approaches to writing, including visual-then-verbal invention and drafting heuristics. Although still rudimentary (Childers et al., 1998; E. H. Hobson, 1990), drawing-leading-to-writing composing strategies help my visually dominant students who do not gravitate to the more abstract, verbal bastions of the humanities. Such visual-based writing activity, likewise, has much to offer verbal learners and abstract thinkers. The challenge is in facilitating their exploration of this unfamiliar territory.

It makes pedagogical sense to bridge the artificial gaps that have been demarcated between the verbal and visual arts. These arts rely on similar compositional algorithms to allow artists and writers to craft their desired messages. As teachers like Bruce Bobick, for instance, demonstrate every day in their classrooms and studios, their students have much to gain from considering and exploring composition methods from disciplines other than their home. Instead of distantly related methods, visual and verbal compositions can be allies in helping students develop the visual-verbal literacy skills they win need to function successfully in the visually saturated culture that surrounds them.

If we look at drawing from this perspective, the composing processes that drive the creation of the plastic and two-dimensional arts have much to offer those charged with teaching writing to students cut from various cloths. Although we have tended to segment them to separate corners of the curriculum and to separate corners of our lives, drawing and writing are not alien, antithetical activities. Visual artists write and verbal artists draw (Hjerter, 1986). Writers who draw and visual artists who write use these media as tools for making their intended statements as effectively as they can. What this type of crossover offers them is the power contained for making knowledge in the processes behind these means of communication. There has been a long history of this crossing over and cross-pollination, even if it has not always been highlighted or used as an argument for incorporating elements from each in the teaching of the other. Our students, too, can use this versatility to their advantage, making writing a more productive, less frustrating, and/or less alien communicative activity.

REFERENCES

Bonwell, C. C. (1998, October). *Active learning and learning styles: Making the connection.* Faculty development workshop, Albany College of Pharmacy, Albany, NY.

Childers, P. B., Hobson, E. R., & Mullin, J. A. (1998). *ARTiculating: Teaching writing in a visual culture.* Portsmouth, NH: Boynton/Cook.

Ernst, K. (1994). *Picturing learning: Artists & writers in the classroom.* Portsmouth, NH: Heinemann.

Fleming, N. D., & Mills, C. (1992). Not another inventory, rather a catalyst for reflection. *To Improve the Academy, 11,* 137–155.

Gardner, H. (1983). *Frames of mind: The theory of multiple intelligences.* New York: Basic Books.

Golden, C. (1986). Composition: Writing and the visual arts. *Journal of Aesthetic Education, 20,* 59–68.

Graves, M. (1977). The necessity for drawing: Tangible speculation. *Architectural Design, 6,* 384–394.

Gutin, J. A. C. (1996). A brain that talks. *Discover, 1,* 83–90.

Hjerter, K. (1986). *Doubly gifted: The author as visual artist.* New York: Abrams.

Hobson, E. H. (1990). The writer's journal and the artist's sketchpad. *Writing Lab Newsletter, 14,* 1-3, 14.

Hubbard, R. S., & Ernst, K. (Eds.). (1996). *New entries: Learning by writing and drawing.* Portsmouth, NH: Heinemann.

Hurd, P., & Hobson, E. H. (1999, July 6). *Pharmacy students' learning style profile: Course and curricular implications.* Paper presented at the meeting of the American Association of Colleges of Pharmacy, Boston.

Jensen, G., & DiTiberio, J. (1989). *Personality and the teaching of composition.* Norwood, NJ: Ablex.

Lawrence, G. D. (1993). *People types and tiger stripes.* Gainesville, FL: Center for Application of Psychological Types.

Myers, I. B. (1990). *Gifts differing* (2nd ed.). Palo Alto: Consulting Psychologist Press.

Olson, J. L. (1992). *Envisioning writing: Toward an integration of drawing and writing.* Portsmouth, NH: Heinemann.

Zimmerman, M., & Marsh, H. (1989). Storyboarding an industrial proposal: A case study of teaching and producing writing. In C. B. Maralene (Ed.), *Worlds of writing: Teaching and learning in discourse communities of work* (pp. 203–221). New York: Random House.

8

Images Across Cultures: Exploring Advertising in the Diverse Classroom

Roy F. Fox
University of Missouri–Columbia

Teacher:	I like this "Milk Likes You" ad.
Lim:	I see Kristi Yamaguchi in same kind of ad.
Kayla:	Who is Kristi Yamaguchi?
Lim:	Japanese ice-skater—ugh!
Kayla:	Is she very beautiful?
Lim:	*No* Japanese beautiful!
Teacher:	That's not true, Lim. . . .

This conversation occurred within a Missouri high school English as a Second Language (ESL) classroom with 12 students from nine different countries. Kayla asked about the woman featured in an American ad. Lim, an intense, serious boy from Korea, replied with an unwarranted generalization about Japanese people. His teacher countered. This cultural and gender issue arose naturally from a conversation about specific magazine ads.

Although their conversation surfaced within an instructional context, these students were not "performing" to address the prescribed "lesson of the day," nor were they answering canned questions from the end of a textbook chapter. Instead, they exercised nearly complete ownership of what they were examining, thinking, and discussing. It was a ripe, teachable moment. Most conversations throughout this exploratory study of advertising, conducted as an informal experiment in a high school ESL class, were not this pointed. Yet many exchanges were like this one—natural, substantial, and honest. Overall, whether analyzing or creating ads, these students generated effective thinking and language.

This chapter describes what happened when this diverse group explored contemporary advertising. Their teacher, Betty Belcher, and I wanted to examine how these students constructed meaning when they were immersed in selected, contemporary, powerful ads. We wanted to observe their critical thinking within the context of their literacy development. We wanted to know (a) how students communicated about the ads' topics and issues, (b) how they read and interpreted advertising's printed and visual texts, (c) how they wrote about ads and their related issues, and (d) how they designed their own ads and what they thought about them.

WHY USE ADVERTISING TO DEVELOP CRITICAL THINKING AND LITERACY?

The study of advertising—especially the evocative, highly visual magazine and TV advertising—provides many rich opportunities for learning and teaching. Students should study ads for a flood of reasons. First, advertising instantly places all students on a level playing field: Most students have been exposed to thousands of ads. This deep pool of knowledge and curiosity makes it easier for them to think, speak, and write when responding to ads. Advertising's topics, characters, situations, styles, products, and appeals are limitless. Second, ads easily elicit student responses because students know that ads represent real messages with specific purposes and audiences. Yet studying advertising is not easy. Most students have seldom analyzed ads or their responses to them. When students react to visual messages, they articulate their thinking (orally and in writing) more willingly and quickly than they often do when responding to print material. This allows teachers more opportunities to extend and build on this thinking and language.

Third, students should study advertising because it is America's most ubiquitous type of public discourse, relentlessly selling objects, services, political candidates, lifestyles, attitudes, values, and beliefs. The average American sees 32,000 TV commercials per year (Considine & Haley, 1992). Fourth, students should study advertising because it is America's most powerful type of discourse. Hugely expensive productions, ads skillfully synthesize words, voice-overs, graphics, images, music, and special effects. Using small focus groups, mass survey techniques, and computerized equipment (e.g., the eye-scanner and analog machine), ads are thoroughly field-tested and crafted to *hit* their *target* audiences. (Note advertising's common use of military metaphors.) Students, then, must learn to decode, analyze, evaluate, and create media—print as well as electronic.

Fifth, students should study advertising because our learning is visual—as much as 80% according to some researchers (Davies, 1996). If learning is anchored in imagery, then it stands to reason that imagery influences thinking and verbal literacy skills. Students construct meaning by interacting with images, just as much as they do with language (e.g., Arnheim, 1986; Eco, 1976; Fleckenstein, 1996; Karl, 1994; Paivio, 1990). In summary, whether we receive them, send them, or think in them, images represent the most common and unifying element of language, media, and mind (Fox, 1994).

Finally, by engaging in intelligent resistance to ads, students develop several kinds of health: (a) *physical health*—by learning about tobacco, drugs, nutrition, and exercise; (b) *emotional health*—by gaining perspective on media-imposed definitions of beauty, sexuality, maturity, and problem solving and by exploring such issues as instant gratification; (c) *social health*—by exploring how ads communicate attitudes, values, and ideologies, including those of consumption, competition, and materialism; and (d) *cultural health*—by exploring if, when, and how ads present groupings of people, such as examining stereotypes of gender, race, and class (Fox, 1996). Students must control advertising lest it control them.

PROCEDURES

This chapter focuses on only seven of the students enrolled in this first-level ESL class. Kayla, a sophomore from Iran, was very quiet in class. Lim, a studious junior from Korea, was living in America while his parents served as visiting university faculty members. Juan, an exchange student from Mexico, was vocal and energetic. Simone had grown up on a sloop in Paris. Monica, a junior from Ecuador, was engaged to be married. Kiema, a junior from Iran, was sent by his family to the United States to earn a diploma and experience American culture. Finally, Carlos, newly arrived from Brazil, was less proficient in English than his classmates.

At the time of this study, their teacher was enrolled in an evening media literacy course, which I was teaching. Throughout this 4-week study, we discussed the project and made small adjustments. The chapter's findings are based on the following data: (a) the ads I initially selected for classroom use, (b) students' oral comments and written responses to ads, (c) the ads created by students, along with their reflective responses, and (d) Betty's daily reflective journal. Students viewed, discussed, wrote about, and created print ads from magazines. Following is a summary of the four phases of the inquiry-based procedures used during this study.

Students began by examining their own TV-viewing habits—content, length of time, and reactions to programs. Because they were asked to compare American TV with TV in their own countries, they often explored cultural differences. For instance, Simone did not own a TV, and the students from climates that are mild year-round spent more time outside after school than did their Missouri counterparts. Next, students read, discussed, and wrote about Linda Ellerbee's "When Television Ate My Best Friend," responding to such questions as, "When do you watch TV? What kinds of programs do you enjoy? Has TV ever affected you the way it did the girl in Ellerbee's article? If so, explain."

In Phase 2, students brought in three newspaper or magazine ads that they judged to be effective. These ads could come from their own country or the United States, and they had to promote different products (e.g., cars, food, cosmetics). All ads were displayed around the classroom and discussed. The teacher then picked an ad and demonstrated how she would complete this assignment by responding to these items: (a) Describe your ad, (b) What is the message (focus on words as well as visuals)? and (c) Why do you like this ad? Afterward, the students picked their favorite ad and responded to these items in writing. During the next two classes, they examined and analyzed ads, focusing on whether each ad would be effective in each student's native country, explaining why or why not. To help them analyze ads, students also applied Rank's (1982) guidelines.

In Phase 3, students created their own ads. They chose (or invented) products or services and then determined the ad's target audience, format, and verbal and visual elements. Students worked on their ads for one class period and finished them at home. During the next two classes, they presented their ads, addressing the following questions: (a) What is this ad trying to do? (b) How is the ad trying to do this? (c) Who is the intended audience of this ad? (d) What do you like about this ad? (e) Would this ad be more successful in the United States or in your country and why? (f) What might need to be changed in this ad? In the final phase, students explored creative ads that had been distributed around the world by companies based in the United States, Great Britain, Germany, Brazil, Denmark, Switzerland, China, and Italy. Such ads often employ little or no language. The ads for Bally Shoes, for example, rely only on the inventive use of the shape of a footprint.

Students examined overhead color transparencies of these ads before choosing two and explaining why they liked them. Next, students selected a single ad and wrote their responses to these questions: (a) What is the story behind these pictures (fictional account presented in ad)? (b) What are you thinking about when you look at each picture? (c) What product or service do you think this ad is selling? (d) What do you think the creator of this ad is trying to make people think? Again, before students began writing, the teacher modeled this process, thinking aloud as she composed on an overhead transparency. Students' final drafts were copied and distributed to all class members. Each writer read his or her paper aloud as the others silently read along, noting questions and strengths.

FINDINGS

The following sections discuss some representative findings from this study. The first section, Critical Thinking About Ads, includes students' focus on audience and purpose, gender and cultural stereotyping, language manipulation, emotional appeals, appropriateness for another culture or gender, and conflicting versus multiple interpretations. The next section, Critical Thinking and Ad Imagery, includes thinking focused on images as well as thinking *with* images, such as identifying and interpreting line, color, shape, size, repetition, association, omission, space, and proximity, and how the visual connects to the printed text. The third section, Critical Thinking While Creating Ads, explores how students generated verbal and visual text.

Critical Thinking About Ads

The following vignettes illustrate how students questioned, hypothesized, speculated, analyzed, synthesized, evaluated, and connected the local and global elements of advertising.

Students Generated Their Own Questions About Ads. Students would often ask their own questions (as Kayla does of Lim, at the opening of this chapter). While examining a black-and-white ad from China, Simone requested that her teacher ask a Chinese student in another class about the myth behind the ad's illustration. Also, while discussing the ads that students brought to class, they inquired about the meanings of words, such as *shadow, seal, evaporation, logo, perspiration, critical,* and *against.* One question often prompted others. When Simone posed questions about a public service ad for an eye bank, Carlos questioned her religion, which elicited much discussion. He even asked Mrs. Belcher if she was a Christian and if she planned to donate her organs, too. This discussion resulted in another interpretation of the ad. This active inquiry occurred naturally and within the context of a single, simple ad.

Observations About the Small Details of Ads Led to Consideration of Larger Issues. A basic tenet of critical thinking is that students connect the global with the local: They link the generalization with the specific detail, the abstract concept with the concrete example (S. I. Hayakawa & A. Hayakawa, 1990). The class examined an ad depicting a Michael Jordan-like basketball player, and two other athletes. They were praying on bended knee and with hands clasped together or over the heart. Each panel of this ad looks like a church's stained-glass window. A ball from each sport (basketball, soccer, and tennis) serves as a halo around each athlete's head. The ornate print above the ad states, "The Temple of Nike," followed by "Hours of Worship: Mon–Sat 10–7 PM. . . ." An excerpt from the extensive discussion about this ad follows:

Juan: Look at the balls—soccer, basketball, baseball. . . .

Simone: I think some people don't like this—some people would think is blasphemy.

Lim: (Looks around room and counts the Nike shoes; all the boys were wearing Nike athletic shoes.) Where you get your shoes, Mrs. Belcher?

Teacher: Wal-Mart. And my shoes are as good as Nike shoes.

Lim, Juan, and Carlos: No, no, no. Cannot be!

Teacher: God shoes, huh?

Through their own natural questioning, these students learn that their teacher disagrees with the "worshipping" of name brands, as the ad suggests—a larger, more complex topic than where the conversation began. In her journal, the teacher noted that the two girls laughed at her comment, but the boys did not. (Alas, the larger topic suggested, blasphemy, was not developed here.) However, in quick order, two complex, substantial issues arose—without the teacher lecturing or preaching—for students to explore in language. Consequently, the students remembered this name-brand issue when it resurfaced later in another context—when the class examined a subtle British ad for Hush Puppy shoes. The teacher described this discussion:

> The Hush Puppies ad made everyone smile. Somehow, a discussion began about who had how many dogs, cats, turtles, guinea pigs, etc. Everyone in class except Kayla had various pets. Carlos asked, "What is Hush Puppies? Truck?" He was surprised to hear it was a kind of shoe.
>
> "You know—quiet—like the good Nikes," Lim told him.
>
> "Right, Lim," I teased, "not like these Wal-Mart shoes that make lots of noise."

> Everyone laughed. This was a good sign that the students were understanding the concepts and conversation.

Here, Mrs. Belcher gently steered the conversation back toward the larger issue of name brands and their hefty prices. The class then continued this discussion. However, this occurred on the heels of a long, animated conversation about pets, which was not the study topic, but a topic that the teacher recognized as a valuable and context-rich use of spontaneous language for her ESL students. This serendipitous and natural discussion may not have happened without the stimulus of the ads. In some of the following sections, notice that students, too, sometimes move conversations from details of ads to larger issues.

Students Explored the Cultural and Gender Issues of Ads. Throughout this project, students often focused on issues of gender and culture—differences as well as similarities. These interactions created a natural opportunity for the teacher and other students to provide additional viewpoints or balance. When their teacher modeled how to write a "story behind the pictures" for an ad from *Sport Magazine*, she described a man in the ad as a Japanese athlete, striving for an Olympic gold medal. Lim, the Korean student, promptly told her that she was "wrong"—that the person she identified could not be an Olympic athlete, that, in effect, the Olympian could not be Japanese. Later that day, his teacher made the following journal entry:

> I told him [Lim] that I saw the ad in a different way than he did, and that was okay. I wondered if his comment stemmed from the fact that I made the main character Japanese. I told everyone that there could be no wrong answers to these questions—it was how each person saw the ads.

Considering Lim's previous comments, the teacher is probably right. Although this is a sensitive issue, Lim is shown that ads are open texts that carry several possible interpretations. Also, this issue of discrimination occurred in a safe, natural context: The ad elicited the issue—not Lim and not the teacher. Consequently, authentic learning occurred. Also, to his credit, Lim questioned the teacher's authority and offered a second interpretation. He was thinking!

When Lim wrote a fictional story behind the pictures of the "Temple of Nike" ad, he synthesized cultures:

> There were three famous sportsmen in the world. Each of them played tennis, basketball, and soccer. Strangely, they were raised at Temple, which located in Korea. Actually, their father participated in Korean War, that's because they were left in Korea and raised, even if they were foreigners. Of

> course, their religion is Buddhism. They tried and tried. Eventually they represent Korea National Olympic team. At the year of 1988 at Seoul, they played for their country for the first time. So before the first game, they were praying at the temple. That time, their sponsor was Nike Company.

Lim controls the ad message by transforming it to mesh with his own culture, providing a realistic scenario of how two cultures merged. His approach demonstrates a positive, unifying point of view by envisioning Michael Jordan as Korean. Also, note that Lim places Jordan in a Buddhist temple—not a Nike or "commercialized" temple. Lim seems to have modified his earlier stance about name brands, when he defended the superiority of Nike shoes. Lim later wrote that, "Nike is like sacred. The creator want to remind like this slogan. So that to sell Nike goods more and more." Lim shifts away from his earlier, automatic acceptance of the brand, and toward the advertiser's motivation.

Throughout this unit, gender differences frequently surfaced. The international Bally shoe ads employ footprints in different contexts, much like the international Absolut liquor ads use the shape of its bottle. Although these ads appear quite similar, the boys preferred the Absolut ads and the girls the Bally images. Of course, culture and gender can be very closely linked, as in this example about Kiema and Kayla, the boy and girl from Iran. The first day of the unit, students discussed how they spent their free time at home, including watching TV. When the issue arose of how safe it was for students to be outside their homes after school, Kiema (male) said, "In Iran, very dangerous. You know if you on street with friends, the police stop you and say, 'What are you doing? Go home now.' One time I arrested because I had Walkman. You must stay home in Iran or you be in jail." Lim then added, "In Korea, after school you must study, not watch television. You in school from seven to ten or eleven at night. Students do not get make choice; must study always." On hearing this, Juan and Carlos interjected, "What? In school eleven at night? No!" Because the class had just heard from the Iranian boy, the teacher instinctively turned toward Kayla, the Iranian girl. Yet as the teacher noted in her journal:

> When I looked at Kayla, she avoided my eyes. I knew she didn't want to speak about this. Sometimes, if Kiema [the boy from Iran] had voiced an opinion, Kayla would not talk. I respected this and looked at Simone.

Several days later, the teacher asked students to write about one of the international ads that they had discussed earlier. Kayla chose a black-and-white ad that depicted a Chinese myth. According to the teacher's journal:

> This made Kiema furious. He said something in Persian to Kayla that was very harsh and gruff. Kiema then chose another ad and returned to his seat.

> A few minutes later, Kayla slowly returned the Chinese ad and selected a second advertisement. Then, Kiema happily jumped up and claimed the returned ad. He in no way acknowledged Kayla's actions—not a look in her direction, not a kind word, not a thank you—nothing. This was expected. I reminded the class that two people may choose the same ad, but Kayla knew better than to try to reclaim her first choice.

Near the end of the unit, Kayla read her writing aloud, stating, "I don't think the product is trying to sell something. It is a feeling of a young man and the picture of this ad is trying to say, 'Just don't think about yourself—think about other people. . . ." Although Kayla rejects the ad's sales purpose, she thinks independently, ascribing her own meaning to the illustration. What was most remarkable, however, was described by her teacher: "This was the first time in eight months that I had heard Kayla defy a male in any way. The class applauded at the end of her reading." Ads elicit responses based on the reader's personal experiences. Kayla's interpretation may have allowed her to express her feelings toward Kiema and possibly others—feelings she could not openly verbalize.

Critical Thinking and Ad Imagery

> When I look at these pictures, I immediately think of the sadness of the girl's face. Then I see that it is not sadness but maybe concentration. I also think of the way that some people think that winning is everything, that nothing is more important than being number one. The [fencing] mask seems to be dark, strong, and secure, giving someone the power to be number one.

In this visual, Monica engages in critical thinking by closely observing the girl's face and then ascribing symbolic meaning to the mask. Monica and her classmates not only thought about images, they also thought *with* and *through* images when the image was not present. Although Monica's analytical response here differs from American students' typical initial responses to ads (Fox, 1994), overall, these ESL students' initial reactions were similar to their American counterparts. For instance, after viewing many of the international ads—most of which contain little or no language—Carlos would always exclaim, "Ah! I like!" During a discussion of TV commercials, Juan imitated all of the ad's voices. In short, students were usually involved and energetic when responding to ads.

Observations of Small Visual Elements Led to Consideration of Larger Issues. The reading of an ad's visual elements (e.g., identifying and interpreting line, color, shape, size, repetition, space, and proximity) often led students to the larger issues of an ad's message, purpose, and audience. An Australian ad tried to communicate the durability of its swimwear with a photograph of a dead shark on a ship. The shark is splayed open and its guts are spilled out, but the swim trunks, amid the gore, remain unscathed. The entire class groaned at this ad's gruesomeness, but none of the students turned away. Kiema jumped up to point out a human arm within the shark's messy entrails. Kayla observed a skull within the organs. The arm and skull were difficult to identify, whereas the advertised swim trunks were easy to spot. After Kiema and Kayla made their sharp observations, the class could better grasp how the visual effectively conveyed the durability of the product.

These students perceptively interpreted color and contrast. One hair color ad that Lim chose showed a model's golden hair cascading down her back. Lim noted that the gold color of the model's bracelet enhanced the gold highlights of the model's hair. In an American milk ad, Lim and Simone observed that the darkness surrounding the lone model, as well as her dark clothes, intensified the whiteness of the woman's "milk moustache." The discussion then focused on, "Why would the creators of these ads emphasize *these* shades and colors?"

Students Often Relied on Association to Interpret the Meanings of Ads. Like all media, advertising is highly intertextual. One sign or symbol—pictures, words, or music—can suggest others. The Absolut Vodka ads reminded students of footprints in the Bally shoes ad. Of course, this same ad could just as easily elicit other meanings—a vacation in Switzerland, a novel, or the film, *Jurassic Park.* Associating one thing with another is a common way in which people respond to images, as well as think through or with images (Eco, 1976; Paivio, 1990). The students in this study were no exception.

One series of international IBM ads employ only the company's logo—the letters *IBM,* constructed with blue and white stripes. These ads are filled with nature scenes, such as a close-up of roses on a trellis. Yet within each scene is one structure that is colored with blue and white stripes (like the logo), such as a footbridge or the trellis behind the roses. Responding to these ads, Lim said, "Looks like the flag—same colors as the American flag." (Neither their teacher nor I initially made this link.) Then Monica added, "I think it says if you use IBM computer, you have time to do these things." Both students associated the meanings of one sign or symbol with another, although Monica further extended her interpretation of it.

Similarly, a series of international ads for Hush Puppy shoes is also devoid of verbal text, except for a line of small print above the image, which reads, "Be comfortable with who you are." The large images in this series show one person with a dog or two. In one ad, a man lies on his back, at work under a car, as his dog sprawls beside him, facing the camera. In another ad, a large dog sits up and alert in a small convertible's front seat, while the relaxed owner's crossed legs stick up out of the backseat and rest on the trunk. After viewing these ads, Monica wrote that,

> The maker of this ad is telling us that if you buy that kind of shoes you will get a comfortable life, as the life of the dogs. And you will feel the connection between the shoes and your feet as the connection that you can have with your dog.

Monica makes a perceptive observation. Instead of picking up on the print's suggestion about self-acceptance or positive identity, she generalizes that owning Hush Puppies leads their owners to eternal relaxation. However, Monica's linking of the foot/shoe relationship to the owner/pet relationship is more complex. What's more, she constructed this analogy from the image without the intertextual knowledge that many American readers might bring to this ad (that the terms *puppies* and *dogs* can refer to feet and that to live carefree is to lead a "dog's life").

The most intellectually vigorous discussion occurred when students disagreed with each other's interpretations—especially those based on associations from images. Their discussion was so intense that they even challenged their teacher. Mrs. Belcher described one such class in her journal:

> Using my "milk moustache" ad as a model, I answered four questions about my ad. Simone had a cow when I compared the composition of the ad to the "Mona Lisa." She thought it was blasphemy, although Juan and Lim supported my observation. Several students objected to my message derived from the ad. Yay!!!! They were right with me, thinking and challenging. I let them talk, refute, rebut, revise their oral language. . . . Wow. The oral language I heard used was thoughtful and insightful.

Critical Thinking While Creating Ads

To become truly media literate, students must comprehend media messages, as well as compose them—for any product or service, any purpose, and any audience. Often working collaboratively, students applied the principles of design, language, and persuasion that they had been exploring through the American and international ads. Personally invested in these projects, students devoted much time and effort to them. Lim's ad grew out of an experience with his teacher and Carlos. Lim asked Mrs. Belcher if he could borrow her watch, a fake Rolex, to use as a model for his ad. The teacher recorded their conversation in her journal:

> "Hmm. You have a Rolex? Very expensive," Lim told me.
>
> "Yeah?" Carlos asked, breaking away from his work and examining the watch with Lim, while the other students continued working.
>
> "Where you buy this?" Carlos was obviously aware that Wal-Mart shoes and a Rolex watch usually are not on the same body.

"Mexico," I answered.
"Yaah?" Carlos laughed.

Lim's ad (see Fig. 8.1) employs a side-by-side comparison of his teacher's watch and Carlos' watch, using visuals and verbal text, labels of important features, and a testimonial from another student.

In his written reflection, Lim stated that:

> This watch has special functions like TV and telephone. So especially business people will be use this watch more than normal people. And also this ad is compare with watch's rival company. I like my ad because it has a lot of detail things. It will be successful with countries because Korea and States have a lot of business men or something like that.

Lim's ad about the fake and real Rolex demonstrated his attempt to incorporate—within the confines of one ad—what he has learned about advertising's manipulation of images and words. The following section summarizes a few observations about students engaged in thinking and language while creating their own ads.

Students Integrate Their Own Viewpoints Into Ad Messages. By connecting to themselves, their family, or their native country, students gained ownership of their work, devoting considerable time and energy to it. Juan's ad was a simple cartoon comparing an overweight person to a

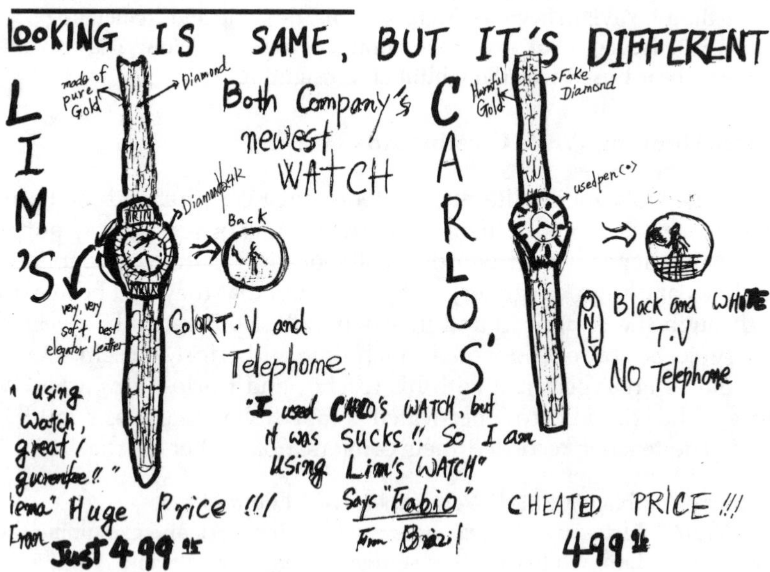

FIG. 8.1. Lim's Rolex watch ad.

thin one, extolling the virtues of Diet Coke over Diet Pepsi. Although this ad was relatively uninspired, his written reflection on it showed a deeper level of thinking:

> I try to sale Diet Coke because I think that Diet Coke is better than Diet Pepsi, and my ad means that if you drink Diet Pepsi, you will feel horrible, and if you drink Diet Coke, you will feel good and look better. . . . Because I don't know how in USA, but in Mexico a lot of women are worry for her body, and if you write your ad like mine, you will sale much.

Juan's goal is to help readers associate intangible qualities with his product. Also note that Juan's written syntax—his use of subordinate clauses embedded within a compound sentence—reveals thinking and fluency in his second language. Finally, Juan's focus on Mexican women's worry over their body image may have been influenced by prior class discussions about how advertisers employ beautiful models to sell their products. Here, Juan may be perpetuating the exploitation of women, an issue that this advertising unit placed on the table for exploration. Many teachers (including me) would question Juan's capitalizing on women's "worry for [their] bodies." However, the larger point is for students to become aware of such messages. And Juan indeed demonstrates an awareness of at least two sides of this issue. To censor part of his view would likely negate much of what he has learned. Such issues, though, could be addressed further by anonymous student evaluations of the ads, or by a conference between the student and teacher.

After abandoning her bread idea, Kayla constructed an ad for a computer to express her own viewpoint. The only text stated, "I'm waiting." In her written reflection, she stated that:

> My ad is trying to sell computer. This computer is for adult and teenager. I try to show the picture of the computer and what can the computer do. I think this ad will be more successful in the United States. Because in my country, is few people know "what is computer and how to use it."

Kayla considers the possible appropriate audiences: both adults and teens in Iran and the United States. The line, "I'm waiting," can speak for both audiences—for the American who is simply waiting for a new computer, as well as for the Iranian—including Kayla, herself—who is waiting for *her* first computer. Kayla's message satisfies her own need as well as her audience's.

Kiema focused almost exclusively on the visual in his pen-and-ink Visa Card ad (see Fig. 8.2). Initially, he wrote, "Never leave home without Visa." When the teacher questioned the originality of this line, he replied, "This is my idea. This is what I think of when I think of city." He later changed this line to, "What is the smartest thing to have in this city?" This

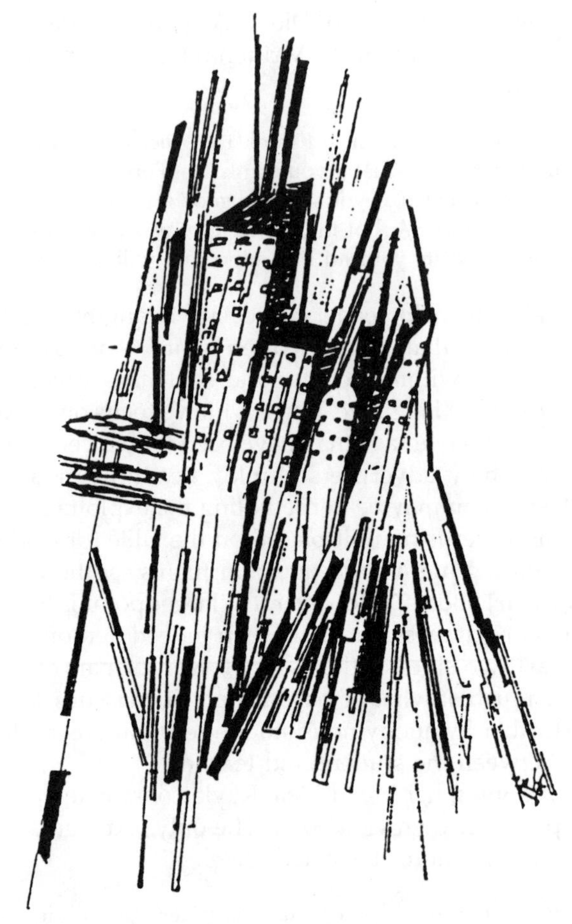

FIG. 8.2. Kiema's credit card ad.

revision is a question and more open and inviting for readers—similar to the international ads.

Although Kiema changed the borrowed line, his theme reminded the reader of the appeal to fear from a popular American series of MasterCard TV commercials. He wrote that:

> My ad try to show large and smokey city. You can see factories and cars and lots of people. And it is not safe to have check and cash, the only thing is to have card and I use visa card. My ad is for people do business. My ad try to show in the city life New York if you want to have money the only way is to have credit card.

Kiema's original drawing of New York City is striking: Its black-and-white contrasts communicate a kind of stark reality—its hard edges and jagged, sharp angles clash with each other. Kiema created a loud, bustling, harsh city—which accurately reflects his intentions, theme, and verbal text in an effective, original manner. Kiema connects the visual to the verbal.

CONCLUSIONS

During this study, students constructed meaning from their personal interactions with images, which are mediated by language—a process that resides at the core of thinking and literacy development. When students construct meaning, the products and processes of images are just as important as the products and processes of language. After the course ended, the classroom teacher and I agreed that students' motivation, thinking, and language (spoken and written) benefited from their study of advertising. Despite their diverse cultural backgrounds, they had considerable experience with advertising. From the outset, students were confident in using English to express their thoughts, feelings, and questions about advertising, as well as about their own culture and social issues. Students expressed ideas that they had seldom, if ever, verbalized, including topics that might have been taboo in their own cultures.

In their second language, students articulated abstract, incomplete thoughts about complex issues, such as gender and culture. This in turn often elicited further thinking and language from others, creating an authentic, social context for growing ideas, for developing language and literacy skills. Although this is desirable for all students, ESL writers must learn to think and explore and discover in their second language and not merely translate already familiar material. Reading, interpreting, and creating ads helps students become better thinkers by developing their spoken and written language, their visual perception and thinking, and their ability to connect verbal and visual text. No matter how many different ways I look at the study of advertising in the classroom, I end up thinking the same thing that Carlos concluded about a Pepsi ad he admired: *Very, very cool.*

REFERENCES

Arnheim, R. (1986). *New essays on the psychology of art*. Berkeley: University of California Press.

Considine, D., & Haley, G. (1992). *Visual messages: Integrating imagery into instruction.* Eaglewood, CO: Teacher Ideas Press.

Davies, J. (1996). *Educating students in a media-saturated culture*. Lancaster, PA: Technomic.

Eco, U. (1976). *A theory of semiotics*. Bloomington: Indiana University Press.

Ellerbee, L. (1991). When television ate my best friend. In *Move on: Adventures in the real world* (pp. 79–82). New York: Putnam.

Fleckenstein, K. (1996). Images, words, and narrative epistemology. *College English, 58,* 914–933.

Fox, R. F. (Ed.). (1994). *Images in language, media, and mind.* Urbana, IL: National Council of Teachers of English.

Fox, R. F. (1996). *Harvesting minds: How TV commercials control kids.* Westport, CT: Praeger.

Hayakawa, S. I., & Hayakawa, A. (1990). *Language in thought and action* (5th ed.). San Diego: Harcourt.

Karl, H. (1994). The image is not the thing. In R. F. Fox (Ed.), *Images in language, media, and mind* (pp. 193–203). Urbana, IL: National Council of Teachers of English.

Paivio, A. (1990). *Mental representations: A dual coding approach.* New York: Oxford University Press.

Rank, H. (1982). *The pitch: How to analyze ads*. Park Forrest, IL: Counter-Propaganda.

9

Technologizing the Word: William Blake and the Composition of Hypertext

Gregg Hecimovich
Seattle University

None could break the Web, no wings of fire.
So twisted the cords, & so knotted
The meshes: twisted like to the human brain
—William Blake, "The Book of Urizen" (1970/1704, p. 82)

Behind every writing occasion is a technological vehicle; behind every word committed to paper or an electronic chip, the innovations and limitations of medium have their say. Students usually do not recognize the full impact of this truth. No doubt, they think: "What does technology have to do with me?" Beyond writing a paper with the assistance of a computer, most students think very little about the impact technology has on the process of composition. The trick is to get students to *see* the truth, to practice a wider vision of composition, a vision that no longer regards the technology of writing as transparent, but instead regards the process of writing as an ideographic art. In my advanced composition course, I take Blake's *The Marriage of Heaven and Hell* (1704, 1970) as the exemplar text and his vision of words serves as our model for the power of technical writing in the modern age.

Composition comes from the Latin *com-*, which means "together," and the Latin *poner*, which means "to place," "to put down." Put in its broadest terms, composition involves a whole network of etymologies: disposing, imposing, interposing, opposing, proposing, and supposing. William Blake's *Marriage* serves as a model for this work. In his "Illuminated" *Mar-*

riage, Blake drew together verse, prose, drawings, and color to give body to his vision of political, psychological, and philosophical truth. The composition of ideas, as Blake well knew, finds its inspiration in forms and figures as well as in the traditional language arts. In an age of multimedia and the Internet, the future rests in a wide range of composing skills. We undertake the cultivation of these skills in the class.

Blake integrated the technological process of art with the act of composition to produce a "Composite Art" (Blake, 1970/1801, p. 74). As he noted in *Marriage:* "But first the notion that man has a body distinct from his soul, is to be expunged; this I shall do, by printing in the infernal method, by corrosives, which in Hell are salutary and medicinal, melting apparent surfaces away, and displaying the infinite which was hid" (p. 39). Blake was concerned about the disembodied voice that print threatened to champion. An art that separated the body of the speaking subject from the energy of its expression was an art of dead matter. Blake attacked such a conception of art and the world it represents by "printing in the infernal method." Blake developed his "infernal method" to bring together passion, activity, intellect, and imagination, hence the interactive nature of his process and the variety within the copies he produced.

Marriage has always been the seminal work for Blake studies—the work that articulates most sharply Blake's artistic vision. Because the work approaches a wide range of themes and subjects, I begin the course with a study of its primary challenges. For Blake, sexual and social morality, backed by the apparatus of religion and law, restrains energy, passion, and genius, condemning humanity to a spectral half-existence. In such a world, men and women accept a worldview that believes in an objective truth to which we must conform ourselves (Damon, 1988). Rank and wealth determine power, and existence becomes the half-life of people seeking to measure and define their lives according to dead objects. Instead, Blake celebrated the opposing forces of passion, activity, intellect, and imagination. For Blake, vision and art come together to challenge a life based on dead things. Blake's *Marriage* serves as his *Principia,* a revolutionary text that deconstructs traditional beliefs. In *Marriage,* Blake upset a common stock of associations, challenging the received positions of reason as right, church as father, law as order. The vision is sketched through a series of mental encounters called "Memorable Fancies," as well as the famous "Proverbs of Hell," an inspired vision delivered to the poet, not at the top of Mount Sinai, but among the smoldering fires of his engraver's shop.

To frame Blake's vision and his "Composite Art," I begin the course with a discussion of oral, written, and digital forms of communications. I ask students to draw three columns on a sheet of paper marked *oral, written,* and *digital.* I then ask them to recount under each an instance of an important, vivid, or memorable communication they have received within each medium. While students prepare their responses, I draw the same columns on the board. In our class tally, invariably, students observe under *oral* moments like being cursed, praised, or told stories, as well as courtship rites. *Written* communications include letters of acceptance to college, bills, semester grade reports, books, newspapers, and speeding tickets. Among *digital* communications, students usually cite e-mail exchanges with friends and family, online purchases, and music or digital media. We then proceed to compare and contrast the different types of communication that we receive according to the different forms.

Our discussion of the assembled lists allows us to extrapolate the primary qualities associated with each. The items included under *written,* we note, are traditionally allied with permanence, rational reflection, and the dissemination of content widely over the material contexts of time and space. In its reproducibility and embodiment of a fixed physical form, these written communications function as stable and permanent texts, removed from the circumstances of direct interaction (letters of acceptance, bills, grade reports, speeding tickets). In contrast, the items listed under *oral* demand the immediate presence of a speaking subject and an audience. Direct human presence, we note, often leads to communications we associate with immediacy, spontaneity, and a passionate expressiveness (oral stories, jokes, and requests for dates). In facing this dichotomy, digital media holds a middle ground. Digital interchange, such as e-mail, and asynchronous "chat" software, resists the temptation to conform to the conventional oppositions of written and oral forms. Such digital forms, we note, practice communication as a mediating power, one that attempts to incorporate the conventions of both writing and speech, literacy and orality, and thereby fully engage with the complex and polyvalent dimensions of language as a whole. Digital interchange can even invite the immediate and direct exchange of images and colors, as well as words (hypertext, digital drawings, graphics, pictures, and digital music/multimedia).

In his incorporation of the oral tradition into his printed texts, I suggest, Blake demonstrated a prescient glimpse of digital composition in its multivalent dimension. Blake aimed for a method of interchange that invited permanence, rational reflection, and dissemination, as well as immediacy, spontaneity, and passionate expressiveness. A close study of Blake's infernal method in the context of recent advances in technology provides a unique opportunity for tracing the ways in which oral traditions shadow print traditions in the rising arts of digital communication. In a series of lectures, to this end, I direct the class's attention to (a) Blake's vision of words and his use of "digital" technology, and (b) print history and our participation in that history as we move forward into the digital age. I augment the lectures with an "illuminated" assignment designed to draw students into imaginatively practicing the concepts presented. Such lessons prepare students to think more critically about the role of digitization in computer-based culture. The parallels also prepare us to see—as Blake did—the possibilities technology holds for integrating language and images.

BLAKE'S VISION OF WORDS AND THE COMPOSITION OF HYPERTEXT

Blake's works are oddly situated between the mass-produced form of the printed book, altered forever in the 19th century with advances in paper and print production, and the more individualized forms of digital dissemination, in which the author holds formal control over his or her medium. His books are printed from copper plates and a rolling press and therefore utilize many sophisticated aspect of 19th-century book production. Yet all dimensions of their production—the writing, etching, printing, coloring, and distribution—are undertaken by Blake alone; labor is not divided among author, printer, and bookseller. In their curious mix of technological sophistication and their self-conscious control of the transmission of the writing product, Blake's literary productions provide important insights into the nature of both print and digital technologies.

To demonstrate how Blake's illuminated works extend our understanding of writing and technology, I emphasize Blake's artistic process and the uneasy relationship it holds to the history of oral and print culture. In a dream, his brother Robert appeared to him and suggested the "Illuminated Process" that would become his trademark. Blake characterized this vision in *Marriage* as his "infernal method." The process involves a letter or image to be raised from the surrounding metal rather than being etched or engraved into it. The letter or image then stands up in relief against the flat plain of the copper plate to be inked and printed (see Fig. 9.1). Blake took the practice further. He developed a method of creating words and images in a single operation. He worked directly from the copper plates using the plates as an artistic medium (Ackroyd, 1996). Blake's first step was to cut out plates from a large sheet of copper, using a hammer and chisel, and to prepare the surface. He made out a rough design with white or red chalk and, with the chalk as a guide, he used a camel-hair brush to paint the words and images upon the plate with a mixture of salad oil and candle grease. The mixture resisted the *aqua fortis,* or acid substance that bit into the surrounding plate for 3 or 4 hours. The "bite" was usually achieved in two stages so that Blake could check on the prog-

FIG. 9.1. Blake, *America a Prophecy* (1793): fragment of relief-etched copperplate. Plate 81 (Copy D), relief etching, c. 1804–1820. Reprinted by permission of the Houghton Library, Harvard University.

ress of the operation. After that time the words and images stood up in relief as part of one coherent design (Ackroyd, 1996; see Fig. 9.2).

The most important technical complication that Blake faced was that he had to write his words backward with his quill so that when the image was printed in reverse they would be the correct way around. To help students visualize the process, we follow the procedure through a series of digital slides. These slides include illustrations of the instruments Blake used to provide variety to his designs—among them quills, brushes of various thickness, as well has his own stock of engraving tools.

FIG. 9.2. "The Lamb," Plate 8, detail of copper plate.

To complete the process, Blake still needed to bring his infernal method through the printing stage. When the acid had provided the proper bite, Blake used a conventional printer's ball of cloth to ink the plate with burnt walnut oil or burnt linseed oil; the plate was then printed on Whatman paper (Ackroyd, 1996; see also Viscomi). The operation resembled the process of woodcut engravings that came into vogue in the 19th century. In woodcut engraving, blocks made from the endgrain of boxwood became the medium. Boxwood is hard enough to let the artist use fine details, and it could withstand the force of the mechanical presses. In class, to demonstrate the process I use an ink stamp pad, cloth, and paper. With advances in mechanized printing, I explain, the process of relief illustrations became increasingly popular, occupying a central place in the books, newspapers, and periodicals of the print revolution. In the commercial era that followed, labor was divided: Artists produced the drawings, and engravers incised them on woodblocks. Stereotyping and later electrotyping made available multiple copies of the same block for high-speed presses (Mitchell, 1988). Blake's vision of "Illuminated" printing foresaw such advancements—with a difference. Blake controlled all aspects of his "labours vast with his Chisel & the mallet" (Blake, 1797/1970, p. 390).

Blake's process was part chance, part artistic strategy. If Blake's "Illuminated" printing prefigures the advancements of 19th-century print technology, it also emphasizes the spontaneous nature of composition—a spontaneity usually associated with oral forms. At each stage Blake wished his composition to be unprompted, an immediate and altering engagement between author, medium, and intended audience. His incorporation of the immediacy of the oral tradition into his printed texts demonstrates one of the earliest uses of interactive print technology. By processing images, words, and design elements simultaneously within his medium, Blake fashioned an early model of technical writing for the digital age.

Digitization is not a notion confined to electronic devices, but a technological norm that operates across a spectrum of materials and processes. It is essential to underscore this truth, and Blake's work demonstrates the point. The organizing principle behind Blake's "Illuminated" process and that behind digital technology hold important parallels. In both, complex operations are mechanized by being broken into simpler operations. In many cases, divisions that are more efficient depend on some binary or digital segment by which all things can be reduced to two bits, 0–1, on–off. Relief printing is just such a technology, with the raised text functioning as a "1" or "on" and the relief area as a "0" or "off." Twenty-six letters in the Latin alphabet, plus 10 numerals and a few accidentals, extend the range of information stored in the two bits of "1–0" and "on–off." By providing alphabetic technology as moveable type, two bits begin to hold the power of all written expression. Like typesetting or the division of all words into a small group of uniform letters, Blake's relief etchings practice the power of digitization, only for Blake digitized content is conceived and executed as an integrated visual field (Eaves, 1993).

Like software design, segmented packets of meaning are arranged and processed in a fashion that looks forward to the "Composite Arts" of the digital age. The lecture on Blake and his "Illuminated Process" concludes with the point that Blake's work with iron and acid foreshadowed the "Composite Arts" of digital media. The two lectures that follow explore 19th-century print history and the subsequent print technologies that make possible the invention of Hypertext and the World Wide Web. Here, too, I observe Blake's infernal method as a model for realizing the power of technologizing the word. Together, these lectures help prepare the class for the culminating "Illuminated" assignment.

19-CENTURY PRINT HISTORY AND THE COMPOSITION OF HYPERTEXT

The year 1798 is best known to literary history as the date of *Lyrical Ballads*. Because 1798 is also the year of Wordsworth's famous Preface, it is often taken to mark the beginning of the English Romantic period. Yet the date has another significance for literature and especially for its dissemination. Two events occurred in that same year to transform printing from what was essentially an industry of hand production to a mechanized industry such as we know today. In 1798, Lord Stanhope invented the iron printing press—the first major advance since the printing press was introduced. In the same year, Robert, a Frenchman, took out a patent for a paper-making machine. For centuries, sheets of paper had been made by hand dipping a mat or wire frame into a vat of wet pulp, the chief component of which was rags. Robert's machine supplanted this slow and costly method, providing the second essential step in the mechanization of print production (Hayden, 1983, p. xvi; see Fig. 9.3). Within 25 years, half of all paper in England was machine produced, and mechanized printing gave rise to a golden age of periodical literature: Journals, newspapers, pamphlets, and books appeared in a readily obtainable form. From 1700 to 1750, an average of 93 books were published each year in England; by 1790–1800, that number had more than quadrupled to an average of 372 books; from 1800 to 1827, the average increased to 588; and by 1853, the number of books published was more than triple that in 1827 (Hayden, 1983). In 1797, the circulation of the major monthly reviews and magazines was between 3,250 and 5,000, which, compared with the average run for a book, was quite large. By 1847, the sheer numbers overwhelm—over 50,000 individ-

FIG. 9.3. Hopkinson's improved Albion press. From *A History of Wonderful Inventions* (London: 1849). Reprinted by permission.

ual titles were in circulation according to a recent estimate (Kent, 1984). The combination of the new technology, the population explosion, and rapidly rising literacy rates signaled a shift away from oral culture. Oral culture's singular hold on folk tradition began to wane. Suddenly, oral forms found new life in print.

Less than 200 years later, in 1989, a different print-related technology reached a significant milestone. Berners-Lee of CERN, the Swiss particle physics institute, proposed the basis of the World Wide Web initially as a means of sharing physics research. Berners-Lee's proposal extended the vision of Stanhope's and Robert's advancements, allowing simpler, more consistent, and inexpensive ways to share and produce texts (see Fig. 9.4). Indeed, Berners-Lee's work can be viewed as the logical extension of the innovations built on Stanhope's and Robert's work. His goal was to take advantage of existing technology to produce a seamless way in which data from any source could be arranged, produced, and uniformly disseminated. The World Wide Web did this, encompassing all existing infosystems such as FTP, Gopher, and Usenet without alteration. Like Stanhope and Robert, the innovation proved revolutionary. The World Wide Web was born.

Three new technologies are incorporated into the new design: (a) Hypertext Markup Language (HTML) serves as the programming language used to standardize the components within a document, (b) Hypertext Transfer Protocol (HTTP) provides the operating function used to transmit the pages, and (c) a Web browser client software program receives and interprets data and displays the results. In practice, the invention proves a new way of effecting the advances of Stanhope's and Robert's inventions re-creating for the digital age the 19th-century print revolution.

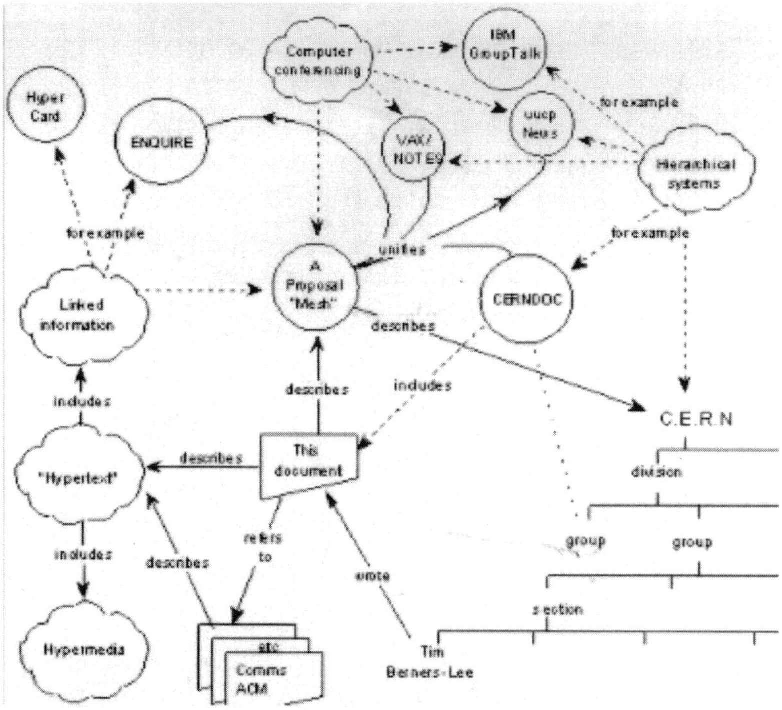

FIG. 9.4. A concept map from Berners-Lee's original World Wide Web proposal, a Hypertext system called the "Mesh," presented in 1989. Available: http://www.w3.org/History/1989/proposal.html.

The parallels are instructive. HTML serves as a more powerful letter- and image-casting device, an extended Hypertext version of moveable type. HTTP serves to digitally process the manufacture of text and images, like Stanhope's Iron Hand Press 200 years earlier. Finally, the Web browser client software functions as a powerful receiver and medium, displaying on an open field the final product. Now instead of exchanging wet rags for processed paper, digital screening exchanges the paperless environment of the computer monitor for processed paper. The comparatively labor-intensive work of paper printing and the physical distribution of printed text is transformed into the hypermechanized processes of HTTP and HTML, used in association with Graphical User Interfaces (GUIs) or client browser software such as Netscape and Microsoft Internet Explorer (see Fig. 9.5). The result is as striking today as the flood of periodical literature was in the 19th century. In 1998, a hundred years after the birth of mass print culture, the new form of digital literacy, the World Wide Web, reached a hallmark. In the fourth quarter of that year, the number of web pages reached 320 million, with 1.5 million web pages being produced

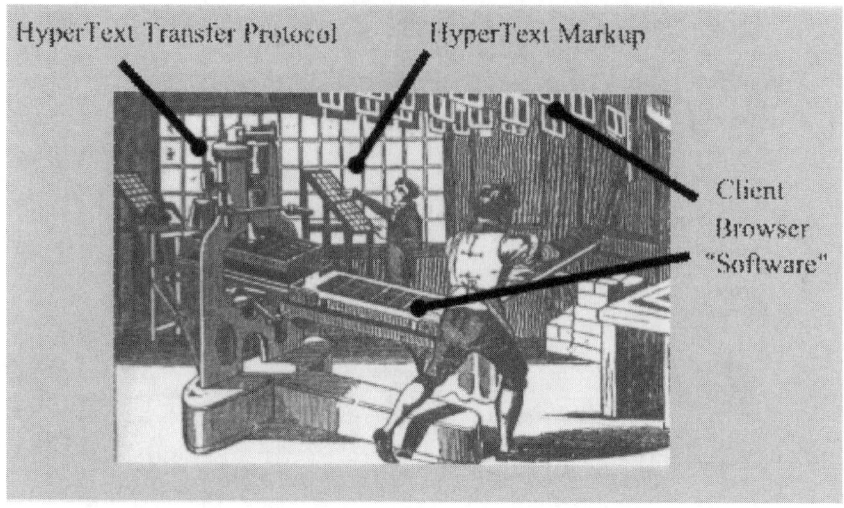

FIG. 9.5. The Stanhope Iron Hand Press. From *The Pictorial Gallery of Arts* (London: 1846). Reprinted by permission.

daily. The percentage of registered domains increased by 118%, traffic over the Internet doubled every 100 days, and the estimated number of Web users in the United States stood at 57,037,000 and worldwide at 147,800,000. Growth of the World Wide Web continued to balloon even beyond the predictions of the most optimistic observers. Internet Service Providers, numbered at a mere 130,000 at its inception in 1989, reached 36,739,000 by July 1998. The extraordinary growth finds its analogy only in the print revolution of the 19th century. The same is happening now as literate forms find a new expression in digital media (Gromov, 1998; Treese, 1999).

Blake, I note, already contains the seeds for both revolutions, print and digital. Like Blake's copper designs that provide the efficiency of reusable and interchangeable parts, a similar principle holds for the uniform programming of web design and the chase orientation of linotype printing (see Fig. 9.6). With web design, the digital etching or two bits, 0–1, on–off commands of HTML are stored on a host server, ready to be retrieved, processed, and freshly displayed on the monitor of the computer that recalls the information and images. In designing a web page, an author must code language and images with uniform tags that can be recognized by any Web browser. For instance, to code a design that will include an image of a lamb and a small shepherd boy, along with the text "Little Lamb God bless thee, / Little Lamb God bless thee," a Web designer will have to provide "1" and "0," "on," "off," two-bit information, not unlike

FIG. 9.6. Type in chase from a Linotype machine from the 1970s.

those created by Blake with his copper, *aqua fortis,* salad oil, and grease (see Fig. 9.2). Such a design will tag and turn "on" and "off" the features of the design according to a reusable script. Design tags will be invisible to the viewer, but are in fact "hyper" language being processed beyond the viewer's eye (see Fig. 9.7). For instance, an image tag that assigns an image

FIG. 9.7. William Blake, "The Lamb," detail.

file and positions it within the field of a browser may appear as "<p align= 'middle'> <img src='lamb.jpg'>," and so forth. Such tags remain hidden from view, but function beyond the field of vision in a fashion not unlike Blake's relief etching. For Blake, too, a matrix of carefully placed lines are sequenced and written onto a medium (in this case iron), and the orchestrated whole is processed to produce a design that can be altered by the user or person executing the design.

Blake clarified the philosophy behind his conception of such "Composite Art" on Plate 11 of *Marriage*. Here Blake (1970/1793) told how "the ancient Poets animated all sensible objects with Gods or Geniuses, calling them by names." However, "a system was formed, which some took advantage of, & enslav'd the vulgar by attempting to realize or abstract the mental deities from their objects" (p. 38). Adams pointed out that the activity of "the ancient poets" was "the creation of language," but that "the poetic verbal universe that holds subject, deities, and objects together is destroyed by a competing idea of language that claims for itself only the power to point outward toward *things*" (Hilton, 1983, pp. 67–68). Blake was emphasizing in *Marriage* the ability of words to disclose a unity between subject and object, body and soul, medium and performance. Accordingly, his "infernal method" melts away "apparent surfaces" and "displays the infinite which is hid" by seeing language as an energy and a process, extending "the organs of the sense" and "Expand[ing] [the] Eyes of Man . . . [into] the depths of wondrous worlds" (Blake, 1970/1797, p. 406).

"ILLUMINATED" ASSIGNMENT

To illustrate Blake's vision of "Composite Art," print history, and their ability to "Expand [the] Eyes of Man," I assign students an "Illuminated" project as we complete this section of the course. Students are asked to invent a digital printing process out of the materials they can gather in their dorm rooms or from their homes. The assignment forces students to rediscover the digital technology behind all print. Students are forbidden to use pencils, pens, markers, printers, or computers; rather, they must develop their own "infernal method" using everyday materials. Each student is assigned the task of "Illuminating" a political, psychological, or philosophical truth in a reproducible manner. The difficulty of the assignment is part of its intent. To shape a meaning worth reproduction is to face the singular challenge of invention. Part of their task, I tell them, is to discern a "truth" by composing it, and then reproducing it for others to perceive. I advise students to figure out the means by which they will express themselves, and then develop their expression by allowing the process to help determine their design. As Blake's work demonstrates, the act of composition is the act of seeing ideas performed in the technological processes of composing.

The students who succeed best prove to be those who are most inventive with their medium. Take, for instance, the project of a student from a recent class. Using thick dental floss, toothpaste, candle wax, and mouthwash, he developed a process he called "Illuminated Dentistry." By modeling recognizable images of sports utility vehicles from candle wax and including the relief lettering of dental floss hardened in toothpaste, he depicted a series of satirical prints, "The Proverbs of Halitosis." These hardened plates were then washed with the red stain of Scope and pressed on heavy bond paper to fashion a series of "truths." Written in the spirit of Blake's "The Proverbs of Hell," the project proved a memorable indictment of U.S. energy policy. Spelling out ironic and sinister mottoes like "No Boundaries," "Extreme Power for Extreme Pleasure," "Conquer Any Jungle—Including the Concrete One," and "Work Hard—Be Successful—Go Someplace Where None of that Matters," the project demonstrated Blake's artistic principles. Every student received a copy, and every copy held a different cast to the bulky figures of vehicles set off by the altered "bleed" of their mottoes. As the student explained to the class, he wanted to underscore the bad taste of thoughtless consumerism: The noxious gases attributable to the sports utility vehicle are the noxious gases fostering environmental halitosis. Student projects such as "The Proverbs of Halitosis" help to reinstate the power of print technology in fashioning ideas.

CONCLUSION

Blake's "Composite Art" of language challenges the classical conception of written language as a corrupting technology and seeks to demonstrate the power of language conceived as ideographic word objects. For the Greeks, the same word *techne* is used for both craft and art; the craftsman and the artist are called by the same name: "technites." Yet for Blake, *techne* never signifies the action of making. The *techne* schema reinforces the very intelligible/sensible schema Blake wished to displace. Accordingly, *techne* involves an artist/artisan who sees with the mind's eye and apprehends the intelligible thing that will be expressed in a sensible medium. *Techne* is misleading in such a formulation. For Blake, the technical practice of composing language and art denotes rather a mode of knowing. To know means to have seen, in the widest sense of seeing, which means to apprehend what is present, as such. When *techne* is considered the bringing forth of an intelligible vision *(eidos)* into a sensible form *(aussehen),* as the Greeks considered it, *techne* does not signify the power of poesis, or making. The task of composition—Blake suggested—is the task of seeing ideas performed in the act of composition. The *techne* of his work's coming-in-to-being holds true to the "processive" nature of technology where the bodying forth of intelligible vision *(eidos)* into sensible form *(aussehen)* occurs synchronically.

In his prospectus "To the Public" (1970/1793), Blake devoted his introductory remarks to the new technique of "Printing both Letter-press and Engraving [i.e., texts and designs] in a style more ornamental, uniform, and grand, than any before discovered, while it produces works at less than one fourth of the expense" (p. 692). His emphasis on the medium calls the public's attention to the means of production as an essential aspect of the work's expression. Essick (1985) noted this aspect of Blake's work:

> The processes used to create an image, whether pictorial, ideographic, calligraphic, or typographic, form a matrix that determines the character of that image. Media are often manipulated to overcome or disguise their inherent properties, and familiarity decreases our awareness of limitations and silent directives, but the determinism of a medium never disappears. When an artist makes a small alteration in the methods of producing an image, it may go unnoticed, since it will have only a slight impact on the product. But if he introduces a major change—for example, from letterpress texts illustrated with intaglio engravings to words and pictures etched together in relief—the audience will suddenly become aware of the new medium itself, not just its content, and may be discomfited by its unfamiliar limitations and unreceptive to its special virtues. (pp. 834–835)

Thus, in 1793, when Blake advertised his new books in a prospectus that may have been printed in the new medium, he emphasized their technical features. For Blake, the public must understand technology as a precondition to the meaning a work performs. To "technologize the word" is to be received into the "Composite Art" of self-discovery. Blake's infernal method proves an apt lesson for the digital age.

REFERENCES

Ackroyd, P. (1996). *Blake.* New York: HarperCollins.

Blake, W. (1970). *The complete poetry and prose of William Blake* (D. V. Erdman, Ed.). Garden City, NJ: Anchor.

Damon, S. F. (1988). *A Blake dictionary: The ideas and symbols of William Blake* (Rev. Ed., M. Eaves). Hanover & London: University Press of New England.

Eaves, M. (1993). *The counter-arts conspiracy: Industry in the age of Blake.* Ithaca, NY: Cornell University Press.

Essick, R. N. (1985). William Blake, William Hamilton, and the materials of graphic meaning. *ELH, 52,* 833–872.

Gromov, G. R. (1998). *Growth of the Internet statistics* [Online]. Available: http://www.internetvalley.com/intvalstat.html.

Hayden, J. O. (1983). Introduction. In A. Sullivan (Ed.), *British literary magazines: The romantic age, 1789–1836* (pp. xvi–xxviii). Westport, CT: Greenwood.

Hilton, N. (1983). *Literal imagination: Blake's vision of words.* Berkeley: University of California Press.

Kent, C. (1984). Introduction. In A. Sullivan (Ed.), *British literary magazines: The Victorian and Edwardian age, 1837–1913* (pp. xv–xxv). Westport, CT: Greenwood.

Mitchell, S. (1988). Wood engraving. In S. Mitchell (Ed.), *Victorian Britain: An encyclopedia* (pp. 870–871). New York & London: Garland.

Treese, W. (1990). *The Internet index* [Online]. Available: http://new-website.openmarket.com/intindex/99-05-s.htm.

10

Technology, Symbol, and Discourse: Writing Within the Information Overload

R. Mark Smith
Valdosta State University

Like their classical counterparts, contemporary writers search for "places" from which to secure information. However, instead of the mental trek through a pre-Gutenberg catalogue of schemes, tropes, and commonplaces, today's rhetor often identifies electronic *loci* on a computer monitor and manipulates both alphabetic and nonalphabetic symbols to access information externally.

Similarly, most contemporary writing instructors emphasize topical, socially relevant writing that demands both familiarity with new information sources and analytical acumen. Certainly, the proliferation of electronic information has revitalized the relevance of topical writing and the role of our students as social entities. This information can also expedite timely social discourse, allowing the learner to probe beneath political or media spins and genuinely research-relevant social issues. However, the Internet's by-product, information overload, which can be both overwhelming and soporific, can also lead student writers to submit work that is woefully deficient of the anticipated critical inquiry:

> I think that the President's health care plan is a good thing. Every year, millions of people die because they have no money and cannot go to the hospital. The health care plan will give everyone good health care. No one will die because they cannot get into the hospital. The health care system will become better because right now, only rich people can afford health care and poor people cannot get it.

This excerpt is simply an aggregate of maxims with no internal logic or transition. The writer has modified the classical maxim—originally intended as tool for logical argument—into a simple rhetorical ornament.

We have long encouraged our students to move beyond the superficiality of flat, expository writing that portrays experience as detached and objective. Schooled in process approaches and social constructionism, we encourage writers to acknowledge and interpret their lived experience. We hope that our students, with their world as their text, will recognize themselves as social individuals and exit the writing class understanding that writing is consequential to life. However, when we encourage students to write about world events—most of which are played out in the electronic media—we often find that their discussions are actually collections of maxims and redundant, circular assertions as exemplified in the previous sample. Part of this problem lies in the singular, symbol-driven nature of electronic discourse that encourages proverbial writing. Certainly, teachers have always contended with aphoristic writing. However, the emergence of electronic symbols as rhetorical commonplaces can challenge relevant student prose.

From the fuzzy specters of Burns and Allen on black-and-white televisions to the vivid images of Bill Clinton and Elian Gonzales on color monitors and high-definition screens, the image is seminal to electronic communications, primarily because communicators are vying for a slice of a diminishing public attention span. Advertisers, newswriters, and other architects of electronic information must quickly captivate the preoccupied psyche, or the window of opportunity shuts. Consequently, communicators must resort to bountiful, yet elemental, symbols for a shorthand code. Furthermore, these messages must be conveyed in a potent, succinct format that evokes instantaneous impressions. As Toffler (1970) observed some time ago, "In an effort to transmit even richer image-producing messages at an even faster rate, communications people, artists, and others consciously work to make each instant of exposure to the mass media carry a heavier informational and emotional freight" (p. 149). The result has been a cornucopia of images: Product logos, celebrity faces, and familiar landscapes and landmarks are reproduced and disbursed in advertisements and newscasts through both electronic and print media. Unfortunately, immersion in a zeitgeist of symbols threatens to engender a new type of unexamined and cliched writing.

Cicero encouraged his listeners to be informed citizen/orators. Even today, being well informed suggests a certain trendiness as such events as "Live Aid" and MTV's 1996 "Rock the Vote" couple social issues with entertainment. Indeed, my students are cursorily familiar with many news topics. Their journals contain brief entries about health care, AIDS, Bill Clinton's ups and downs, and rising fuel costs. However, students' knowledge of and commentary on current events are often superficial because news and information are presented to them rapidly and repeatedly as "factoids," exemplified in CNN's recapitulations of the world's events through visually provocative sound bites and summaries in which the viewer is bombarded with periodic updates with little backgrounding or detail. The popular print media such as *USA Today* employ a similar printed format with charts and full-color pictures and graphics around which the text is wrapped. Through such technical refinement and repetition, cultural symbols have become excessively benign and user-friendly, reduced to interchangeable icons constructed for passive consumption (Flanigan, 1980).

Langer's (1942/1979) aesthetic theory clarifies somewhat the psychological dynamics of symbol-driven discourse in news and advertising, suggesting that when an action occurs "without inner momentary compulsion"—which can happen when acted repetitiously—the action is abstracted from the originating emotion to become merely a gesture. Langer said that "Genuine acts are completed in every detail unless they are forcibly interrupted, but gestures may be quite abortive imitations of acts, showing only their significant features" (p. 152). Furthermore, repetition often confines these gestures to a static signification in that "they are no longer subject to spontaneous variation, but bound to an often meticulously exact repetition, which gradually makes their forms as familiar as words or tunes" (pp. 152–153). In short, as symbols are displayed and reinforced electronically, they become decontextualized and abstracted gestures, strengthened in the consciousness and subconsiousness through repetition. However, interpretative analysis, as described later, can enhance our students' understanding of the dynamics of popular media by teaching them to read symbols as acts rather than as gestures.

Recent media events exemplify Langer's gestures. For example, the coverage of Princess Diana's death several years ago was supplemented by her endless image, accompanied by that of Elton John and other icons of the curious British royalty/popular culture hybrid. Still earlier, O. J. Simpson's face became a universal symbol, as did the formerly unknown images of Johnnie Cochran, Robert Shapiro, and the white Ford Bronco. All these symbols transcended their immediate context and emerged as public spectacle, representing the pervasive attributes of celebrity, wealth, sex, and power.

For the news industry, such images engender a sense of both urgency and sympathy that keeps the public glued to the television and running to the newsstands. As described later, the advertising industry likewise employs symbols to reinforce a product—and its contingent attitudes and lifestyles—in a consumer's awareness. Especially potent are symbols that have evolved into cultural fixtures such as Nike's "swoosh," CBS's eye, and the McDonald's arches. These symbols are no longer accompanied by textual annotations, thus becoming what Ewen (1988) termed "aesthetic[s] of abstract value" (p. 176). Reader-response theory suggests that active reading of electronic texts requires a reading that reaffirms the text's active nature. For a generation now, teachers and theorists have spoken out against writing as a static, product-oriented activity, but electronically generated symbols present a particular problem because they can be easily repeated, tiring the viewer and eroding critical cognizance.

Excerpts from Ann Landers' (1994) annual Christmas column illustrate how trivialized, maximic factoids cast as social issues can comprise a printed text:

> Although our universities are once again places of higher learning, racism abounds on many campuses. . . . While alcohol is still the most abused drug of all, marijuana and stronger substances like crack cocaine are commonplace in junior and senior high schools. . . . Suicide is the third most frequent cause of death among young people in this country . . . venereal disease is epidemic, and now there is AIDS, for which there is no vaccine and no cure.

This next excerpt is by a student seeking to refute gun control efforts:

> Guns don't kill people. People kill people. If guns are outlawed, there will be no decrease in the murder rate. Actually, there will be an increase in the murder rate because people will not be able to protect themselves. Law-abiding people like me will have to give up their guns, and lawbreakers will keep theirs and then use them [their guns] against us. People who want us to give up their guns do not know what they are asking.

Certainly, none of the "facts" in either of these excerpts imparts any new information. Neither is there any evidence of critical thinking or creation of knowledge among these static precepts. Nevertheless, students understandably feel comfortable writing as such because such generalities appear self-evident, autonomous, and logically unassailable, reflecting the images that often accompany them in the public arena.

We can recognize many of the characteristics of electronic symbols as facets of secondary orality, existing as both public and private icons that are repeated and reinforced electronically instead of verbally. As discussed at length by Ong (1967), secondary orality most fully emerged with the advent of electronic media and is identified by its hybridization of the communal, participatory characteristics of classical orality with the "silent," individualizing qualities of print. Lanham (1992) argued that electronic communications resurrect the classical topics, a rhetoric of "preformed arguments," fostering "an aesthetic of collage" now common in visual arts. Furthermore, these revised *topoi* facilitate the destruction of the canonical nature of objects while, simultaneously, bringing them into self-consciousness (pp. 231–232). Likewise, Welch (1990) said that secondary orality has brought full circle the "public" nature of orality in that both forms speak to large audiences. Welch described the synthesis of orality's inclusive traits and electronic discourse's isolating properties: "performance has reemerged in a powerful way as people communicate on film or videotape with actual or perceived simultaneity of performance and reception . . . the isolation brought about by writing and reading has reemerged as people decode the texts of electronic discourse either alone or with a small group" (p. 153). Because interpretation of information so often occurs in relative isolation, the receiver loses the social interplay that constructs meaningful discourse. Furthermore, as stated earlier, the receiver, in an attempt to sort and process the information, quickly trivializes that which is not immediately relevant.

Technology has emancipated human beings from ancient cultural stasis. At the same time, electronic culture has manufactured its own deities: Media icons replace the need for homage to Zeus, Caesar, or Jehovah. However, electronic icons are not public icons in the oral sense but are fashioned largely for passive, one-way communication, demanding little in the way of response, interaction, or homage from their subjects. Ong (1967) said that "the genuine spoken word relates person to person. Mass media, we are urged to believe, do not do so even when they are sound media such as radio or television. . . . They know no true person-to-person contact" (p. 290). Another important difference between primarily and secondarily oral cultures is that the former relied on such apparatuses as schemes and tropes because the culture lacked any means of retrieving or storing information. Repetition and commonplaces simplified and managed information to be conveyed orally. Yet, electronic technology has facilitated the storage of vast amounts of data. Consequently, modern writers are not limited by a dearth of information. However, visual commonplaces remain and propagate as images that are, according to Ong (1971), "fitted to short-term goals" (p. 299).

The innovative writing class supports a context in which users of electronic discourse may enter an active dialectic with the electronic symbols often designed for passive reception. Developing writers need a procedure for deconstructing the cultural symbols that have become freestanding, self-evident aphorisms, and for understanding that symbols, like texts, have their own cultural and social underpinnings. Welch (1990) postulated an agenda in which "the decoder will undergo an activity that leads to reconceptualization. . . . When students are made aware of the varying constraints imposed by each symbol system . . . they are able to engage the symbol system in active ways" (p. 155). A pedagogical model for Welch's reading can be found in Lazere's (1994) writing course based on a General Semantics model of "definition, denotation, and connotation" (p. 38). Although Lazere desired largely to attune writers to the innate politics of language, his model also applies to analyses of media symbols. Lazere aspired to raise the order of thinking to become interpretative rather than simply receptive. In this sense, the successful writer can discern and analyze the biases within all stimuli. Learning to read the uniform and incessant siege of symbols empowers writers to actively participate in discourse.

Welch's theory and Lazere's pedagogy suggest several classroom heuristics useful to initiate students to the rhetoric of images. Generally, students do not recognize the symbol-based nature of electronic texts. Therefore, I introduce all my freshman writers to the ubiquity of symbols and the ensuing potential for decoding and interpretation by having them collect samples of ads from popular magazines from the 1940s and 1950s, comparing them to ads from contemporary issues of the same magazine. Almost without exception, the students discover that the older ads contain much more printed copy and foregrounding of the product itself. Students note that the contemporary ads often contain little print, relying more on single, *pathos*-laden symbols as the predominant image. Some students immediately recognize the subtle persuasive properties of symbols: Color, facial expressions, seemingly indiscriminate props all work together to create a metaphorical or ironic impression to sell the product. The students' reflections on the contrast between the text-based and graphics-based ads vary. Some acknowledge the impact of the images; others appreciate the irony often inherent in symbols (see Chamberlain, 1989). In the illustration that follows, one student compared two ads for life insurance companies. One ad was from a magazine from the 1940s, featuring a testimonial from a business executive whose suit-clad likeness occupied half of the page. The other ad was from a recent issue of the same magazine and was dominated by a close-up of a firefighter's dirty, soot-stained face. The student was quick to note that, for him, each ad's impact was directly related to the prominence of the images:

> This [recent] ad is especially eye-catching because of the firefighter's face. It is realistic and makes me appreciate the danger of the real world and the need for life insurance. After all, who needs life insurance more than a firefighter? . . . I can relate to this ad's message much more than the [older] ad. . . . [The older] ad is full of fine print that I would never consider reading. I do not have time or the interest in reading the fine print in an ad. Therefore, if the picture does not catch my attention, the ad is wasted on me. . . . The image of a man in a suit does not make me think about needing life insurance. Instead, it makes me think of banking or accounting or some other profession where people wear gray suits.

After discussing the image-based nature of advertising, we move to analyzing an ad itself. I employ Glasgow's (1994) analytical exercise that critiques advertising images, revealing the consumers' susceptibilities to the influences of preformed images. Glasgow's students collect and analyze magazine or newspaper advertisements through a multistep process, first addressing the ad's literal components such as color, shapes, and typography. The second step entails an "inferential comprehension" that addresses the ad's "stories, metaphors, or cultural codes." The student describes these "codes" in terms of "personal needs, cultural values and lifestyles, and advertising appeals." In the final analysis, the writer investigates the ad's implications through a historical, psychological, sociological, or anthropological approach (p. 496).

My adaptation of the assignment encourages students to identify the ad's predominant image and then identify and explicate the image's underlying narrative, devoting particular attention to the narrative's inherent social and cultural codes. If successful, such an explication will aid in reading the images as *acts* rather than simply as *gestures* (as defined by Langer, 1942/1979).

My assignment is paraphrased as such:

> First of all, describe the image—its color, positioning, context, its overall "look." Then, describe the "story" behind the ad. What can you say about the people in the ad just by their appearance? What do you think is supposed to be happening before and after the picture or drawing was made? Finally, what attitudes and values are portrayed in the image's story? What assumptions does the ad make about the reader, and how is the reader expected to react to the image? How do you think this image is supposed to influence you to buy the product?

Although 1st-year writing students are unfamiliar with the concept of narrative, with some prompting they can easily deconstruct the image to reveal its "story," distinguishing the image as depicting an ongoing cultural narrative that they can distinguish.

One student was particularly intrigued by the ads sponsored by the Milk Association that featured a dirty, tousled Steve Young, then the San Francisco 49ers' quarterback. This student's observations revealed not only his immediate response to the ad but also the surreptitiousness sometimes inherent in advertising:

> The ad is noticeable because it features a large picture of a celebrity I am familiar with because I am a football fan. However, the fact that he is wearing a milk mustache makes him look silly and somehow takes Steve Young out of his usual context. Professional football players are not supposed to look

> silly; they are supposed to look macho. However, it is the silliness that caught my attention. . . . It is obvious to me that Young has just finished a game and is having some richly-deserved refreshments. However, a football player does not usually drink milk after a game. He drinks Gatorade or something like that. . . . The people who made the ad are trying to show us how even Steve Young likes milk, a kid's drink. I am supposed to believe that if a great football player drinks milk, then I should too because I want strong bones and a healthy body. . . . Seeing Steve Young with a milk mustache does not make me want to run out and buy milk because I really do not think that he drinks milk after a game. However, I will think of the ad the next time I am in the milk section.

This writer comprehends how celebrity images influence his perception of products and has identified the advertisers' goal of abstracting a familiar image so that it can assume a context beyond its antecedent. More important, he has identified the irony so often fundamental in symbol-driven advertisements. Indeed, irony is a most effective tool because it relies almost wholly on a subtext discernible only to those who recognize Steve Young. The ad's meaning is lost on anyone not familiar with the face in the ad. Thus, the symbol has allowed the advertiser to create, single-handedly, an instant elite, an in-crowd, an enviable feat for most advertisers, who seek to make their target market feel exclusive by purchasing a product. Furthermore, in his final line, the writer makes an acute yet inadvertent commentary on the subversive and eerily indoctrinate nature of the symbol-based irony often found in modern advertising. That is, although the ad does not categorically inspire the writer to purchase the product, it does initiate an implicit, Pavlovian response that is of greater duration and impact than an explicit, hard-sell suggestion.

Another student composed an especially perspicacious analysis of an ad for a "2000 calorie mascara":

> This ad features a glamorous woman being made up by a man whose face can barely be seen at the edge of the picture. The woman is wearing a fancy, black boa, and it seems that she is getting touched up for a photo shoot. I can image that she lives in a fine house in Beverly Hills and is driven to and from the set in a limousine. She has a fun and exciting life with lots of friends and things to do. . . . I think that this ad is supposed to appeal to women who want to feel like movie stars with their own makeup artist. . . . However, I was most interested by the slogan that read "2000 calorie mascara." The ad writer was being ironic because women are not supposed to buy high-calorie foods. However, the ad implies that we can indulge ourselves in high-calorie mascara that "fattens lashes 200 percent." No woman ever wants to hear the word "fat," but every woman wants "fat" eyelashes. . . . This ad, which was in a popular women's magazine, plays on the stereotype that women are supposed to desire to be glamorous movie stars and that we

> are most qualified for jobs that involve our looks. Even the mascara's name is set in a star like one would see at that theater in Los Angeles. . . . Although show business is a job that would seem exciting, it catches women in a trap of basing their lives on their looks. . . . I have selected computer science as a major because, in that field, no one cares how I look if I can program a computer.

This student has effectively decoded the ad by recognizing both the symbols' primacy in establishing an impression and the cultural assumptions inherent in the visual narrative. Furthermore, she has used her own understanding and misunderstanding of cultural icons (as in her reference to "*that* theater in Los Angeles") to recast the symbols as *acts* rather than simply *gestures,* as described by Langer (1942/1979). The writer has exemplified both the image's role as a cultural commonplace as well as its narrative unity.

As with all our objectives in the writing class, however, we should aim our energies at writing that ultimately involves the plural constructs of voice, purpose, and audience. The successful learner realizes that writing is inherent to full personal and cultural participation and, furthermore, that images are intrinsic in our electronic culture. As the writing class progresses, then, I look for an imagistic awareness in writing that goes beyond that of the teacher as audience. Fortunately, many students have produced ensuing writing that evinces a heightened consciousness of electronic images.

Much of this kind of writing comes from a follow-up assignment that is based on Burke's (1966) theories of symbols and humans as "symbol-using animals." Burke's proposition that symbols are seminal to reality underlies an understanding the primacy of symbols:

> Take away our books, and what little do we know about history, biography, even something so "down to earth" as the relative position of seas and continents? What is our "reality" for today . . . but all this clutter of symbols about the past combined with whatever things we know mainly through maps, magazines, newspapers, and the like about the present? . . . And however important to us is the tiny sliver of reality each of us has experienced firsthand, the whole overall "picture" is but a construct of our symbol systems. (p. 5)

In this particular assignment, the writer is asked to write a letter to a close friend. The writer is to assume that she has just inherited a million dollars from a deceased relative, but, until the estate is settled, she is not to mention the inheritance to the friend. Although condensed, this excerpt demonstrates that the writer does indeed acknowledge an inherent symbol system:

> I have thought a lot about what it will take to make me happy. I used to think it would be great to be able to have all the clothes I wanted. However, the other day, I saw a family in the park the other day getting out of their mini van. Have you ever noticed that only families drive mini-vans? I mean, it would be uncool to see a group of girls our age driving around in a mini-van. That thought reminded me that only old people drive Cadillacs and Lincolns. Young people drive BMWs and Mercedes.

This writer is assessing the symbols of contentment. Her inability to reveal her newfound fortune forces her into a reflective mode, and she makes some astute observations about those in our culture whom we perceive as materially prosperous.

In a similar assignment, a student is asked to assume that he has just murdered someone in a robbery attempt and must then describe a walk down a city street, again with the admonition that he not mention the crime. In this excerpt, the description is replete with symbols:

> I notice a cross in one of the stained-glass windows. I have gone to church all my life and have always found solace in the large brick building. In particular, the cross is supposed to represent peace and hope, but these feelings are unfamiliar to me now. . . . For some reason, I notice signs of authority. Red lights at street corners make me queasy, and when I see someone in a police or military uniform, I break out in a sweat. I now understand those people who always run when they see the police.

This excerpt is not as conscious as the first of electronic symbols common to popular, mainstream culture. However, the writer does reassess his social position by viewing common cultural icons through a different terministic screen.

This particular assignment supports my larger goal of incisive, compelling, socially relevant writing by forcing the writer to consider the primacy of symbols in a symbol-driven culture. By concealing their overriding gestalt, these writers challenge the accepted forms of expression and look from the inside out to assess themselves and their culture. Such a peculiar and difficult perspective prevents the purely superficial, preconceived discourse that often emerges from the acute passion of personal exigencies.

Some social theorists have welcomed technology as a harbinger of a new democracy in which more people than ever have access to information and, consequently, greater control of their lives. Others doubt technology's capacity to better the human condition. For instance, Postman (1992) denounced the Information Age as disjointed and chaotic: "Information has become a form of garbage, not only incapable of answering the most fundamental human question but barely useful in providing coherent direction to the solution to even mundane problems" (pp. 69–70). Postman and others envision technology as representing an ethical predicament in which humans are stripped of their moral compasses by the increasing commodification of information.

I find Postman unduly pessimistic. Despite some fiascoes and genuine catastrophes, humankind has generally managed ultimately to behave rather prudently in the face of technological paradigm shifts. Similarly, after the initial enamor, the Information Age will likely settle into its appropriate context, managed by both the free market and governmental regulation. But, with all its promise to exacerbate a progressive and user-friendly classroom, information technology nevertheless threatens to weaken student discourse through trivialization. As we reexamine and redefine "good writing" and "literacy" in a technological context, we must seek new ways to present and evaluate electronic texts. The preeminence of electronic symbols reaffirms the classroom's role as a forum of critical thought and active inquiry.

REFERENCES

Burke, K. (1966). *Language as symbolic action: Essays on life, literature, and method.* Berkeley: University of California Press.

Chamberlain, L. (1989). Bombs and other exciting devices, or the problem of teaching irony. *College English, 51,* 29–40.

Ewen, S. (1988). *All-consuming images: The politics of style in contemporary culture.* New York: Basic Books.

Flanigan, M. C. (1980). Composition models: Dynamic and static imitations. *Theory Into Practice, 19,* 211–219.

Glasgow, J. N. (1994). Teaching visual literacy for the 21st century. *Journal of Reading, 37,* 494–500.

Landers, A. (1994, December 25). My annual wish for my readers: Have the best year that's possible. *The Atlanta Constitution,* p. M5.

Langer, S. K. (1942/1979). *Philosophy in a new key: A study in the symbolism of reason, rite, and art.* Cambridge, MA: Harvard University Press.

Lanham, R. A. (1992). Digital rhetoric: Theory, practice, and property. In M. C. Tuman (Ed.), *Literacy online: The promise (and peril) of reading and writing with computers* (pp. 221–243). Pittsburgh: University of Pittsburgh Press.

Lazere, D. (1994). Teaching the political conflicts: A rhetorical schema. In G. Tate, E. P. J. Corbett, & N. Myers (Eds.), *The writing teacher's sourcebook* (pp. 35–52, 3rd ed.). New York: Oxford University Press.

Ong, W. J. (1967). *The presence of the word: Some prolegomena for cultural and religious history.* Minneapolis: University of Minnesota Press.

Ong, W. J. (1971). *Rhetoric, remance, and technology: Studies in the interaction of expression and culture.* Ithaca: Cornell University Press.

Postman, N. (1992). *Technopoly: The surrender of culture to technology.* New York: Vintage Books.

Toffler, A. (1970). *Future shock.* New York: Random House.

Welch, K. E. (1990). *The contemporary reception of classical rhetoric: Appropriations of ancient discourse.* Hillsdale, NJ: Lawrence Erlbaum Associates.

IV

VERBAL VISION

11

Calling All RadioGirls: Talking to a New Image

Mary P. Sheridan-Rabideau
Rutgers University

In this chapter, I focus on verbal imagery, not the privileged poetic devices such as poems, but everyday, conversational verbal imagery. Like its literary sister, everyday verbal imagery provides participants with a sense of place, people, and practices, shaping us as we shape them. As everyday verbal imagery permeates spoken discourse to the point of its own invisibility, it exercises a kind of hegemony over us. Despite its very real power, however, verbal imagery is not wholly deterministic. Spoken images might norm, but they can also offer possibility. Through repeated, detailed language, everyday verbal imagery can create an alternative, even an idealized (if unrealized) potential that can position participants in ways we might not readily recognize. It is this space between the ideal and the real that is a site for agency (see Butler, 1993). By invoking and enacting these images, we can alter them and our positions in relation to them, opening up agency where once agency seemed denied. Whether in the community or in the classroom, this opening is a rich site for teaching and learning.

To examine how the play among the meanings of any verbal image can be a rich source for agency, a site to examine discursive possibilities and the material constraints that shape and are shaped by these discursive possibilities, I focus on one verbal image, "RadioGirl." First, I outline part of Probyn's (1994) analytic framework that, according to Probyn, highlights how speaking oneself in certain ways allows for theoretical maneuverings that foster distinct positions and new alternatives for experiencing the self. I argue that part of speaking oneself is to create verbal images of oneself in everyday talk. Reflecting on these verbal images may help us imagine different ways to be in the world and in the classroom. Second, I map Probyn's framing onto a concrete verbal image, "RadioGirls." RadioGirls are pre/adolescent girls who, along with their moderator, host and produce a biweekly radio program. Through their on-air talk, RadioGirls create verbal images of themselves that complement and compete with typical, more limiting verbal images of pre/adolescent girls.[1] Third, I connect lessons from this community organization to the classroom. The verbal images we create about our classrooms can powerfully impact our students and ourselves. For example, verbal images of students as deficient or gifted or as active or passive clearly impact the learning and learners of the classroom. By attending to the social and material implications of repeated, conversational verbal imagery, my analysis of RadioGirl can inform our classroom practice, in particular the ways we use verbal imagery to construct the participants and activities of our classrooms. I conclude by positing general questions teachers can ask about their pedagogy and then ground this discussion in a concrete assignment sequence.

VERBAL IMAGERY

Reacting to the backlash against feminism (see Faludi, 1991) and noting the many crimes against girls and women because they are girls and women (e.g., the 1989 killing of 14 women at the University of Montreal), Probyn (1994) believed feminism is in a bind: It is being vilified at the same time it is desperately needed. A large part of Probyn's project is to find a way out of this difficulty. She called feminists to think about politically useful images of themselves and then to discursively enact these images so that they provide new ways of making sense of the world. I argue that verbal imagery is one way to construct selves and to put these selves into discourse. Through detail, description, and repetition, verbal imagery can position people and practices in such a way as to limit or expand a person's options. In other words, verbal imagery can act as an opportunity space, a space that sets the scene and shapes who and what seem viable in that (discursive and material) scene. In our own classrooms, the rec-

[1]Though I focus on two prevalent verbal images of pre/adolescent girls (as agentive and as contained), these are not static, mutually exclusive, nor the only verbal images available at RadioGirl. Nonetheless, these images do have distinct characteristics that shape the opportunities girls see for themselves. Therefore, I separate and highlight these images for analysis.

iprocity between verbal imagery and activities we foster can coconstruct both students and teachers and how we engage each other. As a way to conjure possibilities, verbal imagery can help us simultaneously imagine and enact what we consider to be more beneficial classroom practices (guided inquiry). In this way, verbal images can act as an entry point for creating this change. In the next section, I analyze how this change occurred in the hands-on learning at RadioGirl.

RADIOGIRL

Dominant discourses—as interpretive schemas for making sense of the world and a person's place in that world (see Bakhtin, 1981)—often offer verbal images of girls in ways Pipher (1994) described as destructive and limiting. Although these discourses vary, through sexist assumptions they typically provide limiting verbal images of girls (in schools, see American Association of University Women, 1991, 1992, 1994a, 1994b, 1998; Mincer, 1994; M. Sadker & D. Sadker, 1984, 1986; and in pop culture see Carroll, 1997; Nilsen, 1993; Pipher, 1994). For example, pre/adolescent girls receive verbal images depicting women as passive whereas men achieve and women as valued for being sexy but men for being successful (Nilsen, 1993). The material and embodied consequences of these limiting images can be seen in primary socializing agents, such as schools, that too often offer girls less attention, have biased curriculum and tests, and make conflicting demands on girls such as "be successful, yet act feminine" and "defer to men" (Marklein, 1993). As this research highlights, too often the material consequences of these everyday verbal images limit what options girls and women see available for themselves. Clearly, girls need alternative verbal images.

RadioGirl[2] was created explicitly to counter these limiting verbal images. This biweekly radio program was sponsored by the community radio station (WEFT) and a feminist grassroots organization (GirlZone) devoted to providing girls with hands-on workshops that encourage girls to challenge limiting societal stereotypes about what pre/adolescent girls (could) do. GirlZone and RG sought to "provide girls with the tools [such as verbal images] to consciously examine the constraints of socialization which define female roles" (GirlZone grant proposal, p. 2). In other words, RG wants to challenge dominant images and their related social relations by offering girls alternative images of what it means to be a pre/adolescent girl.

[2]Participants at RadioGirl often referred to themselves as RadioGirls. To avoid confusion, I refer to the girls as RadioGirls and to the radio program as RG.

Ayleen,[3] the adult facilitator of RG, knew that as first-time "airshifters," RadioGirls would construct their on-air images in large part by relying on what images others offered them. Consequently, through vivid, repeated language, Ayleen created a verbal image of RadioGirls that challenged the more limited images of pre/adolescent girls. Summarizing and framing their disparate work, Ayleen described the RadioGirls:

> The RadioGirls grace the airwaves with force every other Sunday from 10–11 a.m. Topics covered have included: the controversy of the Crayola color Indian red; the movement to eliminate the Chief as a symbol of the U of I; celebrating Black History Month: African American musicians and the saga of Dr. Martin Luther King, Jr.; celebrating women of various backgrounds for Women's History Month, including mothers and local women; poetry they [RadioGirls] have written, short stories, and much more. Interviews with: the founders of GirlZone, Gina and Aimee; women involved with a local resource book for women geared at incoming freshmen students of the U of I; a teacher from the Howard school who is from England; a woman U of I hockey player who is anti-chief; Susan Hofer, a local jazz vocalist; a woman from A Woman's Place who organized weekend workshops on rape awareness around Take Back the Night. And if you are a regular listener of the show, you know many other topics as well. Their interests are diverse and they want to be active. (RG show, July 4, 1999)

Ayleen portrayed the 6- to 13-year-olds who write, research, and host RG as agents, interested and engaged in social action. Through this depiction, Ayleen challenged typical verbal images of pre/adolescent girls so that girls might imagine themselves as something other than what traditional images offered. To Ayleen, an active activist/inquirer is one verbal image that, if embodied, could have positive material consequences. Ayleen used this verbal imagery in her everyday life as one way to offer the girls the promise of a more politically useful self.

Not only did Ayleen offer RadioGirls an alternative verbal image, she also offered them a place to safely enact that verbal image. In this space, RadioGirls could explore and possibly take up verbal images not traditionally associated with girls this age. For example, at RG, talk about science and world events was relevant and of interest, whereas this same talk in another setting (i.e., in school) was not. Ayleen explained:

> They've got these ideas that other kids their age aren't necessarily talking about, like science and what's going on in Kosovo, and they are finding that nobody around them really wants to hear about it so they can't get in discussions at school cause people would be like, "Oh, why are you talking about

---

[3]Several participants requested to use their own name instead of a pseudonym. I honored their requests. However, some participants requested pseudonyms with only first names. To keep consistency, I refer to all RG participants by their (real or pseudonymous) first name.

> that," "Who wants to hear about that?" But yet, when it's presented as part of the radio show, it's like an important piece, because they are pieces for the show and all of the sudden, it becomes more, it kind of gives them a space to talk about ideas that they don't necessarily have [a place] to talk about somewhere else. (personal communication, May 26, 1999)

By providing an image and a place where girls could enact this image, RG became an opportunity space where girls could engage in activities and explore possibilities other than the ones they typically found available to them. In this way, RG reinforced the reciprocity between opening possibilities through verbal imagery and providing safe spaces to experiment with how to viably enact these possibilities.

The RadioGirls enacted this alternative image in part through the verbal images they made public on RG. For example, Mudita and Brittany wrote and read a poem on-air about what it meant to be a RadioGirl:

> "R" Responsible for everything we do
> "A" Attitude, strength, and health
> "D" Determined to reach our goals
> "I" Intelligent as we come
> "O" Outstanding, unique, and talented
> "G" Girls are as equal as anybody
> "I" Inside and out filled with beauty
> "R" Respectful to others
> "L" Living our lives up
> "S" Sisters with attitude
> And that spells RadioGirls. (RG show, August 29, 1999)

The boldness of the girls' voices and the unusually loud volume of this poem indicate the RadioGirls' enthusiasm for and alignment with the poem they wrote. They are acting as what Goffman (1982) would call principals, speakers "whose position is established by the words that are spoken, someone whose beliefs have been told, someone who is committed to what the words say" (p. 144). Through writing and broadcasting this poem, RadioGirls both repeated and ratified the verbal images that Ayleen has offered. However, they used their own verbal imagery to portray themselves as agentive preadolescent girls. In doing so, they embodied the verbal image of a RadioGirl.

As Probyn (1994) highlighted, there are material consequences of (verbal) images; the ways a person speaks herself allow for certain theoretical maneuverings that may foster alternative ways of experiencing the self. At RG, the consequences of "speaking oneself" as an inquisitive, activist RadioGirl shaped and was shaped by the participants. For example, 7-year-old Cyan strongly self-identified as Native-American. Ayleen encouraged her to research and discuss discrimination against Native Americans, leading to Cyan's further involvement in Native-American causes.

This, in turn, informed RG segments as Cyan spoke about antiChief rallies and plugged Native-American artists and activists. Similarly, Ayleen encouraged RadioGirls to research and report on-air about community causes (e.g., Take Back the Night Rallies) and community activists. Because of her contact with these activists, preteen Sevhilla became one of the youngest participants in a Southern States Feminism Conference and Sevhilla is currently active in a local alternative school, the School for Designing Society. For these pre/adolescent girls, embodying Ayleen's agentive verbal imagery has had important material consequences in their everyday worlds. Called to imagine alternative verbal images and provided the opportunity space to experiment with these images, RadioGirls highlight the potential for verbal imagery to facilitate change and to foster agency.

This potential, however, is not utopic. As the RADIOGIRL poem illustrates, Mudita and Brittanys's depiction of a RadioGirl illustrated the potential of verbal imagery to help girls claim attributes they are frequently denied (i.e., attitude, talent, intelligence), *as well as* the recognition that RadioGirls did not have free rein to create their own images. Referencing a dominant image of preadolescent girls that had become so pervasive as to seem the norm, this poem indexed more stereotypical images that RadioGirls were reacting against (i.e., beauty as a superficial and exterior thing, girls as subservient). Part of the invisibility of these normed images comes from the fact that these images make up larger narratives that shape the way participants view themselves and their world. As Weedon (1997) noted, "What an event means to an individual depends on the ways of interpreting the world, on the discourses [and, I would add, the verbal images that make up these discourses] available to her at any particular moment" (p. 76). Just as Weedon focused on the discourses that foster or constrain what verbal images seem viable, Davies (1992) analyzed the power of these narratives and believed that people have a hard time imaging alternatives to these (often limiting) images and narratives. Everyday verbal images provide an expected pattern of interaction that assigns participants specific roles. Davies argued that the roles assigned to women are too often limiting. Similarly, Haraway (1989) argued that dominant stories have boxed women into "supporting roles" and have thwarted women's agency to alter these limiting stories. Part of Haraway's goal is to point out these limiting images and narratives. By highlighting these biases and by positing alternatives, Haraway attempted to create new verbal images and thus new meanings and roles.

For Haraway, as for Ayleen, verbal imagery can and does have material consequences, such as helping women and girls have more agency. Haraway's goal of exposing the limitations of dominant imagery about girls and women (and in doing so, encouraging new images and subsequent practices) resonated with Ayleen's goals for RG. Ayleen used the vivid, concrete, and repeated image of a RadioGirl to serve as what Haraway (1997) would call a figuration—an image that we live as we see it work, in this case, an image that girls live as they say and do it. The verbal image of a "RadioGirl" countered the limiting imagery that permeates culture to the extent that it is almost invisible. RadioGirl imagery counteracted the limiting images of preadolescent girls that dominate our culture. This verbal image, then, became the opportunity space, a space that is impossible to open without that verbal image. The image and the opportunity occur simultaneously.

The limiting images Ayleen reacts against are also lived and reinforced through imagistic language (and behavior) in the classroom. As earlier research noted, everyday verbal imagery in the classroom (e.g., girls as passive or as science/math/computer-phobic) affects our students (e.g., girls receive less attention or less often encouraged to take science/math/computer classes). In the next section, I argue that the verbal imagery we offer and the ways our students take up, modify, and reject this imagery can have important material consequences for the ways our students recognize who they want to be. After questioning how we, as teachers, can facilitate more positive (what Probyn, 1994, might call more politically useful) images of our students, I conclude by offering an assignment sequence to ground this discussion.

PEDAGOGY

Teaching Considerations

Examining our often tacit imagery and encouraging our students to do the same is not easily accomplished. Through teacher lore, anecdotal and formally written, we know how even our best intentions may not translate into successful practice. Within discussions of gender, class, and/or race issues, cautions abound about how the differences between and within teachers' and students' verbal imagery can impact the classroom (Finders, 1999; Gutierrez, Rymes, & Larson, 1995; Heath, 1982, 1983; Romano, 1993; M. Sadker & D. Sadker, 1994). These different ways of seeing the people and practices of the classroom dramatically impact the teaching and learning occurring there. Consequently, as teachers, we need to create classrooms that foster reflection and analysis of this imagery.

Critiquing everyday verbal imagery can help our students and ourselves become aware of the often tacit constructions and expectations of ourselves and of our students. We can ask our students to articulate the competing images of students or teachers they find in everyday print or radio/TV "talk." How do they find themselves multiply positioned within these images? As teachers, we can examine how we have constructed our classrooms as evidenced in the implicit or explicit images of our students and ourselves in our course syllabi, our assignment sheets, and our own classroom talk. In part, this requires we interrogate imagery prevalent in our teacher lore by asking what images of ourselves and our students are we creating in the interactions we encourage. For example, in liberatory pedagogies we could ask how our verbal imagery of the classroom positions who is liberating (from what? for whom? at what cost?) and who is being liberated. In pedagogies of empowerment or equality, how do our images account for the complexity that surrounds invoking positions of power both inside of and outside of the classroom? We can examine how our classroom practices have been informed by institutional structures as outlined in our school handbooks, teacher talk, and merit raises. How do our images we glean compare to each other's and to students' own images? Finally, what do these images tell us about the learning and teaching that go on in our classrooms? Reflection on questions such as these can shape the imagery and classroom practices that construct our students and ourselves.

If, as I argue, verbal imagery is an often overlooked site of production for both people and practices, then critique of everyday verbal imagery in the classroom can be an important site of change. To foster this change, we need to both offer "politically useful" images (as we or our students define them) and transform our classrooms into opportunity spaces that encourage students to see themselves as agents who can take up these images. In other words, we need to attend to the reciprocity between the verbal imagery and the scene where behavior validates this image. By recognizing verbal imagery as a means to change the people and practices in our classrooms, we expose the need for our classrooms to become opportunity spaces where both occur simultaneously. Assignment sequences based on Literacy Narratives can provide opportunities to do this by fostering reflection upon (a) the verbal imagery prevalent in everyday imagery surrounding "literacy" and "student" and (b) the practices that stem from assumptions built into these images.

Sample Assignments: Literacy Narrative and Follow-Up Analysis

One goal of composition courses is for students to become aware of academic conventions. By understanding the unspoken rules that govern much of academia, students better understand how these conventions position and serve them. In my composition courses, I encourage students to recognize the conventions of academic literacy (from writing conventions to interaction conventions) and the ways these conventions are supported (from institutional requirements to assumptions about material resources). Within this context, I assign a Literacy Narrative and Follow-Up assignment sequence in part to facilitate students' reflection on everyday verbal imagery. Most literacy narrative assignments ask students to describe/narrate/analyze either: a) how they came to/developed academic literacy or b) what role literacy has played in their lives or in the lives of a group that the student chooses to study (perhaps a friendship group, a church group, or an online group). This essay usually takes a traditional academic form and could be used in many courses (e.g., an English-education or a world literacy course). In first-year writing courses, this assignment has many sequencing options, from the first assignment, as a way of reminding students of their already vast literacy skills, to a midsemester assignment, after students are familiar with potentially new academic conventions but before students explore their own research interests, to the last assignment sequence, as a culmination and reflection on academic privileging of certain types of literacy.

In the Follow-Up assignment, students examine how the (dominant) stories about literacy constructed the "student" or "literacy" of the first essay. This assignment asks students to formally analyze their previous work as well as tie this analysis to larger discourses that shape people and practices in certain ways. In this Follow-Up assignment, I emphasize how everyday verbal imagery about "students" and "literacy" articulates relationships that warrant examination if not critique. Similarly, I encourage students to reflect upon how alternative images may facilitate new ways to make knowledge. These everyday verbal images may parallel writing conventions that facilitate certain meanings and not others. Consequently, students may write this Follow-Up essay as a traditional essay or in an alternative form. One example of an alternative form could be a web page with links to style manuals, university documents, Presidential candidates' speeches about the current state of education/literacy/students, grrrl e-zines, or other forms of atypical literary publications. Another alternative assignment could be an analysis of a three-dimensional object of the student's own making (e.g., a student-created book based on their version of *Closing of the American Mind* or *Why Can't Johnny Read;* a treasure map indexing what the student identifies as the treasure of literacy and the informing literacy myths/facts). As with other pedagogical advice, creating this space is dependent on a teacher's own style. For example, writing assignments that examine textual relationships (e.g., form-content) and encourage students to explore "alternative" textual options vary widely, from highly structured examples (e.g., the Open Essay described in Covino's *Forms of Wondering,* 1990) to experimental examples (e.g., the Grammar B in Weathers' *An Alternative Style,* 1980) to technologically diverse options (e.g., web essays that foreground the image/text/navigation relationships where students must first analyze the design relationship between form and content before designing their argument and presentation of links). A teacher's pedagogy will predispose her or him to a particular "alternative" essay, though the goal of critiquing tacit verbal images and of imagining alternative ones may be quite similar.

In these essays, whether traditionally or alternatively argued, students analyze the detailed, repeated verbal imagery about (student) literacy, examine what policies or institutions foster this imagery, and argue what the implications of this (and possibly alternative) verbal imagery may be. By examining the real-life instantiations of these verbal and material images and by being allowed to conjure alternative images and instantiations, students are encouraged to do the difficult work of critiquing what is given and seeking what they desire. They are, in part, exploring their own imagery in the space between the real and the ideal verbal images they see available to them. This is a lesson we can all learn.

DISCUSSION

Everyday images and their material consequences shape the people and practices of learning. Though many associations with everyday images have become tacit, their material instantiations drive our classrooms as evidenced by the practices we foster and by the people we expect our students and ourselves to be. This call may sound familiar, but I argue its complexity is too seldom heeded. As a case study, RG touched on this complexity. To fight the norming pressure dominant verbal imagery exerts, Ayleen offered girls alternative verbal images. Intuitively recognizing Goffman's (1982) point that the acceptability of any utterance [or image] is determined by the situational context, Ayleen provided girls both alternative situational contexts (e.g., RG) and alternative verbal imagery (a "RadioGirl"). The resources these social settings provided encouraged verbal images not publicly enacted elsewhere, such as research and writing about science or world events. In this way, RG highlights how we teachers need to (a) critically examine the (dominant) verbal imagery of our students and ourselves and (b) continually create our classrooms as opportunity spaces for students to pursue alternative verbal images. To facilitate examination of everyday verbal images, teachers can create classrooms as opportunity spaces where students can engage in purposeful experimentation. In this space of experimentation, a space between the real and the ideal, attention to verbal imagery is one way teachers can hope to foster active engagement in the classroom.

REFERENCES

American Association of University Women. (1991). *Shortchanging girls, shortchanging America.* Washington, DC: Greenberg Lake Analysis Group.

American Association of University Women. (1992). *How schools shortchange girls: A study of the major findings of girls and education.* Washington, DC: AAUW Educational Foundation.

American Association of University Women. (1994a). *Schoolgirls: Young women, self-esteem, and the confidence gap* (1st ed.). New York: Doubleday.

American Association of University Women. (1994b). *Shortchanging girls, shortchanging America.* Washington, DC: Greenberg Lake Analysis Group.

American Association of University Women (AAUW). (1998). *Separated by sex.* Washington, DC: AAUW Educational Foundation.

Bakhtin, M. M. (1981). *The dialogic imagination* (C. Emerson & M. Holquist, Trans.). Austin: University of Texas Press.

Butler, J. (1993). *Bodies that matter: On the discursive limits of "sex."* New York: Routledge.

Carroll, R. (1997). *Sugar in the raw: Voices of young Black girls in America.* New York: Crown.

Covino, W. (1990) *Forms of wondering: A dialogue on writing for writers.* Portsmouth, NH: Boynton/Cook.

Davies, B. (1992). Women's subjectivities and feminist stories. In C. Ellis & M. G. Flaherty (Eds.), *Investigating subjectivity: Research on lived experience* (pp. 53–78). Newbury Park, CA: Sage.

Faludi, S. (1991). *Backlash: The undeclared war against American women.* New York: Crown.

Finders, M. (1999). Raging hormones! Stories of adolescence and implications for teacher preparation. *Journal of Adolescent & Adult Literacy, 42,* 252–263.

Goffman, E. (1982). *Forms of talk.* Philadelphia: University of Pennsylvania Press.

Gutierrez, K., Rymes, B., & Larson, J. (1995). Script, counterscript, and underlife in the classroom: James Brown vs Brown v Board of Education. *Harvard Educational Review, 65,* 445–471.

Haraway, D. (1989). *Primate visions: Gender, race, and nature in the world of modern science.* New York: Routledge.

Haraway, D. (1997). Modest_Witness@Second_Millennium.FemaleMan© _Meets_ OncoMouse™ : Feminism and technoscience. New York: Routledge.

Heath, S. B. (1982). What no bedtime story means. *Language and Society, 11,* 49–76.

Heath, S. B. (1983). *Ways with words: Language, life and work in communities and classrooms.* Cambridge, England: Cambridge University Press.

Marklein, M. B.(1993). Learning to give girls equal classroom attention. In V. Cyrus (Ed.), *Experiencing race, class and gender in the United States* (pp. 242–243). London: Mayfield. (Original work published March 13, 1990, *USA Today*)

Mincer, J. (1994, January 9). Boys get called on. *The New York Times,* Education Special Section, p. 27.

Nilsen, A. P. (1993). Sexism in English: A 1990s update. In V. Cyrus (Ed.), *Experiencing race, class and gender in the United States* (pp. 159–165). London: Mayfield. (Original work published 1990, *The Gender Reader*).

Pipher, M. (1994). *Reviving Ophelia. Saving the selves of adolescent girls.* New York: Putnam.

Probyn, E. (1994). *Sexing the self: Gendered positions in cultural studies.* London: Routledge.

RadioGirl. (1999, July 4; 1999, August 29). Champaign, IL: WEFT.

Romano, S. (1993). The egalitarian narrative: Whose story? Which yardstick? *Computers and Composition, 10,* 5–28.

Sadker, M., & Sadker, D. (1984). *The report card on sex bias.* Washington, DC: MidAtlantic Center for Sex Equity.

Sadker, M., & Sadker, D. (1986). Sexism in the classroom: From grade school to graduate school. *Phi Delta Kappa, 67,* 512–515.

Sadker, M., & Sadker, D. (1994). *Failing at fairness: How America's schools cheat girls.* New York: Scribner's.

Weathers, W. (1980). *An alternative style: Options in composition.* Rochelle Park, NJ: Hayden Book.

Weedon, C. (1997). *Feminist practice and poststructuralist theory* (2nd ed.). Cambridge, MA: Blackwell.

12

Seeing Ourselves as Others See Us: The Maternalization of Teaching in Everyday Talk

Christy Friend
University of South Carolina

> *The thing I liked best about her [a high-school English teacher] was that she really spiced up what could have been bland material. She made learning literature a real treat.*
>
> —Interview data (my italics)

> *The most rewarding thing to me is to see my 27 "kids," my students, blossom and grow and discover things about the world around them, because I know that they depend on me.*
>
> —BancOne commercial

> *Only the . . . women who taught freshman composition part-time took the work seriously. [C]ollectively we were known to the male full-time faculty as the "Heights Housewives."*
>
> —Bloom (1992, p. 818)

Teachers as chefs, teachers as gardeners, teachers as housewives. These passages—the first from a college freshman's recollections of a favorite teacher, the second from a bank advertising campaign featuring a teacher, the third from a personal essay that appeared in a major composition journal—illustrate the rich verbal imagery people in our culture use to talk about teachers and teaching. It is not surprising that our language about teachers is so evocative and complex. After all, teachers work within a basic social institution where most Americans spend extended periods of their lives, and their function is at the center of current public debates over educational reform. The teaching profession is a vital one to our culture, and our understanding of it is part of what Bruner (1990) called our "folk psychology," the everyday, commonsense representations that structure our mental processes and our ways of understanding the world. A basic source of these representations, as W. Taylor (1998) and others have argued, is figurative and metaphoric language. Verbal imagery, Taylor said, is not "just the business of the poet or the literary critic" but a key means by which cultural knowledge is produced and preserved (p. 20).

Most of the chapters in this volume discuss the ways in which images enrich our experience of the texts we read and write in the classroom. However, my interest is in those images, like the three examples cited earlier, that shape our understanding of the teaching profession itself. Surprisingly, few scholars have examined verbal imagery related to teaching. W. Taylor (1994) analyzed the ways in which teachers have been portrayed in canonical literary and philosophical texts. Bauer (1998) recently critiqued portrayals of teachers in popular contemporary film. Several scholars in rhetoric and composition have discussed prevalent images of teaching practice (Flynn, 1989; Miller, 1991) and the teaching profession (Hairston, 1992; Reichert, 1996) in academic discourse. However, little attention has been paid to how nonspecialists talk about teachers in everyday conversation, even though these "everyday" images potentially reveal important cultural meanings. As J. Taylor (1989) argued, images used in ordinary or everyday language tend to be more closely tied to people's experiences and behavior than do those used in expert discourses. These everyday images, furthermore, are the ones that students bring to the reading and writing courses we teach. They ground students' understanding (and our own) of what teaching and learning, reading and writing involve, and they shape the ways in which we approach our work in the classroom. What exactly are these images, and what are their implications? Do these images adequately account what we do when we teach? Are they consistent with the relationships and processes we want to build in our classrooms? And if they are not, how can we work to reshape these perceptions? This chapter explores these questions.

I begin by introducing the work of Lakoff (1987), who argued convincingly for the importance of popular metaphors to understanding cultural and individual meaning systems. Then I describe a pilot study I conducted that collected data from individual interviews and focus groups to investigate how people talk about teaching in everyday settings. The verbal images that emerged from these data, although diverse, are interrelated in systematic, motivated ways that suggest a fundamental cultural association between teaching and mothering—an association with serious implications for teachers of reading and writing.

LAKOFF'S THEORY OF METAPHOR

Lakoff (1987) was among the first to recognize the important role figurative language plays in the construction of cultural knowledge. Traditionally, linguists have focused most of their attention on the literal correspondences between language and objects in the "real world," relegating nonliteral meanings to the margins of their study. Lakoff, however, argued that imaginative and figurative linguistic constructions embody powerful meaning-making processes. The reason for this, he said, is that human knowledge "arises from, and is tied to, our preconceptual bodily experience: the spatial perceptions, experiences of cold and hear, hunger, and so on, that are universally shared" (p. 267). Abstract concepts not experienced bodily take on meaning when humans relate them to these basic experiences through verbal images such as metaphor.

Metaphor, according to Lakoff, links emotions and other abstract concepts with areas of universal physical experience, providing a basis for shared understanding. Thus, for example, a metaphor may describe being in love by comparing it to the physical experience of falling down, "head over heels" (Lakoff & Kovecses, 1987). Metaphoric images, Lakoff stressed, not only provide ways of understanding and making predictions about the concepts they describe, but also can generate inferences to new domains of knowledge—and thus they are powerful sources for exploring the ways people define and understand teaching.

THE PILOT STUDY: METHODS AND DATA

Because the purpose of my study was to investigate and begin to describe shared cultural models of teaching, I collected data from several groups of participants using methods designed to approximate everyday conversation. First, I conducted a series of individual interviews with 16 university students, including 4 graduate student teaching assistants, at the University of Texas at Austin. Second, I conducted three focus-group sessions with 15 adults from the Austin, Houston, and Lake Charles (Louisiana) metropolitan areas. The interviews and the focus-group sessions all focused on the same three prompts:[1]

---

[1]I conducted, tape-recorded, and transcribed the individual interviews, which lasted from 30 minutes to an hour, during the 1994–1995 and 1996–1997 academic years. Interview participants were all middle-class Whites; 12 were attending the University of Texas as 1st-year undergraduates; the other 4 were graduate student/teaching assistants majoring in English. Seven interviewees were men and 9 were women. More information about procedures and data are available from the researcher.

- Talk about some of the best teachers you've had.
- Talk about some of the worst teachers you've had.
- What expressions or slang terms do you or your friends use to talk about school or teachers?

The analysis that follows is based on information collected from these two sources. I first noted occurrences of verbal imagery, eventually identifying over 300, then looked for patterns and recurring images. I gathered all figurative expressions that occurred more than twice and grouped the resulting list into what I saw as common themes. Although the resulting list contains expressions *commonly* used to talk about teachers and teaching, not all are *strictly* "about teaching." However, it is not surprising if talk about teaching shares linguistic constructions with other jobs that involve similar relationships and processes. In other words, metaphors about teaching may be mediated through other domains of knowledge, and vice versa. As Lakoff and Johnson (1980) showed, such mediated expressions are common. Because figurative expressions often generate associations across several domains, to limit my study to teaching-exclusive expressions would slight the richness and complexity of participants' cognitive models of teaching. In addition, examining the domains that tend to be connected with teaching potentially reveals important information about its position in our culture. Of course, it is equally important to eliminate expressions that are idiosyncratic or not commonly used to describe teachers; this is why I include in my analysis only those expressions that showed up at least twice.

Participants' talk about teaching relied largely on three central metaphors of education: education as a journey, education as a transfer of knowledge, and education as nurturance. Each of these metaphorical frameworks enables us to understand the relationships between teacher, student, and the educational process in different ways.

For each focus-group session, all of which were conducted during the 1994–1995 academic year, a research assistant distributed the prompts to the group, read procedural instructions, and tape-recorded the sessions, but left the room during the participants' discussion. I transcribed the sessions from the audiotapes. The 15 focus-group participants (5 in each session) included a diverse range of ages (18–57), educational levels (ranging from participants who had not finished high school to one with a PhD), occupations (including homemakers, laborers, clerical workers, and professionals in the public and private sectors), and ethnicities (including 1 African American, 3 Mexican Americans, 1 Chinese American, 1 British citizen, and 1 participant from India). Seven focus group participants were men and eight were women.

TEACHING AS A JOURNEY

In this basic metaphor, participants described education as a journey in which students, led by the teacher, progress toward the goal of knowledge. This image emphasizes the role of the student, who moves along the educational path. Students' educational experiences were therefore described metonymically in terms of the various degrees of progress they make along the way: successful students **go far, expand their horizons,** and **new worlds open up to them**. Less successful students may, in contrast, **get off track, drift, get lost,** or reach an educational **dead end**. Although the student's progress is the focus of this metaphor, corresponding expressions describe the teacher's function in terms of her position in relation to the students she leads through the educational process. A good teacher, for example, lets students go first and follows behind to make sure that all stay on the path to knowledge. She **puts students on the right track, pushes students forward,** and **walks them through** the course material **one step at a time**. A bad teacher, however, fails to maintain this ideal position on the journey. She may **ramble** or **go off on tangents**.

Still other expressions highlighted the course and direction of the journey: Students **follow courses of study** as they **continue** their education. Similarly, difficult classes and material can be **rocky terrain** or **heavy sledding**, whereas easy ones are **smooth sailing** that a student can **skate through**. A common elaboration of this metaphor emphasized the direction of the journey. A good teacher, for instance, **sets high standards** to **push students to the next level of learning** so that they will be **promoted** to the next **grade**, whereas a less skilled teacher may talk **above the students' heads**.

TEACHING AS A TRANSFER OF KNOWLEDGE

The second central metaphor participants used, which I call the "transfer metaphor," describes education as the passing of knowledge from the teacher to students, who accumulate and store it. Unlike the journeying metaphor, which focuses on the student's progress, this metaphor is structured in terms of the material to be learned.

Within the transfer model, the knowledge and skills taught in school (abstract concepts) are conceived as concrete entities. A pervasive example occurred in participants' frequent references to **course material** or **"what's in"** a teacher's lecture. A teacher can **pile on work, weighing down** or **burying** a student. Students take a **heavy** or a **light load** each semester, depending on how difficult the class **content** is and how **much** they want to learn. Because knowledge is represented here as a physical substance, a commodity that can be owned by the teacher and/or the student, teachers' and students' minds were often described as storage containers. For example, the **stuff** a student learns in a good class may **fill gaps** in his knowledge or understanding of the subject or **stick in his mind**. Other constructions focused more on the actual process of transfer: how the teacher "sends" information, the trajectory it takes as it goes, and whether students "catch" the information and complete the exchange. A good teacher, for instance, **gets the material across** to the students and makes sure that they **get a grasp** or a **handle** on it.

As Lakoff (1987) showed, the central metaphors that structure a domain of cultural knowledge can be extremely productive, because new inferences, involving new domains of experience, can be mapped onto various aspects of the central metaphor, thus "elaborating" upon it (p. 198). One of the most common elaborations of the transfer metaphor relates teaching to feeding, thus playing out the transfer model's emphasis on teachers as "full" containers of knowledge who deposit pieces of knowledge into students' "empty" minds. For example, good teachers **spice up** material that might otherwise be **bland**, and they keep material **fresh** for the students, who as a result, are able to **digest the material**. Unsuccessful teachers under- or overfeed students, perhaps **cramming material down students' throats** or asking them to **regurgitate** information on a test. Other constructions describe the nutritional characteristics of the "food"—the course material—itself. Thus, students may take useful **meat and potatoes courses**, which are **solid fare** that they can **really sink their teeth into**. Easy classes are "junk food," referred to as **cake, gravy, McCourses**, or **lite** or **gut courses**. As these examples suggest, feeding expressions play out several implications of the transfer model by emphasizing the one-way nature of the learning process and the student's role as a passive receptacle dependent on the teacher.

TEACHING AS NURTURANCE

The third central metaphor suggested by my data conceives of education as a nurturing process, in which the teacher tends intellectually immature students, who, under her protection, develop and grow. Unlike the journeying model, which emphasizes the student's progress, and the transfer model, which highlights the material to be taught, the nurturing model is structured in terms of the teacher—who protects students from mental and emotional harm, creates opportunities for learning, and takes care not to force or warp the student's intellectual growth. The student's role in this model is simply to flourish or wither in response to the teacher's care.

Expressions associated with this metaphor draw on several different domains of nurturing. In one common set of expressions, teachers are conceived of as shepherds or animal tenders, who protect and guide flocks of students until they mature intellectually. For instance, successful teachers know when to **tighten the reins** in the classroom, but also give students **plenty of room to roam**. They **spur** them to learn by **putting them through the paces** or perhaps using the **carrot and stick** method. And, rather than protecting and nurturing students' development, bad teachers may, instead of being good "shepherds," themselves take on the attributes of predatory animals. Thus, difficult or unfair teachers, of course, are **bears, bitches,** or **monsters**. (Many of these expressions can describe nonteaching situations; however, study participants used them explicitly to refer to teaching.)

In another elaboration of the nurturing metaphor, teachers become gardeners and students their plants. Perhaps the most familiar example of this elaboration is "kindergarten" (German for "a garden of children"). Good teachers nurture the **seeds of knowledge** present within each student and **give students room to grow**, allowing them the freedom to **blossom** and **flourish** intellectually. Very strict teachers may even **weed out** students whom they do not believe to be capable of succeeding in a particular course of study.

However, by far the most prevalent nurturing images participants used related teaching to yet another domain of experience: motherhood. In these expressions, teachers—whether male or female—were depicted as breathing life into their students, who were represented as children, no matter what their actual ages. Teaching here becomes a creative "birthing" process. Thus, an effective teacher **makes the class come to life, inspires, enlivens,** and **activates** students. Bad teachers are those who fail to generate this kind of "life," resulting in classrooms that are barren and lifeless: They may **stifle** or **squelch** student interest and their classes may be described as **really dead**. In describing a class that has been "brought to life," some participants represented teachers as childrearers who attend to the emotional, physical, and intellectual well-being of students. For instance, a successful teacher **loves** his or her students and perhaps **treats them like his or her own**. However, like good parents, good teachers, though nurturing, aim at fostering students' eventual independence by teaching students to **stand on their own two feet** and think **for themselves**. Too-easy teachers may **baby** or **spoon-feed** their students. Two of the teaching assistants I interviewed even referred to their students as **"my kids."**

The mothering metaphor is not reflected only in word- and sentence-level expressions, but was also a frequent theme in stories that participants told about favorite teachers. One participant, recounting experiences with a respected teacher, said, "She had the most important quality a teacher can have, and that's that she truly loved her students with her whole heart." Another described the turmoil he felt when he saw a favorite teacher overcome with emotion after a difficult confrontation with another student: "It shocked me to see that he had weaknesses after all. It was like seeing your dad cry, or something—you idolize him so much that you think he's perfect and don't realize that he can break down just like anyone else." One interview participant who was working as a teaching assistant stated this connection perhaps most explicitly: "I don't have any kids of my own, and so I feel like this is part of why I want to teach. I nurture, give something to students that they need to grow as citizens, as thinking people."

A MATERNAL MODEL OF TEACHING

Of course, these three metaphors, the various expressions that arise from them, and their interrelationships do not exhaust the ways Americans talk about teaching. My data did include other metaphors, including some comparing education to military exercises and to carpentry. Nonetheless, the overriding prevalence of the three suggests that they are central to our cultural understanding of teaching. And, indeed, these very images show up frequently in much popular discourse about education. Popular magazines, for example, often feature narrative essays about superlative teachers, many of which draw explicitly on the kind of mothering imagery participants used when they narrated their own experiences. A *Jet* magazine feature story on celebrities' memories of favorite teachers, for example, includes an anecdote by singer James Brown, who recounted that when his seventh-grade teacher died, he "attended the funeral services and signed the guest book 'James Brown, son' " ("Stars Remember," 1991, p. 13). Similarly, the following passage from a *Reader's Digest* piece uses strikingly maternal language to talk about a high school English teacher: "My mother had always dreamed of an education for her children. She couldn't be there when I graduated from Boston University, but the person who came with my father and shared our joy was [teacher] Marjorie Hurd. In later years, she danced at my wedding and cried with me at my father's funeral" (Gage, 1990, p. 80). The ubiquity of these images raises important questions: How does the use of these metaphors rather than possible others shape how teaching is understood and valued in our culture?

The three metaphors complement and reinforce each other to a remarkable degree. Each emphasizes a different part of the educational process: The journey metaphor is organized in terms of the student's progress, the transfer metaphor in terms of the material taught, and the nurturing metaphor in terms of the teacher's role. Yet all encourage similar conceptions of students as passive and of teachers as protective and giving. Whether students are being guided through an educational journey, waiting for pieces of knowledge to be deposited in their brain, or receiving nurturing from motherly teachers, they bear little responsibility for their own learning. Correspondingly, the teacher in all three perspectives is always available, providing emotional and intellectual services for students who are dependent on them. In particular, the mothering expressions, though most closely related to the nurturing metaphor, contain elements of all three—because mothers lead (journey), feed (transfer), and tend (nurture) the needs of children. In sum, these three metaphors may coexist because they share a feminized, maternal conception of the teacher and an infantilized conception of students, a conception that resonates most powerfully in the "mothering" expressions. That these images for understanding teaching in our culture overlap so consistently with our understanding of mothering indicates that the two activities occupy similar positions in our cultural knowledge systems—a connection that has far-reaching pedagogical and social implications.

Some might argue that the apparent connection people make between teaching and mothering is simply a literal one based on the similarities of the duties both perform. Both teachers and mothers socialize young people and many teachers—most teachers at the primary and secondary levels and in college writing programs—are women; thus, comparisons between them could be seen as obvious, even necessary. However, they are not. Teachers are not conceived of as mothers in all cultures, nor have they always been in ours. Other possible metaphors for education, which are peripheral to our own understanding, include several that assign teachers more autonomous and intellectually powerful roles. For instance, Plato's famous "cave" analogy depicts education as a process of initiation, where the responsibility for learning lies with the student, who must endure a descent into darkness and "open his eyes" to knowledge. Another alternate model, developed chiefly in the work of Marxist scholars like Freire (1971), describes education as a process of social and cultural liberation, in which the student is an active participant in political struggle, and the teacher's role is more catalyst than caretaker. Perhaps the most obvious alternate model of teaching would compare teaching to the master–apprentice relationship. In apprenticeship, the master is an artisan who works independently of the student, unlike the maternalized teacher whose work focuses on the student's activities. Likewise, the apprentice has the responsibility of working independently, unlike the student, who in a mothering model is dependent on the teacher's protection and care.

Alternate images of teaching do exist and could potentially ground our cultural understanding of teaching. The fact that the alternatives I discuss herein—all of which propose more active students and more independent teachers—are absent suggests that the mother-child dynamic implied by the three metaphors is fundamental to our culture. The question now becomes how this conception affects the value that the general public places on teaching and the expectations we and our students bring to the classroom.

EFFECTS OF THE MOTHERING MODEL

According to Lakoff (1987), when the metaphorical language about two areas of experience overlaps, people's thoughts and actions about them may also overlap. He gives the example of lust and anger, which share metaphors linking them to hunger, heat, and animals. The result of this overlap, Lakoff proposed, is rape, which occurs when people respond to lust with retaliation, just as they would respond to anger. Does the association between motherhood and teaching also lead people to equate them in problematic ways? This issue is particularly important because of the traditionally low-status, unpaid, nonprofessional connotations mothering holds in our patriarchal culture. Many feminist scholars have pointed out the ways in which motherhood isolates women and restricts their independence (De Beauvoir, 1974). Other feminists document the pervasive social and economic devaluing of motherhood (Chodorow, 1989). Although many women deeply value motherhood and although it draws certain kinds of social recognition, few would deny that mothers are economically and politically marginalized in our social structure.

Do these ways of thinking about and behaving toward mothers extend to the treatment of teachers in the United States? Some scholars have argued that the sexism traditionally directed at any predominantly female workforce has perpetuated the low status—both social and economic—of teaching as a profession (Miller, 1991). Plenty of evidence seems to support this possibility: Public school teachers are certainly underpaid, and their actions are restricted by more administrative controls than those of most professionals. For instance, teachers at the elementary, high school, and even some college levels are regularly tested to prove their competence, allowed little freedom in deciding what to teach and how to teach it, and sometimes denied basic workplace amenities like a telephone, clerical help, and a private work space. Even at the college level, where research faculty enjoy relative autonomy and prestige, teaching staff suffer many of the same indignities. Bloom (1992), for example, lamented that as a part-time writing instructor in a prestigious university, she was delegated to share a teaching assistant's office where she had to "sit on the floor next to the kitty litter" while her literary colleagues' focus on publishing scholarship merited them plush private offices (p. 821). In short, teachers—especially those who value teaching over scholarship and research—are too often not treated as professionals. But can these injustices be linked to the mothering imagery that pervades both academic and popular discourse about pedagogy?

Perhaps. Many scholars have documented that teachers, even of college-level students, are expected to adopt maternal behaviors in the classroom. Miller (1991) noted that 1st-year college writing students "are, despite their actual maturity, sentimentalized as innocent—preeconomic, presexual, prepolitical" (p. 47). Such perceptions reflect not only the expectations and language of the general public or school officials, but also the ways in which teachers envision themselves. A recent textbook on teaching writing, for example, advises new instructors that "the challenge for you as a writing teacher is to create a writing environment that feels safe so that students can bloom as writers" (Friend, Hairston, & Ruszkiewicz, 1996, p. 16). A prominent composition specialist idealizes the teacher of writing as "a midwife, an agent for change," saying that "the teacher's role is to nurture change and growth as students encounter individual differences" (Hairston, 1992, p. 192). And a similar nurturing orientation prevails in recent critiques that propose that politically charged teaching methodologies may traumatize students, who need a more nurturing classroom environment (McCarthy & Fishman, 1996). These statements suggest that our popular model of teaching contains within it a sufficient stock of metaphors and associations with motherhood that can actually provide a kind of "rationale" for devaluing and patronizing teachers in many of the same ways we devalue and patronize mothers (Lakoff, 1987, p. 415).

LIMITATIONS AND UNANSWERED QUESTIONS

Although these preliminary connections between teaching and mothering are provocative, the limited nature of my pilot study precludes me from pushing these arguments too far. Perhaps most important, because the study involved a relatively homogeneous group of mostly White, mostly middle-class, mostly college-educated participants, it is not clear how widespread these verbal images are. Do the participants in my study perceive teachers in the same way that low-income Chicano/a youth in Los Angeles do—or might they see the school system and its employees as more alien, more "expert," and perhaps more intimidating to the community they serve than in more affluent communities? Are African-American children in Mississippi, who come to school with the awareness of a long history of institutionalized racism, as likely to see teachers as nurturing figures? What about Appalachian students in rural West Virginia, Vietnamese Americans in East Texas, or affluent White students who attend military academies on the East Coast? In short, without further research involving a wider diversity of groups, it is difficult to tell whether the meaning patterns my subjects shared are in fact regionally, ethnically, and socioeconomically specific rather than culturally universal.

However, my data do suggest that even if they are not universal, the images that people use to describe teachers in everyday talk are more than mere words. The metaphors that connect teaching with mothering are expressions of an underlying system of meaning that may shape how many people in our culture engage in teaching and in learning. These images come not from educational institutions themselves, nor from academic theories, but are embedded within everyday language and popular culture. Unfortunately, in associating teaching primarily with motherhood, we emphasize the teacher's availability and generosity to students at the expense of more independent qualities like skill and artistry. And even more disturbing, pairing teaching with mothering may rationalize and help perpetuate the low social and economic status of the profession. Yet, if we admit that figurative language shapes our thinking and behavior in powerful ways, how can we use this knowledge to our advantage? In short, is it enough to be aware of these metaphors' limiting and potentially harmful associations, or should we actively strive to replace these metaphors with more positive ones?

First, as teachers we must remember that educational approaches based on nurturing are not entirely negative. In fact, as Reichert (1996) pointed out, many feminist educators embrace these approaches precisely because they validate students' needs and students' voices—in contrast to traditional, authoritarian pedagogical approaches. Composition specialists like Bridwell-Bowles (1995) emphasized that "feminine" approaches to writing, which emphasize collaboration, personal writing, and a nurturing classroom community, create spaces where students from traditionally marginalized groups feel comfortable to express their ideas in a variety of ways (p. 43). As Reichert put it, to wholly refuse the "feminine identity" associated with the mothering metaphor could "restrict the efforts of . . . pedagogies which want to recognize the powerful ways writing (and teaching writing) can work against an oppressive patriarchy" (p. 155). That is, in situations when these metaphors validate our efforts to empower students through their reading and writing, we should feel free to embrace them.

However, as Fleckenstein reminds us in the introduction to this volume, we must also remember that at some point all metaphors break down. Whatever its pedagogical virtues, to the degree to which the mothering model encourages students to see themselves as passive receivers rather than active producers of text or to treat teachers as service providers rather than as writers and intellectuals on their own terms is the degree to which it provides an inadequate vision of what we hope to achieve in the classroom. Thus, we should resist it, by drawing students' attention to its limitations and consciously drawing on new images in our class discussions, writing assignments, and daily activities. Metaphors like apprenticeship, quest, and liberation not only encourage students to think in new and empowering ways about their own reading and writing—they also offer us new, empowering visions of our own work.

REFERENCES

Bauer, D. (1998). Indecent proposals: Teachers in the movies. *College English, 60,* 301–317.

Bloom, L. Z. (1992). Teaching college English as a woman. *College English, 54,* 818–825.

Bridwell-Bowles, L. (1995). Experimental writing within the academy. In L. Wetherbee Phelps & J. Emig (Eds.), *Feminine principles and women's experience in composition and rhetoric* (pp. 43–66). Pittsburgh: University of Pittsburgh Press.

Bruner, J. (1990). *Acts of meaning.* Cambridge, MA: Harvard University Press.

Chodorow, N. (1989). *Feminism and psychoanalytic theory.* New Haven, CT: Yale University Press.

De Beauvoir, S. (1974). *The second sex.* New York: Vintage.

Flynn, E. (1989). Composition studies from a feminist perspective. In *The politics of writing instruction: Postsecondary* (pp. 137–154). Portsmouth, NH: Boynton/Cook.

Freire, P. (1971). *Pedagogy of the oppressed.* New York: Methuen.

Friend, C., Hairston, M. C., & Ruszkiewicz, J. J. (1996). *The instructor's resource manual: Creating a community of writers.* New York: Harper.

Gage, N. (1990, June). The teacher who changed my life. *Reader's Digest,* pp. 77–80.

Hairston, M. (1992). Diversity, ideology, and teaching. *College Composition and Communication, 43,* 179–192.

Lakoff, G. (1987). *Women, fire, and dangerous things.* Chicago: University of Chicago Press.

Lakoff, G., & Johnson, M. (1980). *Metaphors we live by.* Chicago: University of Chicago Press.

Lakoff, G., & Kovecses, Z. (1987). The cognitive model of anger inherent in American English. In D. Holland & N. Quinn (Eds.), *Cultural models in language and thought* (pp. 195–221). Cambridge, England: Cambridge University Press.

McCarthy, L. P., & Fishman, S. (1996). Teaching for student change: A Deweyan alternative to radical pedagogy. *College Composition and Communication, 47,* 342–366.

Miller, S. (1991). *Textual carnivals.* Carbondale: Southern Illinois University Press.

Reichert, P. (1996). A contributing listener and other composition wives: Reading and writing the feminine metaphors in composition studies. *JAC: A Journal of Composition Theory, 16*(1), 141–157.

Stars remember their favorite teachers. (1991, September 9). *Jet,* pp. 13–15.

Taylor, J. (1989). *Linguistic categorization.* Oxford, England: Clarendon.

Taylor, W. (Ed). (1984). *Metaphors of education.* London: Heinemann.

13

Textual Vision: Moving Beyond "Same"/"Other" in Reading African-American Literature

Demetrice A. Worley
Bradley University

Students studying literature often either resist or have difficulties engaging with African-American writers' literary texts, and, by failing to engage with the texts, they fail to evoke the lived-through experience that defines literature (Rosenblatt, 1983). Telling my students about the importance of African-American literature and the connection it has to their lives does not make it real to them. They have to experience it for themselves. As Janie tells Phoeby, "It's uh known fact, Pheoby, you [*sic*] got to *go* there tuh *know* there. Yo' papa and yo' mama and nobody else can't tell yuh and show yuh" (Hurston, 1937/1990, p. 183). Thus, a major goal of a teacher of an African-American literature class populated predominantly by White, middle-class students is to evolve strategies that will enable readers to engage with African-American literary text worlds. A large part of the problem in resistant reading is that many students are unable to respond to the vivid textual images and metaphors so characteristic of and so vital to literature in general and African-American literature in particular. Confused by the unfamiliarity of African-American imagery, they respond by either blocking the imagery or recasting images of difference as images of the same.

As an African American/womanist/teacher/scholar/poet, I consciously present students with a variety of classroom activities to provide them with (a) alternative ways of interpreting texts that are different from the traditional ways (a middle- or upper class White male perspective) and (b) a variety of ways of meaning making to meet the diverse learning styles of my student populations (Oliver, 1994). To enable my students to experience the literary world woven of textual images and to help them overcome a desire to see other as same, I have evolved a spiral process that begins with a text's verbal imagery, progresses to students drawing their interpretation of that imagery, and concludes with students creating their own texts that serve as a meeting point between literary metaphors and graphic image.

WEAVING THE THREE STRANDS OF IMAGERY

In *Their Eyes Were Watching God,* Hurston (1937/1990) began with two vivid textual images:

> Ships at a distance have every man's wish on board. For some they come in with the tide. For others they sail forever on the horizon, never out of sight, never landing until the Watcher turns his eyes away in resignation, his dreams mocked to death by Time. That is the life of men.
>
> Now, women forget all those things they don't want to remember, and remember everything they don't want to forget. The dream is the truth. Then they act and do things accordingly. (p. 1)

These textual images, of men and women's lives/dreams, are connected to Hurston's character Janie's growth at the end of the novel. When my students read Hurston's text, they are, for the most part, able to interpret what these metaphors mean in a broad sense. But, when I ask them to interpret the meaning of these metaphors as they apply to the life of a Black woman character in the 1930s, many of them experience cognitive dissonance.

When I ask them to create written texts that explain their understanding of African-American texts, they attempt to give me what they think I want: dry academic prose. I agree with Purves' (1994) assertion that students know that academic writing will help them succeed at the university so they produce the models of writing that surround them. The writing that students see given validity is text that has order and an appearance of reasonableness. However, as Purves pointed out, "[The] most powerful prose stylists of the nineteenth and twentieth centuries broke away from that kind of style and moved toward a prose of images and metaphors" (p. 27). For our students, who have been raised on a diet of visual images (cartoons, video games, print advertisements, movies, videos, and MTV), it is imperative that we help them learn how to "read" images.

In relationship to reading, Levy (1985) reported that when we read, visual thinking plays an important role in "[m]aintaining an integrated story structure, appreciating humor and emotional content, deriving meaning from past associations, and understanding metaphor" (pp. 43–44). When students read verbal texts, imagery serves as a bridge between "affect and cognition, affect and text world, text world and real world" (Fleckenstein, 1989, p. 253). To grow as readers of texts and as writers of text, it is imperative that our students become comfortable with reading and creating textual images: "It is no exaggeration to say that comparisons [textual images/metaphors] are the basis for growth and progress. Our very survival depends on our ability to integrate the new with the old by means of comparisons" (Bartel, 1983, p. 45). Because visual imagery is so essential to both the experience of the text world and the meaning of that text world, all students, but especially students from a culture other than that of the text world, need strategies that offer them bridges to difference that retain that difference. Shifting from verbal imagery to graphic imagery and returning to verbal imagery offers such a bridge.

When students create their own visual metaphors of images in the text and rewrite these metaphors by tapping both the text and drawing, they connect text lives and their lives (Rosenblatt, 1983). Drawing allows "the recording, storage, manipulation and communication of images" (Adams, 1986, p. 92). According to Sigel (1978), picture comprehension (i.e., coming to know pictures) is "analogous to reading the printed word, where, in each case, the 'reader' must transform a set of symbols or signs from one system to another. It is only through a process of transformation that comprehension can begin" (p. 94).

As students create their own visual images of the text and write about these images, or of aspects of the texts, Rosenblatt (1983) contended that they make connections between the texts they have read and the lives they live, thereby enabling them to transform vague thoughts into meaningful words and symbols. According to Yancey (1998), the writing aspects of the activity call on students to read reflectively by structuring the reading and inviting accounts of their reading process. Claggett (1992) stated that writing also enables students to work with the same types of tools, such as metaphor, as the authors they are reading, allowing them to "become authors themselves, with an internal awareness of the writer's craft" (p. 77).

When students do engage in this spiraling process, they are better able to engage with their evolving text worlds without reducing the crucial difference of the Other to a mirror of the Same. Multiple ways of knowing and making meaning are power. This open weave of imagery becomes a space where students can share in African-American writers' "imaginative words." Morrison (1992) stated: "The imagination that produces work which bears and invites rereading, which motions to future readings as well as contemporary ones, implies a shareable world and an endlessly flexible language. Readers and writers both struggle to interpret and perform within a common language shareable imaginative words" (p. xii).

STUDENTS READING/DRAWING/WRITING TEXTUAL IMAGES

White students, from two upper-level contemporary African-American literature courses at two historically predominantly White, midsize, private postsecondary institutions, created the drawings and written responses that I discuss in this text. These students fit the general profile of White students I have encountered in my African-American literature classes. Most of the White students self-identified themselves as middle- to upper middle-class and fairly well read. Whereas many of the students say that they are well read, many of them have never read African-American literature. In both classes, women made up over 80% of the class and students of color made up less than 20% of the classes.

For the most part, the White students in my classes are familiar with analyzing literary texts; they are familiar with literary tools such as metaphor, simile, analogy, and figurative language. However, they sometimes have a difficult time understanding how or why these literary tools are used by African-American writers or they believe that the way that African-American writers use them are invalid. The students from my two classes were not resistant to the African-American literary texts we read, but they were reluctant to create drawings in a literature course. This reluctance is one that I often encounter in my classrooms. Many students' reluctance to draw is the result of drawing being excluded from students' creative processes in middle and high school, and for the most part from their undergraduate education (Gardner, 1980; Worley, 1994). After reassuring my students that it was "OK" to draw in a literature class, I told them that their drawings would be accepted regardless of their drawing ability. The students created a wide range of drawings that included, but were not limited to stick figures, realistic images, geometric shapes, swirls of colors, and collages. I stressed to the students that even though they would share their drawings in small-group discussions, they were to consider the drawings purely writer-based, not reader-based texts.

TEXTUAL IMAGES IN BLACK AND WHITE/AND COLOR

In the opening pages of Morrison's (1987) *Beloved,* Sethe suggests to her mother-in-law, Baby Suggs, that they move to another house in order to escape the "ghost" that haunts their house. Baby Suggs responds, "Not a house in the country ain't pack to its rafters with some dead Negro's grief. We lucky this ghost is a baby" (p. 5). This "ghost" fits Western ideas of a ghost: It can move or break objects, and it is invisible—"merely looking in a mirror shattered it. . . . two tiny hand prints appeared in the cake" (p. 3). However, Morrison's "ghost" behaves in ways that do not fit with our standard Western ideas about ghosts: It takes the physical form of a woman. The "ghost" Beloved describes the moments when she became flesh:

> I come out of the blue water after the bottoms of my feet swim away from me I come up I need to find a place to be the air is heavy I am not dead I am not there is a house there is what she whispered to me I am where she told me I am not dead I sit the sun closes my eyes when I open them I see the face I lost Sethe's is the face that left me (p. 213)

This "ghost" is interested in more than haunting a house; she has taken a physical form to get back what she "lost."

When teaching about the "ghost," I present an interpretation of Beloved as an embodiment of the Haitian/Yoruba deity Erzulie. This interpretation does not fit with my White students' Western concept of ghosts. However, after reading Morrison's (1987) textual images about Beloved, creating their own graphic images, and then creating their own textual images about their drawn images, students are able to bridge their Western cosmology with the African-American/Haitian/West African cosmology that Morrison presented in the novel. For example, Julie created a drawing with a filled-in black circle. Above the circle she drew figures of three humans (Paul D, Sethe, and Denver, respectively) in green, blue, and yellow. Below the black circle, she drew five black lines. Then, citing passages from *Beloved* that describe Beloved's desire for sweets (p. 55), her demands for Paul D's sexual attention (pp. 116–117), and her endless demands for Sethe's love (pp. 239-243), Julie created the following textual image:

> Beloved is a black hole pulling in everything around it. A black hole is a greedy and self-serving anomaly, just like the West African spirit of the Erzulie, just like Beloved. Beloved is never satisfied. She has tantrums, and begs for more sweets, more love, and sexually cannot be resisted, just like the Erzulie. The black hole is a non-physical way to represent this constant taking for self. These two spirits, like the black hole, do as they like, absorbing everything they can and occasionally spitting something good back out. This release of something good is neither planned nor intentional, merely an abstract of their consumption.

Julie's textual image is a combination of her understanding of how black holes function and her understanding of Erzulie. Even though scientists have not directly observed a black hole, they have concluded from indirect evidence that at least one exists: Cygnus X-1. Julie's choice of using a black hole as a metaphor for Beloved/Erzulie seems to indicate her willingness to say that even though we, as readers, do not know for a fact that Beloved is Erzulie, Morrison presented enough indirect evidence to indicate that Beloved could be a physical representation of Erzulie.

STUDENT TEXTUAL IMAGES

The following three examples of students' visual and textual images were created in response to reading journal prompts about the role of motherlines and the search for self in Hurston (1937/1990) and Morrison (1987).

Hurston (1937/1990) presented numerous textual images connecting Janie to nature. One of the earliest images in the novel compares Janie's life to a tree: "Janie saw her life like a great tree in leaf with the things suffered, things enjoyed, things done and undone. Dawn and doom was in the branches" (p. 8). One student, Holly, chose this textual image as a metaphor for Janie's search for self. In response to a reading journal prompt about Janie's search for self, Holly created a drawing of a tree with a brown trunk and thin branches filled with green, yellow, red, brown, and blue leaves. The leaves had words and phrases related to significant moments in Janie's life written on them: "Nanny," "first kiss," "hurricane," "Jody's death," "the Muck," "love," and so on. Several leaves are on the ground at the tree's base. Holly used the aforementioned quote to open her written response:

> The tree I have sketched represents the various stages of Janie's life experiences. I have highlighted seven "leaves" to indicate some of the key events in her life. I have divided her life into four stages and used the symbolism of the four seasons and the development and colors of a tree and its foliage. The fours stages are as follows: Janie's time with Nanny in West Florida; her marriage to Logan Killicks and the farm; her marriage to Jody Sparks and Eatonville; her marriage to Tea Cake and the Muck; and her return to West Florida. . . . Janie's life was cyclical and like a tree as it changes with the seasons, Janie may drop her leaves but as her life continues, she will bud and bloom again. Her life experiences made her a strong person. Like a strong tree that leafs anew with each passing season.

Holly, a nontraditional student who was married and the mother of two teenagers, drew on her knowledge of life experiences in her written response. Unlike the majority of 20- to 22-year-olds in the class, she has experienced some of the cyclic nature of life, beginnings and endings: love, marriage, children, and work. She combined her knowledge with Hurston's textual image to create an image of a tree that reflects the cyclical nature of Janie's life and the cyclical nature of the novel (its beginning is its ending; its ending is its beginning).

Sometimes students use several textual images from a novel to create their own textual image. In response to the reading journal prompt about Janie's search for self, Sara selected several of Hurston's textual images as inspiration for her response: Janie packing away her "self" from Joe Starks (p. 68), Janie as ruts in the road (p. 72); Janie's shadow prostrating itself before Joe Starks (p. 73), and Janie pulling in her horizon (p. 184). Sara created an 18-×-24-inch pastel drawing of a Black woman sitting with her eyes closed. Throughout her long written response, Sara used her interpretations of different aspects of her drawing to illustrate her understanding of Hurston's textual images:

> The area of [Janie's] search that I chose to transpose into my drawing is the dichotomy of her interior and exterior self. This dichotomy allowed Janie to form a veneer that protected her from psychological damage and allowed her to love without fear later in life.
>
> This idea of a hidden inner self is strengthened by the text on page 68: "things were packed up and put away in parts of her heart where [Jody] could never find them." I tried to communicate this idea of an individual that psychologically existed on many levels in my artwork. The grid-like crosshatching on the chest of Janie in the drawing has depth, as the color layers reveal upon a close look, but they also can appear flat and non-dimensional, as Janie's emotions seem at times. . . . The crosshatches also serve as a metaphor for the 'wheels' on page 72: "[Janie] was a rut in the road. Plenty of life beneath the surface but it was kept beaten down by the wheels."
>
> The "shadow of herself" that "prostrates itself before Jody" (p. 73) is also represented in my artwork. The greenish haze surrounding the face in the picture serves as this shadow. I tried to make the color seem to pull the character back into the picture, as Janie's emotions were pulled into herself. I also created a positive shadow to complement the negative: the reddish crosshatching from Janie's left shoulder lighten the picture and creates a pulling out effect. This red crosshatching is also a metaphor for the "horizon" that Janie pulls in "like a great fish net . . . from around the waist of the world" and drapes over her shoulder (p. 184).
>
> I called the work "movement in repose" to capture the idea of an individual alive beneath the surface but closed off to the exterior world. The "movement" of Janie's search for self thus seems less pro-active and more circular—she is progressing, but not in a linear manner. She is completing her return to a self whose identity exists separately of men or society. . . . However, it is apparent by the coloring and line movement with the picture that there is activity in this "sleep."

Sara was an honors English major and a visual artist. As an honors English major, Sara had had a large amount of experience interpreting texts.

However, she had had limited exposure to African-American texts, and she had never been asked to provide a written interpretation of her own art. The richness and complexity of Sara's textual images reflects her strengths as an English major and illustrate her understanding of Hurston's textual images about Janie's double-consciousness: Janie's experience of living two lives, an inner life of self and an outer life for her home community.

Morrison (1987) presented a textual image of Denver in her green boxwood "room" that illustrates Denver's disconnectedness from her mother and the African-American community. The sweet smell of cologne is Denver's only companion inside the boxwood space:

> Denver's secrets were sweet. Accompanied every time by wild veronica until she discovered cologne. The first bottle was a gift, the next she stole from her mother and hid among boxwood until it froze and cracked. . . . In that bower, closed off from the hurt of the hurt world. Denver's imagination produced its own hunger and its own food, which she badly needed because loneliness wore her out. *Wore her out.* Veiled and protected by the live green walls, she felt ripe and clear, and salvation was as easy as a wish. (pp. 28–29)

Jody used Morrison's textual image of Denver's love for the sweet smell of cologne as the starting point for her interpretation of the motherlines in *Beloved* (see Willis, 1987, on motherlines). Jody created a drawing of a blue, green, and yellow perfume bottle with a black aerator. In her written response, she said that the motherline between Denver and Sethe is an unopened bottle of perfume:

> The picture I have drawn to represent motherlines in *Beloved* is a bottle of perfume. . . . By not sharing the whole story about her other baby girl to Denver, Sethe is keeping a very important motherline from her daughter. This motherline is her family history. . . . This unspoken motherline is a bottle of perfume because like perfume the story will always be there, but if you do not tell it (or spray it), the story and the perfume will just wait, hovering in the mind, and in the bottle. With the telling of the story or the spraying of the perfume, there is a release.

In her textual image of the perfume bottle, Jody built on Morrison's textual image of the pleasure Denver experienced with the sweet smell of cologne in the boxwood. The knowledge that the essence of perfume cannot be experienced unless it is released from the bottle is what Jody brought to her textual image. She connected the image of spraying perfume (an experience she has had), a release of the perfume from the bottle, with Denver being "released" from the stranglehold of her family history.

STUDENTS' REACTIONS TO TEACHING STRATEGY AND TO AFRICAN-AMERICAN IMAGES

Most of my students become receptive to the drawing and writing activities I include in my African-American literature classes. A few students never buy into the idea that drawing and creating their own textual images enhance their understanding of the textual images in the texts, but they do complete their assignments. In their small-group work, when the students share their drawings and written responses with each other, the White students and the students of color are interested in each other's interpretation of the texts. If some students' textual images fall outside of the small groups', or the whole class', perimeter of meaning, other students are quick to ask how students arrived at their interpretations of the text and to ask them to point out the evidence from the text that supports their interpretations.

At the beginning of the semester, many of the White students are not comfortable with African-American textual images. They would prefer to discuss only the universal qualities of the images instead of first discussing the images as being directly connected to the culture of a specific group of people, and then moving to discussing how those images have some universal qualities. By the end of the semester, these students are more comfortable with African-American textual images. The White students' representations of African-American textual images demonstrate that they are coming to an understanding of the texts; they do not dominate the images and change them into a reflection of the "Same." Instead, their understanding becomes a new knowledge that is built on what they already know. In one of Elizabeth's reading journal responses, she discussed how she changed from seeing Janie's development in a negative light—in one of her previous reading journal responses, Elizabeth had expressed her anger with Janie's acceptance of being slapped by Tea Cake (Hurston, 1937/1990, p. 140)—to seeing Janie's development in a positive light:

> [I was taught] from day one that there was nothing a man could do for me—nothing I couldn't accomplish on my own. . . . In order for me to understand Janie, to believe in her, I have to put aside all of the "feminist" propaganda I was nourished on. . . . Judging Janie from a distance allows me to see her growth. To understand how far she had to travel from a girl dreaming of love under a tree to the woman we met walking carelessly through town after a three year absence. She did find her love in Tea Cake and herself while working in fields with him. However, it was in [the] loss of Tea Cake that Janie truly struck out on her own. She gave up her true love in order to save herself as well as saving Tea Cake from himself. I respect the woman Janie became. Now, I understand the lady in the overalls.

Elizabeth was able to arrive at this new reading of Hurston's textual images *after* she had created several drawings and written responses about Janie's search for self and shared them with her peers. Some White students expand and demonstrate their understanding of African-American textual images in their semester papers. Others actively search out additional texts by African-American writers that they want to read for extra-credit projects or add to their "summer reading lists."

CIRCLING THOUGHTS

Encouraging and developing White students' abilities to create their own visual and textual images is one way we can help White students engage with African-American text worlds. As Scholes (1985) pointed out, "the more culturally at home in a text our students become, the less dependent they will be on guidance from the instructor" (p. 27). Like Sethe's circling around Paul D, literally and figuratively, as she tries to tell him about what happened in the woodshed (Morrison, 1987), I circle. I circle as I continue to develop ways, through reading and writing, to help my White students engage with African-American literature. I want my students to move beyond "seeing nature [cultures/literature/this thing called life] . . . in the guise of the Europocentric productionism and anthropocentrism that have threatened to produce, literally, all the world in the deadly image of the Same" (Haraway, 1992, p. 297). I want my students to weave African-American writers' textual images, their own visual images, and their own written textual images. To use their images/their thoughts/ their relationships to words in literary texts/to themselves/to the contexts from which they have emerged to gain a power the character Beloved never gains. Beloved asks, "how can I say things that are pictures" as she tries to describe the place on the other side of the bridge (Morrison, 1987, p. 210). In my African-American literature classes, my White students and students of color learn to use their visual drawings and textual images as they attempt to name and describe their reading experiences.

ACKNOWLEDGMENTS

A National Council of Teachers of English Research Foundation Teacher-Researcher Grant and a Bradley University sabbatical leave provided support for the creation of this text. However, without the assistance from students in Bradley University English 329 and Dartmouth College English 69 Contemporary African American Women Novelists courses, this text would have remained a visual image in the writer's mind.

REFERENCES

Adams, J. L. (1986). *Conceptual blockbusting: A guide to better ideas* (3rd ed.). Reading, MA: Addison-Wesley.

Bartel, R. (1983). *Metaphors and symbols: Forays into language*. Urbana, IL: National Council of Teachers of English.

Claggett, F. (1992). *Drawing your own conclusions: Graphic strategies for reading, writing, and thinking*. Portsmouth, NH: Heinemann.

Fleckenstein, K. S. (1989). *Connections: The cognitive and affective links between expressive writing and aesthetic reading*. Unpublished doctoral dissertation, Illinois State University, Normal)

Gardner, H. (1980). *Artful scribbles*. New York: Basic Books.

Haraway, D. (1992). The promises of monsters: A regenerative politics for inappropriate/d others. In L. Grossberg, C. Nelson, & P. A. Treichler (Eds.), *Cultural studies* (pp. 295–337). New York: Routledge.

Hurston, Z. N. (1990). *Their eyes were watching God*. New York: Harper. (Original work published 1937)

Levy, J. (1985, May). Left brain, right brain: Fact and fiction. *Psychology*, pp. 38–44.

Morrison, T. (1987). *Beloved*. New York: Knopf.

Morrison, T. (1992). *Playing in the dark: Whiteness and the literary imagination*. Cambridge, MA: Harvard University Press.

Oliver, E. I. (1994). *Crossing the mainstream: Multicultural perspectives in teaching literature*. Urbana, IL: National Council of Teachers of English.

Purves, A. C. (1994). People prose. In R. F. Fox (Ed.), *Images in language, media, and mind* (pp. 21–28). Urbana, IL: National Council of Teachers of English.

Rosenblatt, L. (1983). *Literature as exploration* (4th ed.). New York: Modem Language Association.

Scholes, R. (1985). *Textual power*. New Haven, CT: Yale University Press.

Sigel, I. E. (1978). The development of pictorial comprehension. In B. S. Randhawa & W. E. Coffman (Eds.), *Visual learning, thinking, and communication* (pp. 93–111). New York: Academic Press.

Willis, S. (1987). *Specifying: Black women writing the American experience*. Madison: University of Wisconsin Press.

Worley, D. A. (1994). Visual imagery training and college writing students. In A. G. Brand & R. Graves (Eds.), *Presence of mind: Writing and the domain beyond the cognitive* (pp. 133–139). Portsmouth, NH: Boynton/Cook.

Yancey, K. B. (1998). *Reflection in the writing classroom*. Logan: Utah University Press.

14

"Spots of Time"—Writerly and Readerly Imaging With William Wordsworth and Basho

Nathaniel Teich
University of Oregon

Poetry is all around us, we can tell our students; it is in the mass media we see and hear, in the pop music, even in our everyday language. But trying to teach about poetry and its primary component, imagery, is always a challenge. Students, regardless of age, usually consider the analysis of poetry the opposite of enjoying language—like tofu or veggie-burgers: supposedly good for you, but nothing you want to have anything to do with regularly. In response, those teachers and textbooks devoted to stimulating creative writing, and writing poetry in particular, offer many and varied prompts and exercises to engage students' interests and creativity (see Behn & Twichell, 1992; Dunning & Stafford, 1992; Goldberg, 1986; & Sears, 1986).

What happens, however, in the language arts and literature classes essentially devoted to the "study" and "analysis" of "texts" that may or may not be labeled *creative*? I present here a way to treat imagery as the primary component of all verbal modes. From this standpoint, students can be offered a two-part writing task: First, analyze the textual imagery being studied and, second, write about their own experiences using images that they create.

This focus on imagery at its most comprehensive helps break down the artificial distinctions separating what is usually called and taught as "creative" writing from its supposed opposites: expository and analytical modes. Teaching students to understand the primacy of imagery and then craft their own image-based narratives should help them in their discussions of literature, analysis of mass media, and development of their writing abilities. Imagery is the key to presenting students with examples and opportunities to merge the conventional modes by recognizing and using all the devices of "creative" writing in a variety of reading and writing tasks.

In the first part of this chapter, I describe assignments based on Wordsworth's idea of "spots of time" and present examples of students' writings from two different courses. One is the upper-division, specialized course on British Romantic Writers in which I developed the Wordsworth assignment. The other is the lower-division, introductory course on World Literature in which I subsequently tailored the assignment to general students' reading of Basho, the 17th-century Japanese haiku master. I assumed that his travel journals of prose and haiku would be more accessible to these students than the more scholarly context in which I taught Wordsworth.

Regardless of the course, students' goals are, first, to show their understanding of textual concepts and implications of the writer's work. Second, they then make connections with their own personal experiences—enacting the thematic and imagistic concepts of the poetic texts to produce their own analogous imagistic narratives, thus showing self-awareness within the context of the literature. In writing these assignments, I urge students to merge the conventional modes—that is to use their stories and story-making powers to draw upon personal narrative, imagery, dialogue, metaphor, anecdote, and all the other elements we associate with "creative" writing.

In the second part of this chapter, I discuss Romantic ideas of imagery and image making in some theoretical detail, focusing on Wordsworth's development of his "spots of time" idea. Conceptions of imagery formulated by the poets of the Romantic period continue to influence our contemporary ideas and practices of writing. However, I do not intend to dwell on theoretical discussions or definitions of imagery—a slippery and overgeneralized term, which is best illustrated and experienced (as in, "I know it when I see it"), rather than classified and categorized.

Theorists themselves recognize that the term *imagery* includes a range of more or less precise items, from mental pictures, visual perceptions, repetitive patterning, to rhetorical figures of speech (simile, metaphor, metonymy, etc.). Distinguishing between mental and verbal imagery can depend on the orientation of focus: whether on the writer who originates linguistic images in a text, on readers who perceive mental images from the text, or on the text itself, which does have an objective existence as a linguistic artifact (despite those theorists and readers who cannot seem to find texts in classrooms). Though I do not intend to collapse the distinction between verbal imagery and any verbal description, I must stress that in my "spots of time" assignments, students' construction of their own central image is only part of my goal. I am less concerned with assuring that students fully develop a central image than with their developing a relevant personal narrative; and this only after adequately explaining their understanding of the poet's ideas about and uses of imagery in specific texts.

ASSIGNMENTS AND STUDENT EXAMPLES—SPOTS OF TIME FROM WORDSWORTH AND BASHO

Let me identify briefly my title. Wordsworth's idea of "spots of time" refers to recollecting formative experiences from childhood. These experiences provide the "emotion recollected in tranquillity," which he stated in his "Preface" to *Lyrical Ballads* (1800), as the basis for his creative process. As I discuss in more detail in the next section, this recollected emotion culminates in the written evocation of images associated with the experiences. What is remarkable about "spots of time" as a concept is its fusion of both place and time. A spot of time is a point on the space/time continuum, like a photo or a freeze-frame of motion pictures. It is reminiscent, I tell students, of the congruence of motion and stillness in traditional haiku; thus, my association of "spots of time" with Basho for theoretical and pedagogical purposes when teaching non-Western literature. Basho (1644–1694) was the premier haiku master who combined prose reflections and haiku in journals of his travels across Japan. In my research for this essay, I came across a statement by Blyth, in his 1947 Preface to his pioneering four-volume study of haiku in English translations: "Haiku record what Wordsworth calls those 'spots of time,' those moments which for some quite mysterious reason have a peculiar significance" (Blyth, 1949/1981, p. 6). Blyth made a number of comparisons of the Japanese haiku poets and their poetry with the British Romantics and their works (also see Rudy, 1966).

In my classroom applications of "spots of time," I present Wordsworth and Basho as models for students to write personal narratives focused around a memorable image and incident in their lives. My goal is to have students recognize, understand, and practice a wholeness in their writing that is usually separated in school and academic discourse. This is an exercise for interconnectedness—of thought and feeling, cognition and affect, mind and body. Wordsworth served as my first model for asking students to write about a spot of time that they can recall as having a formative influence on their lives or that simply provides them with some solace in their daily lives.

My second model for a similar assignment in a different course, World Literature, a lower-division survey course with a general-student enrollment, turned out to be Basho. He wrote travel journals mingling prose description and haiku on his several journeys: pilgrimages to see people, natural sights, temples, shrines—locations of the ancient cultural heritage throughout Japan. The literal roads he traveled can be taken as an analog, a symbolic image of his seeking the "Way" in Taoist or Zen Buddhist terms. He was engaged in a lifelong process, a spiritual journey seeking enlightenment. Ultimately, he created "an artist's way of life, a reclusive life devoted to a quest for eternal truth in nature" (Ueda, 1991, p. 4).

Basho's travel journals fit the model of the "spots of time" assignment by allowing students to interpret incidents and poems within the context of Basho's life and art, and then to reflect upon and connect the situations with similar experiences and emotions in their own lives. Basho, on the road, reflects his aloneness and continual parting from family and friends. He confronted death of loved ones and the struggle to go on in the face of adversity. Many students, on their own for the first time at college, have felt that they could share Basho's thoughts and emotions.

Also we discussed several quotes by Basho (1966) about the creative process. One comment on his process of observing and writing fresh and interesting description is particularly relevant to the "spots of time" assignment. Similar to Keats' ideas in his 1817 letters about "negative capability" and empathy ("if a Sparrow come before my Window I take part in its existence") (Abrams, 1993, pp. 830–831), Basho discussed a standpoint of negating ego in order to represent nature faithfully:

> Go to the pine if you want to learn about the pine, or to the bamboo if you want to learn about the bamboo. And in doing so, you must leave your subjective preoccupations with yourself. Otherwise you impose yourself on the object and do not learn. Your poetry issues of its own accord when you and the object have become one—when you have plunged deep enough into the object to see something like a hidden glimmering there. However well phrased your poetry may be, if your feeling is not natural—if the object and yourself are separate—then your poetry is not true poetry but merely your subjective counterfeit. (p. 33)

Discussing a comment like this served a similar purpose for the general students in World Literature that a more specialized discussion of Wordsworth's theory served for the students in the British Romanticism course. Students could understand, at whatever their level of sophistication, the two different tasks of the assignment: to write about one's own incident and feelings, but to attempt to put aside the preoccupations with self when describing the images and emotions that the author wrote about in the text. Moreover, even when students wrote about their own images and emotions, I urged them to follow Basho's (1966) dictum of putting aside "subjective preoccupations with yourself" to explore their incident and image in fresh, new ways.

As models for the writing assignment, Wordsworth and Basho provided the means for students to transfer and integrate what are often separated as modes of writing in isolated courses: personal/expressive narration in composition or creative writing as opposed to analytical/expository essays in literature courses. When I asked for combined analytical and expressive writing in a survey course like World Literature or a specialized course like British Romanticism, most students presented better work than their strictly analytical essays. They showed engagement not only with their personal responses, but also with their insights into the literary texts.

Appropriately, the upper-division and graduate students in the British Romanticism course had a more critical and analytical task with Wordsworth than the World Literature students had with Basho. As I illustrate in the next section, I stressed discussion of how Wordsworth's thinking about "spots of time" developed and the extent to which he was successful in communicating his emotions and thoughts through the language and images that he selected. For their papers, only after analyzing Wordsworth's theory and a specific spot-of-time incident from *The Prelude* or one of his short lyrics, were the students to write about their own spot of time.

Here's what some of the English majors in the British Romanticism course wrote, in an honest and often compelling way:[1]

> Gina: The universality of this concept came to me when I applied it to my own life. When I was asked to look inward and search for my own spot of time, I realized that I have values and deeply held beliefs that were largely shaped by seemingly insignificant episodes in my formative years.

> Mary: As I struggled to break myself of the patterns of simply analyzing other's works and reach for my own spot of time, I realized how revolutionary Wordsworth's poetry must have been. Here we have a poet deeply interested in his own feelings and life subjects. . . . I have been programmed to analyze for so long that it appeared difficult to pull a memory from the locked corridors of my childhood. . . . However, granted this new freedom . . . , I realized that some of my most splendid childhood memories, like Wordsworth's, have been waiting for their release. . . . [Her conclusion, after describing an incident working with special needs students in an elementary school:] Now, after working with the children for so long, I feel that I should have done something to help Eddie. This guilt pains me and I realize why Wordsworth feels he must reflect upon his past and judge the actions in his present state. He must cleanse himself, as I must cleanse myself of the sadness of that day I last saw Eddie.

[1]Each student's name has been changed to one of a similar gender.

Here is the writing of a student whose previous analytical essays were Cs and for her first paper a D in mechanics and organization. For this assignment her writing cleaned up and was cohesive:

Jessica: I won the state title for breast-strokers in the 11–12 age division. . . . I have a plaque to prove it. . . . I am sure my mother has them [my plaques and medals] stashed away wrapped neatly in a box somewhere in the attic. She and my father wanted them more than I ever did. I took the race, and I never participated in a swim meet again. I hated competitive swimming. . . . I had proven to myself that I could get through it. No matter how much I disliked it, I could do it to my full potential and walk away with this knowledge. This is the power that surges through my body every time I am confronted with a difficult situation.

MaiLynn: Now, when I begin to feel bogged down, I remember the wonder of that blinding sunrise, new for me every morning, and I consider that God's covenant with me.

Patti: What is helpful to remember about these images is that very same contradiction. In life, there is often more than one feeling present at once; there can be the feeling of ease, but also a bodily awareness of potential for harm. . . . If I let my body remember the sense of being cold; of smelling dew and grass in early morning; and the touch of being physically close and secure in a field of unknown boundaries, my senses create an emotional painting of the experience. . . . Both the sensual and the intellectual recognitions are preset, and together they create a full picture of the events in my life . . . , who I am and what I value, just as Wordsworth's events did for him.

In the World Literature course, the students responded to the universalized themes and images of Basho's haiku. Their first task was to analyze the imagery and emotion in at least two of the haiku, in the context of Basho's life and ideas about writing. Although the context for many of the haiku in his journals was often minimal—he would just record going to a place and then write a poem—I urged students then to discuss general ideas about Basho and the structure of haiku. The students, however, usually devoted more space to their own spots of time.

There were always several students, in the many classes that wrote on this assignment, who responded to Basho's images related to death. It was often their first experience of coming to terms with the loss of a family member. In the first example that follows, the student responded to Basho's image at the grave of a famous poet who died unexpectedly. According to the scholars, Basho may not have known him personally; yet the emotion that Basho's image evokes was perceived as genuine and associated by the reader with the death of her mother. In the second example, Basho had returned home to learn that his mother died, and his brother displayed a lock of her white hair. The student made a direct connection of her sense of loss with the emotional effect of Basho's image.

Move mound of the grave –
From how my voice is weeping
The wind of autumn.

Tami: This poem has special purpose for me, because my mother passed away last February. Since then, last winter and this winter have been hard to endure. When I am depressed and it rains, I feel almost as though the sky knows my pain, and it is weeping for me. On the anniversary of her death I was obviously uneasy, and it happened to snow. The snow was so beautiful and calm, it made me feel serene inside.

If my hand takes them
They would melt from my hot tears –
The frost of autumn.

Jan: He is undoubtedly affected by his mother's death and . . . his words are haunting. I can relate to Basho in this aspect. My father passed way this past October and so I can sense the pain that is in this haiku. It's as if he is afraid that his tears will erase the memories of his dear mother. . . . I have personally experienced the pain of losing memories [associated with images of father].

There were also happy images and emotions. Here the student responded to Basho's images with very different personal images but similar emotions:

Together let's eat
Ears of wheat –
Share a grass pillow at night.

Stephan: Personally this haiku made me reflect on an experience I had this summer on an island in Croatia. I had spent a number of years there as a child and it had been about seven years since I had seen my friends and family there. One evening my cousin, whom I had not spoken to in nearly a decade, and I went swimming. It was about three or four in the morning, and with no one around for literally miles, it seemed as if we had the whole Adriatic to ourselves. We floated on our backs until sunrise and exchanged stories of how differently our lives had become, and I remember realizing that such peace and tranquillity can only be achieved in nature with a true friend.

Finally, a few students communicated remarkable self-awareness and the therapeutic value of their reading, writing, and transformational growth. Although the following haiku by Basho was intended to communicate his desire for solitude for contemplation, with his only companionship from the morning glories around his fence (Ueda, 1991), the student alluded to but changed the image for her own emotional quest and values:

The morning glory –
In daytime the bolt fastens
The gate of the fence.

Maria: Basho's desire for inner peace and honesty did not always lead him down an easy path. At one point in his life he experienced an inward mourning filled with silence. Humans no longer satisfied his need for companionship. He found relations without pretense in Nature. . . . He adopted isolation as a means of coping [and undertaking] self-evaluation that could not occur in the presence of human falseness. . . .

For the past year I have been in search of the "lost" part within me. . . . I continue to unearth my Mexican roots. . . . I am of mixed heritage; my mother is Caucasian and my father Mexican-American. This confusing in-between stage discomforts, eludes, and enlightens me simultaneously. Writing keeps my thoughts open and honest. Reading other artists honestly adds to the clarity I search for in my "cultural balance" journey.

. . . The morning glories speak to me not as physical Nature, rather as aesthetics in general. Books and paintings served as my morning glories as I shut my door tight. . . . Basho's physical journey, in written form, serves as a reminder to me about the importance of words and honesty with one's self and others.

Initially, I was surprised by the results of asking students to select and write about their own "spots of time" images and events. Some college students seemed reluctant, if not paralyzed, when asked in literature courses to write about themselves. The spontaneity and exploratory creativity younger children show more easily in early grades can become deadened or discouraged the further they go through their formal education. And students find that few, if any, academic college courses across the curriculum encourage them to respond personally and creatively. In fact, one student explicitly articulated this problem (see the quote from Mary in the Romantics course). Thus, I found unintended benefits from the "spots of time" writing. Creative students felt liberated and permitted to write from their authentic selves. And others seemed to be loosened up to become more self-aware, to connect what they read with their own lives, and to try out their own verbal images in expressing their experiences.

ROMANTIC IMAGING—WORDSWORTH'S "SPOTS OF TIME"

It has become commonplace for both visual and verbal artists to say that they think in images. However, many people—certainly our students—do not often recognize that imagery can be present in and, indeed, is constitutive of all verbal modes, not just what is commonly called poetry. For example, when beginning a literature survey course, I have recast prose passages into verse form and verse as prose. From this exercise, students see that the images and emotions evoked are not necessarily determined by typographical form and arrangement (of course, we can then see the exceptions in e e cummings and other "concrete" texts).

Our current conception that the constituents and functions of language are independent of mode or genre was anticipated by William Wordsworth in a strikingly modern assertion over 200 years ago. In his 1800 Preface to *Lyrical Ballads*—one of the manifestos of British Romanticism, reflecting the influence of his poetic colleague, Samuel Taylor Coleridge—Wordsworth declared that there is "no essential difference between the language of prose and metrical composition" (1966, p. 24).

Wordsworth's theoretical statements and poetic reflections on his creative process epitomized the growing preoccupation of writers during the Romantic movement in England to analyze the ways that their imaginative visions were transformed into their writings. For Wordsworth, the primary goal of his poetry was to produce pleasure for readers who would share the emotions and thoughts associated with specific images and events from his life experiences. Wordsworth's best-known statement about poetry is usually remembered and quoted as: "all good poetry is the spontaneous overflow of powerful feelings" (1966, p. 42). However, this statement in his 1800 Preface is usually cut off from his extended explanation.

> I have said that Poetry is the spontaneous overflow of powerful feelings: it takes its origin from emotion recollected in tranquillity: the emotion is contemplated till by a species of reaction the tranquillity gradually disappears, and an emotion, kindred to that which was before the subject of contemplation, is gradually produced, and does itself actually exist in the mind. In this mood successful composition generally begins, and in a mood similar to this it is carried on. (Wordsworth, 1966, pp. 57–58)

This theoretical description is poetically rendered in Wordsworth's often anthologized poem about the daffodils, "I wandered lonely as a cloud." It can be regarded as the paradigm of Wordsworth's romantic integration of visual, mental, and verbal imagery. The poem directly claims that, from a specific incident of viewing daffodils, Wordsworth at a later "tranquil" time reflected on the happy emotion and reexperienced something of the original emotion. Then he could write down a verbal equivalent of his states of mind, emotions, and images. Of course, those images and emotions would become something new in their verbal constructions:

I wandered lonely as a cloud
That floats on high o'er vales and hills,
When all at once I saw a crowd,
A host, of golden daffodils;
Beside the lake, beneath the trees,
Fluttering and dancing in the breeze.

Continuous as the stars that shine
And twinkle on the milky way,
They stretched in never-ending line
Along the margin of a bay:
Ten thousand saw I at a glance,
Tossing their heads in sprightly dance.

The waves beside them danced; but they
Outdid the sparkling waves in glee;
A poet could not but be gay,
In such a jocund company;
I gazed—and gazed—but little thought
What wealth the show to me had brought:

For oft, when on my couch I lie
In vacant or in pensive mood,
They flash upon that inward eye
Which is the bliss of solitude;
And then my heart with pleasure fills,
And dances with the daffodils.

Except for the second stanza, which he added for publication in 1815, William wrote the poem in 1804, probably not much sooner than 2 years after his sister, Dorothy, recorded the original experience in her *Grasmere Journal,* April 15, 1802. She provided a different written record of the same scene. Note the striking differences between the two versions, especially in the images and emotional effects. William's dominant image of the daffodils dancing is in contrast to the waves and the poet's lonely detachment, which is likened to a distant cloud. To Dorothy the dominant image of daffodils is similar, but described more fully, plus she had other images filling out the scene in a different narrative of social connections:

> When we were in the woods beyond Gowbarrow park we saw a few daffodils close to the water side. . . . But as we went along there were more and yet more and at last under the boughs of the trees, we saw that there was a long belt of them along the shore, about the breadth of a country turnpike road. I never saw daffodils so beautiful they grew among the mossy stones about and about them, some rested their heads upon these stones as on a pillow for weariness and the rest tossed and reeled and danced and seemed as if they verily laughed with the wind that blew upon them over the lake, they looked so gay, ever glancing, ever changing. . . . There was here and there a little knot and few stragglers a few yards higher up but they were so few as not to disturb the simplicity and unity and life of that one busy highway. (Abrams, 1993, pp. 293–294)

When students compare and contrast the two texts, almost unanimously they find Dorothy's simple, natural language and immediately accessible images forming a more refreshing and genuine description than William's. Even though she used personification, it produces a more tender and cozy image—the fresh and charming contrast of the flowers that "rested their heads" on the "mossy stones" for "a pillow"—than William's hyperbole of the added second stanza. Moreover, Dorothy's vivid and elaborated description of the "road" of lively daffodils creates the immediacy of a happy scene of social unity on the road of life. She took the perspective of an un-self-conscious reporter, in contrast to William's abstracted, self-reflexive, and analytical standpoint. Students are quick to draw these comparisons and contrasts. Accordingly, we discuss that there are various ways to frame the same event and craft the images that communicate the writer's emotions.

Beyond this discussion of the various specific images, I stress to students that it is their responsibility as readers in all situations, not just for the "spots of time" writing assignment, to get beyond the "self." I'm not asking them to negate the self, just control the dominating ego in order to understand what a writer and the text seek to communicate: the images, ideas, emotions that originated from someone else not the self. Although each of us inescapably constructs meanings and feelings personally in terms of our knowledge, experiences, and social conditioning, we gain more the extent to which we can incorporate both our individual responses and the perspectives of others.

In the Romantics course, there is more specialized discussion to provide historical and textual grounding for understanding Wordsworth's development of his "spots of time" idea. The usual reference to the "spots of time" passage is Book 12 of *The Prelude,* published in 1850, shortly after Wordsworth's death:

> There are in our existence spots of time,
> That with distinct pre-eminence retain
> A renovating virtue, whence—depressed
> By false opinion and contentious thought,
> Or aught of heavier or more deadly weight,
> In trivial occupations, and the round
> Of ordinary intercourse—our minds
> Are nourished and invisibly repaired;
> (Wordsworth, 1850, Book XII, ll. 208–215; 1979, pp. 429, 431)

Wordsworth introduced the "spots of time" idea in his long autobiographical poem to refer to the influential boyhood experiences that led him to write elsewhere that "the child is father of the man" (and, for gender balance, we should also now say "mother of the woman"). Moreover, in several places, he made a common Romantic assertion that all people are capable of understanding their experiences and using their imaginations, just like poets and artists do, as evidenced here by the repeated pronoun *our*. Thus, we can focus on our own "spots of time" and re-create our own formative images and experiences, which we could write in poems, journals, or other modes. Accordingly, our personal recollections from childhood will have "renovating virtue" by which we will be mentally "nourished and repaired."

Further in this passage, Wordsworth made an additional, and not uncommon, Romantic assertion that the human mind and its imaginative constructs will dominate external, objective reality. Inseparable from the idea that "spots of time" exist in our consciousness, capable of being remembered, the passage concludes:

> The mind is lord and master—outward sense
> The obedient servant of her will. Such moments
> Are scattered everywhere, taking their date
> From our first childhood. I remember well
> (Wordsworth, 1850, Book XII, ll. 222–225; 1979, p. 431)

Although this claim of dominant power may be controversial, we can certainly grant that a person's psychological reality can exert control, in the dominating sense of Wordsworth's "lord and master" metaphor, over that person's perceptions of externality. However, what is just as interesting to me as Wordsworth's assertion here of the primacy of mind/imagination, is the progressive change that the "spots of time" passage underwent. At this point in the passage, as his general explanation concluded, just prior to introducing a specific incident and its powerful image, Wordsworth changed his earlier wording. He wrote in 1805 (XI, l. 270) that it was his "deepest feeling" that this dominance of mind was true (1979, p. 430). These words were replaced by the greater certainty in 1850 (XII, l. 221) of "Profoundest knowledge," implying a shift from feeling to fact (1979, p. 431).

In contrast, Wordsworth's earliest version of the passage, in his 1799 manuscript, makes a much shorter statement. It does not include reference to dominance, but directly acknowledges the connection of the "spots of time" to "imaginative power":

> There are in our existence spots of time
> Which with distinct preeminence retain
> A fructifying virtue, whence, depressed
> By trivial occupations, and the round
> Of ordinary intercourse, our minds—
> Especially the imaginative power—
> Are nourished and invisibly repaired,
> Such moments chiefly seem to have their date
> In our first childhood. I remember well
> (Wordsworth, 1799, I, ll. 288–296; 1979, pp. 8–9)

Note the emphasis on the centrality of "imaginative power," not just unspecified "mind" in general—as in the later versions when the line about "imaginative power" was replaced by the idea of mental dominance. Note also the organic metaphor "fructifying," which was changed to "renovating" by 1805. As the scholarship about Wordsworth's career demonstrates, the "early" Wordsworth was much more explicit than in his later works about the role of imaginative creativity and his process of composing verbal imagery.

Thus, we should remember that the "spots of time" concept did not originate in 1850, nor even in the 1805 manuscript of *The Prelude.* It dates from the formative *Lyrical Ballads* period when, during the winter of 1798–1799, Wordsworth began drafting what was to develop into his long versions of *The Prelude.* The "spots of time" passage is introduced early in the manuscript that has come to be called "The Two-Part *Prelude* of 1799," rather than near the end of the expanded versions. Moreover, the transition, "I remember well," at the end of the passage in all versions, introduces a different incident in the 1799 manuscript from the one in the later versions. Clearly for Wordsworth, the idea of "spots of time" could apply universally for any formative incident and associated images.

For the purposes of the reading and writing assignments that I have asked students to complete, a spot of time connotes an imaginative construct comprising perceptual, experiential, and communicative elements.

Whether as readers engaging the verbal images of a written text or as writers constructing textual imagery, we find a similar process of linking narrative incidents with their key, emotionally evocative images. Wordsworth described the process more fully by emphasizing the tacit role of emotion. For him, recollected emotions associated with a narrated incident form the basis for his contemplation and then his construction of verbal images that correlate with the original emotions and incident.

However, Wordsworth recognized problems inherent in the interchange of the poet's writing and the readers' understandings. He wrote, near the end of the Preface to *Lyrical Ballads:*

> I am sensible that my associations must have sometimes been particular instead of general . . . ; but I am less apprehensive on this account, than that my language may frequently have suffered from those arbitrary connections of feelings and ideas with particular words and phrases, from which no man can altogether protect himself. Hence I have no doubt, that, in some instances, feelings even of the ludicrous may be given to my Readers by expressions which appeared to me tender and pathetic. . . . To this it may be added, that the Reader ought never to forget that he is himself exposed to the same errors as the Poet, and perhaps in a much greater degree. (Wordsworth, 1966, pp. 59–60)

Thus, writers and readers encounter related problems: the writer trying to construct verbal imagery in a context sufficiently sharable by readers, while maintaining the integrity of the creative vision; the readers recreating the text as a performance of their own, while maintaining the integrity of the writer's particular associations of the images and ideas. As I explain my "spots of time" assignment to students, I stress the transformational potential of reading and writing about literature. Beyond constructing purely personal meanings from texts, students will benefit from getting out of the self to understand and participate in the worlds of others. The two parts of the "spots of time" assignment offer such opportunities.

IMPLICATIONS: "A POEM IS THE VERY IMAGE OF LIFE EXPRESSED IN ITS ETERNAL TRUTH"—SHELLEY, "A DEFENCE OF POETRY"[2]

As I mentioned at the outset of this chapter, for the "spots of time" assignment, I am less interested in theoretical definitions of imagery than having students respond, analyze, and write about images that they have read in the assigned texts or have themselves created. Yet as the student examples

[2] See Abrams (1993, p. 757)

illustrate, there can be relative similarities or huge differences as each of us processes, understands, and subjectively responds to the world, as well as another's writings.

For Wordsworth, given the unique personal vision expressed dramatically in his poetry, he worried that his images and related emotions might be too subjective for his readers to share. That indeed was often the case. And his reputation suffered accordingly with those of his contemporaries who read and judged his work by traditionalist standards and values. Although they attacked his work for being too individualistic and not general and universal enough, this was the era of the Romantic paradigm shift in the psychology of creativity—when, for example, an original genius like Blake would assert: "To Generalize is to be an Idiot. To Particularize is the Alone Distinction of Merit" (1965, p. 630).

Even though *paradigm shift* has become an overused term, it is an apt way of stressing that the emergence of modern Western conceptions of image, imagery, and imagination are inseparable from the development of the Romantic movement in England. Major figures, such as Blake, Wordsworth, Coleridge, Keats, and Shelley, presented new ways of thinking about and producing discourse in general and poetry in particular. Recognizing that there are many differences as well as similarities among the Romantics, I have focused in detail on Wordsworth's theorizing and poetic practices to illustrate one variety of Romantic image making.

Later, Wordsworth (1966) would come to the conclusion, as he wrote in the "Essay Supplementary to the Preface" of his 1815 volume of poems, "that every Author, as far as he is great and at the same time *original*, has had the task of *creating* the taste by which he is to be enjoyed" (p. 182). For readers and writers weaving and following the threads and patterns of textual imagery, the Romantic paradigm still provides inescapable challenges. We must negotiate the oscillations between such opposing constructs as the particular and the general, the familiar and the defamiliarized, personal vision and social standards, self and other.

When Coleridge, in his *Biographia Literaria* (1817), summed up the "plan" that he and Wordsworth had for *Lyrical Ballads*, he said that:

> Wordsworth's . . . was . . . to give the charm of novelty to things of every day . . . , by awakening the mind's attention from the lethargy of custom, and directing it to the loveliness and the wonders of the world . . . but for which, in consequence of the film of familiarity and selfish solicitude we have eyes, yet see not, ears that hear not, and hearts that neither feel nor understand. (Abrams, 1993, p. 388)

Through their original imagery, Wordsworth and Coleridge were turning the ordinary and familiar into the new and astonishing, the self-centered into the empathetic. Coleridge, for his own aim of creating "characters supernatural, or at least romantic," offered his now well-known phrase, which has come to be applied more generally to describe the appropriate readerly perspective for aesthetic participation: "that willing suspension of disbelief for the moment, which constitutes poetic faith" (Abrams, 1993, p. 388). For the process of reading, Coleridge implicitly contrasted the aesthetic experience to the religious believers' affirmation of truth through religious faith. We now take this statement to mean putting aside doubting in order to participate in an act of faith in the aesthetic experience.

Regarding the process of writing, I noted earlier that both Keats and Basho presented the creative process as a negating of one's imposing ego to get out of the self and into the object or the being in focus. This participation in what is "not self" we now label *empathy.* Although there are many theoretical and functional definitions of empathy, Rogers (1980) described it on various occasions as an honest effort to understand the other's thoughts, feelings, and circumstances from the other's point of view. This effort "to perceive the internal frame of reference of another" is to perceive "as if one were the person, but without ever losing the 'as if' condition. . . . If this 'as if' quality is lost, then the state is one of identification" (pp. 140–141). Thus, to Rogers, one does not lose one's identity, but rather enters into a fuller, potentially transformative experience. This is a profoundly ethical stance. In his "Defence of Poetry," Shelley (1821) called it *love:*

> The great secret of morals is Love; or a going out of our own nature, and an identification of ourselves with the beautiful which exists in thought, action, or person, not our own. A man, to be greatly good, must imagine intensely and comprehensively; he must put himself in the place of another and of many others; and the pains and pleasures of his species must become his own. The great instrument of moral good is the imagination; and poetry administers to the effect by acting on the cause. (Abrams, 1993, p. 759)

Can we, as teachers, help our students (and ourselves) to achieve "moral good" by means of imaginative participation in the poetic images we read? Raising such ethical issues of empathic understanding, I believe, does not lead to indoctrination. Rather, it calls for balanced pedagogical approaches that would allow for the subjective and personal expressions of "reader response" strategies as well as the historical and contextual reconstructions for textual fidelity. To strive for this multiple experiencing of verbal imagery—cognitively and emotionally—is to enter one of the transformative paths for human awareness and values. As Shelley said:

> All the authors of revolutions in opinion are not only necessarily poets as they are inventors, nor even as their words unveil the permanent analogy of

things by images which participate in the life of truth; but as their periods are harmonious and rhythmical, and contain in themselves the elements of verse; being the echo of the eternal music. (Abrams, 1993, p. 757)

REFERENCES

Abrams, M. H. (Gen. Ed.). (1993). *The Norton anthology of English literature* (Vol. 2, 6th ed.). New York: Norton.

Basho, M. (1966). *The narrow road to the deep north and other travel sketches* (N. Yuasa, Trans.). London: Penguin.

Behn, R., & Twichell, C. (1992). *The practice of poetry: Writing exercises from poets who teach.* New York: HarperCollins.

Blake, W. (1965). *The poetry and prose of William Blake* (D. V. Erdman, Ed.). New York: Doubleday.

Blyth, R. H. (1981). *Haiku: Vol. 1. Eastern culture.* Tokyo: Hokuseido. (Original work published 1949)

Dunning, S., & Stafford, W. (1992). *Getting the knack: 20 poetry exercises.* Urbana, IL: National Council of Teachers of English.

Goldberg, N. (1986). *Writing down the bones: Freeing the writer wthin.* Boston: Shambhala.

Rogers, C. R. (1980). *A way of being.* Boston: Houghton Mifflin.

Rudy, J. G. (1966). *Wordsworth and the zen mind: The poetry of self emptying.* Albany: State University of New York Press.

Sears, P. (1986). *Secret writing: Keys to the mysteries of reading and writing.* New York: Teachers and Writers.

Ueda, M. (1991). *Basho and his interpreters: Selected hokku with commentary.* Stanford, CA: Stanford University Press.

Wordsworth, W. (1966). *Literary criticism of William Wordsworth* (P. M. Zall, Ed.). Lincoln: University of Nebraska Press.

Wordsworth, W. (1979). *The Prelude: 1799, 1805, 1850* (J. Wordsworth, M. H. Abrams, & S. Gill, Eds.). New York: Norton.

Conclusion: Afterimage: Resources for Imagery Study

Linda T. Calendrillo
Western Kentucky University

Interest in using imagery in teaching has burgeoned in the past few decades, and teachers can tap many rich veins to learn more about the theories behind teaching using imagery and about strategies to help them introduce imagery into their classrooms. This bibliographic investigation presents a starting place for new teachers and experienced teachers who want to acquaint themselves with this area of study. This list does not include citations that appear in our authors' reference lists; it is meant to extend those sources for our readers. Because those of us interested in imagery like to think about words and pictures, I have included text sources and graphic sources. I have also included some organizations, journals, and special-interest considerations for your use. To gather the information listed here, I asked our authors about what influenced their interest and research into imagery. Their insights have given us a substantial collection of material to work with.

INFLUENTIAL TEXTS IN IMAGERY

A list of classic texts in imagery follows. Most of these are theoretical texts. Yet because imagery is the center of discussion, graphic representations are often included and emphasized within. These texts are largely in the area of science, particularly psychology; sources from a humanities perspective follow. (If you are looking for an overview, concentrate on the readings marked with asterisks.)

Finke, R. A. (1989). *Principles of mental imagery*. Cambridge, MA: MIT Press.

Finke, R. A. (1990). *Creative imagery: Discoveries and inventions in visualization*. Hillsdale, NJ: Lawrence Erlbaum Associates.

Kosslyn, S. M. (1983). *Ghosts in the mind's machine: Creating and using images in the brain*. New York: Norton.

Kosslyn, S. M. (1994). *Image and brain: The resolution of the image debate*. Cambridge, MA: MIT Press.

Morris, P. E., & Hampson, P. J. (1983). *Imagery and consciousness*. New York: Academic Press.

Osherson, D. N., Kosslyn, S. M., & Hollerbach, J. M. (Eds.). (1990). *Visual cognition and action: An invitation to cognitive science* (Vol. 2). Cambridge, MA: MIT Press.

*Pinker, S., & Kosslyn, S. M. (1983). Theories of mental imagery. In A. A. Sheikh (Ed.), *Imagery: Current theory, research, and application* (pp. 43–71). New York: Wiley.

Rollins, M. (1989). *Mental imagery: On the limits of cognitive science*. New Haven, CT: Yale University Press.

Humanities sources are somewhat broader, as the following list shows. This listing suggests the range and diversity within the area we are investigating. Sources range across many fields; rhetoric, cultural studies, art, education, philosophy, linguistics, for example, are all represented here, as are many others. (If you are looking for an overview/summary of issues, concentrate on the readings marked with asterisks.)

Allert, B. (Ed.). (1996). *Languages of visuality: Crossings between science, art, politics, and literature*. Detroit: Wayne State University Press.

Barthes, R. (1977). *Image – music – text* (S. Heath, Trans.). New York: Hill & Wang.

Bolter, J. D., & Grusin, R. (1999). *Remediation: Understanding new media*. Cambridge: MIT Press.

Brand, A. G., & Graves, R. (Eds.). (1994). *Presence of mind: Writing and the domain beyond the cognitive*. Portsmouth, NH: Boynton Cook.

Csikszentmihalyi, M. (1991). *Flow: The psychology of optimal experience*. New York: Harper Perennial.

Fiske, J. (1993). *Television culture*. New York: Routledge.

Gaggi, S. (1997). *From text to hypertext: Decentering the subject in fiction, film, the visual arts, and electronic media*. Philadelphia: University of Pennsylvania Press.

Goldberg, N. (1986). *Writing down the bones.* Boston: Shambhala.

Hoffman, K. (1996). *Concepts of identity: Historical and contemporary images and portraits of self and family.* New York: HarperCollins.

Klauser, H. A. (1987). *Writing on both sides of the brain.* New York: HarperCollins.

Lunenfeld, P. (Ed.). (2000). *The digital dialectic: New essays on new media.* Cambridge, MA: MIT Press.

Lury, C. (1998). *Prosthetic culture: Photography, memory and identity.* London: Routledge.

Mitchell, A. (1983). *The nine American lifestyles.* New York: Macmillan.

Mitchell, W. J. (1994). *The reconfigured eye: Visual truth in the post-photographic era.* Cambridge, MA: MIT Press.

Pugh, S. L., Hicks, J. W., Davis, M.. & Venstra, T. (1992). *Bridging: A teacher's guide to metaphorical thinking.* Urbana, IL: National Council of Teachers of English.

Spender, D. (1980). *Man made language.* London: Routledge & Kegan Paul.

Stavrianos, I. (2000). *Images and words: Change and chaos in American culture.* Montreal: Black Rose Books.

*Tye, M. (1984). The debate about mental imagery. *The Journal of Philosophy, 81,* 678–693.

ADDITIONAL READINGS IN SPECIAL AREAS OF INTEREST

The readings listed in this section are important, but somewhat specialized. If you are seeking additional reading in areas that were touched on in the chapters in *Teaching Vision* beyond the sources referred to in the chapters, this is a good place to look for those particular areas. For example, we have reading in theater studies, race issues, feminist theory, primary education, "plastic" artists' works, and other areas of study represented here. This eclectic list was gathered principally from questioning our authors about their particular interests. (Because of the special nature of this listing, there are no sources highlighted in this section.)

Benton, T. H. (1983). *An artist in America* (4th ed.). Columbia: University of Missouri Press.

Boal, A. (1998). *The rainbow of desire: The Boal method of theatre and therapy.* New York: Routledge.

Brennan, T., & Jay, M. (Eds.). (1996). *Vision in context: Historical and contemporary perspectives on sight.* New York: Routledge.

Cameron, J. (1992). *The artist's way.* New York: Putnam.

Davies, B. (1992). Women's subjectivities and feminist stories. In C. Ellis & M. G. Flaherty (Eds.), *Investigating subjectivity: Research on lived experience* (pp. 53–78). Newbury Park, CA: Sage.

Dyson, A. H. (1997). *Writing superheroes: Contemporary childhood, popular culture, and classroom literacy.* New York: Teachers College Press.

Fussell, P. (1965). *The rhetorical world of Augustan humanism: Ethics and imagery from Swift to Burke.* London: Oxford University Press.

Gawain, S. (1995). *Creative visualization.* Novato, CA: New World Library.

Haraway, D. (1989). *Primate visions: Gender, race, and nature in the world of modern science.* New York: Routledge.

Heathcote, D. (1984). *Dorothy Heathcote: Collected writings on drama and education* (L. Johnson & C. O'Neill, Eds.). London: Hutchinson.

Kress, G. (1994). *Learning to write* (2nd ed.). London: Routledge.

Kress, G., & van Leeuwen, T. (1996). *Reading images: The grammar of visual design.* London: Routledge.

McLuhan, M., & Fiore, Q. (1967). *The medium is the massage.* New York: Bantam.

Postman, N. (1985). *Amusing ourselves to death: Public discourse in the age of show business.* New York: Viking.

Rank, H. (1976). Teaching about public persuasion: Rationale and a schema. In D. Dieterich (Ed.), *Teaching about doubletalk* (pp. 3–19). Urbana, IL: National Council Teachers of English.

Stafford, B. M. (1997). *Looking good: Essays on the virtue of images.* Cambridge, MA: MIT Press.

Stafford, B. M. (1999). *Visual analogy: Consciousness as the art of connecting.* Cambridge, MA: MIT Press.

Wilhelm, J. D. (1997). *"You gotta be the book."* Urbana, IL: National Council of Teachers of English.

JOURNALS AND ORGANIZATIONS OF INTEREST

National Council of Teachers of English (NCTE) and International Reading Association sources are vital to any investigation of the kind we are having. To review their journals, visit www.ncte.org and www.reading.

org. Also available are most specialized journals like *Imagination, Cognition and Personality; The Journal of Mental Imagery;* and *Consciousness and Cognition,* all journals in psychology. In English studies, *JAEPL: the Journal of the Assembly for Expanded Perspectives on Learning,* often has articles about imagery; AEPL is an NCTE affiliate, and *JAEPL* is coedited by Kristie S. Fleckenstein and Linda T. Calendrillo. Also, of interest is *Afterimage: The Journal of Media Arts and Cultural Criticism* (http://www.vsw.org/afterimage). The Cultural Environment Movement (CEM), founded by George Gerbner, is an organization dedicated to supporting equality and fairness in media. Organizations dealing with the therapy/healing dimension of imagery include the Academy for Guided Imagery, Association des art-thérapeutes du Québec, Inc. (Professional Association of Quebec Therapist), and the International Association of Interactive Imagery.

VIDEOS

Boihem, H., & Emmanouilides, C. (1997). *The ad and the ego* [Video]. San Francisco: California Newsreel.

Buñuel, L., & Dalí, S. (Writers, Directors, & Producers). (1928). *Un chien Andalou* [Film]. (Available from Facets Video, 1517 W. Fullerton, Chicago, IL 60614, www.facets.org.)

Capra, B. (Director). (1991). *Mind walk* [Film]. (Available from Malofilm Group, Quebec)

WEB SITES

Web sites age quickly. I am including only a few here to get you started. If you do not find these available, try a search of a particular area of imagery you are interested and link to the "edu" sources first. These are your most reliable because they are prepared at educational institutions. You will find some remarkable information on the Web, and graphic imagery is the world the Internet exists within.

Imagination, mental imagery, consciousness, and cognition: Scientific, philosophical and historical approaches [Online]. (2000, October 2). Available: http://web.calstatela.edu/faculty/nthomas/index.htm

Thomas, N. J. T. (1997). Mental imagery. In *Stanford encyclopedia of philosophy* [Online]. Available: http://plato.stanford.edu/entries/mental-imagery/

PERSONAL SOURCES

It may go without saying that often your best sources for teaching ideas are the teachers you know and work with at your institution or surrounding schools. When it comes to imagery, those teachers you discuss matters with and learn the most from may be outside your regular discipline. If you are interested in the psychological aspects of imagery work, talk to the social scientists. If you want to use art and its strategies, talk with the art teachers. Those mathematicians know more about visual and mental imagery than many of us know, and people who have been taking education classes can often talk about learning styles theory adeptly and coherently. Speak to those around you, and learn as you go!

List of Contributors

Linda T. Calendrillo is the English Department Head at Western Kentucky University. She is a rhetoric and composition specialist and coedits, with Kristie S. Fleckenstein, *JAEPL: The Journal of the Association for Expanded Perspectives on Learning*.

Kristie S. Fleckenstein teaches at Ball State University. She is currently working on a book-length project, *The Poetics of Teaching: Imagery in a Writingreading World*.

Roy F. Fox teaches at the University of Missouri-Columbia, where he also directs The Missouri Writing Project. His most recent book is *MediaSpeak: Three American Voices*.

Christy Friend is Assistant Professor and Associate Director of First-Year English at the University of South Carolina. She has recently published articles in *JAC: A Journal of Composition Theory, College English,* and *Rhetoric Review,* and she is a coauthor of *The Scott, Foresman Handbook for Writers*.

Terri Pullen Guezzar is currently the Curriculum Specialist in Information Technology at American InterContinental University in Atlanta, Georgia, where she manages content development in networks, software applications, and databases.

Gregg A. Hecimovich is an Assistant Professor of English at Seattle University. His articles on 19th-century British literature have appeared in *ELH, Victorian Poetry,* and the *James Joyce Quarterly*. He is also author of the upcoming edition of Anthony Trollope's *Phineas Redux* for Penguin Classics.

Catherine L. Hobbs is an Associate Professor of Rhetoric/Composition/Literacy in the University of Oklahoma English Department. She is editor of *Nineteenth-Century Women Learn to Write* and author of *Rhetoric on the Margins of Modernity: 18th-Century Rhetoric and Language,* forthcoming from SIU Press.

Eric H. Hobson, Associate Professor of Humanities at the Albany College of Pharmacy, directs the school's faculty development efforts to improve instructional quality and student learning. Among other publications, he collaborated with Joan Mulling and Pamela Childers to write *ARTiculating: Teaching Writing in a Visual World.*

Debra L. Innocenti earned her MFA in writing at Sarah Lawrence College in New York. Her work has appeared in a number of journals, including *American Literary Review, Prairie Schooner, The Beloit Poetry Journal, Glimmer Train Stories, New Letters, Italian Americana,* and *The Texas Observer* among others. She has received prizes from *American Literary Review, Glimmer Train Stories,* The Center of Texas Studies, and the University of Houston-Clear Lake. Presently she teaches at St. Mary's University in San Antonio.

Sheryl A. Mylan is an Associate Professor of English at Stephen F. Austin State University. She is the coauthor of *Voices and Visions: An Integrated Approach to Reading and Writing* and has written articles on Williams, Kingston, Mailer, and others. Currently, she is working on *Understanding Literature Through Writing.*

Mary P. Sheridan-Rabideau is an Assistant Professor in the English department of Rutgers, The State University of New Jersey. Her research interests include gender, technology, and literacy.

Mark Smith is an Associate Professor of English at Valdosta State University, where he teaches graduate and undergraduate courses in composition, professional writing, and rhetoric.

Nathaniel Teich is a Professor of English at the University of Oregon, where he teaches both literature and rhetoric/composition courses and also serves as director of the Oregon Writing Project for classroom teachers. Publications include *Rogerian Perspectives: Collaborative Rhetoric for Oral and Written Communication.*

Demetrice A. Worley is an Associate Professor of English and Director of Writing at Bradley University, Peoria, Illinois, where she teaches courses in composition, African-American literature, creative writing, and technical writing. She received her doctorate in English from Illinois State University.

Chris Worthman teaches literacy courses in the School of Education at DePaul University and coordinates critical literacy programs for pregnant and parenting teens in Chicago. He continues to work with TeenStreet and its parent organization, Free Street.

Author Index

Subject Index

C

D

P

Q

R

S